ENDORSEMENTS FOR

GOD SPEAKS

"I've long thought a full-length book ought to be written on the implications of essential kenosis for understanding the Bible. And now thanks to Gabriel, we have it! Not only does Gabriel explain the implications essential kenosis has for understanding the Bible, he gives his readers a gift: he writes in a conversational way. This book is insightful and accessible. I'm not great at prognostication (but according to the Bible, God's prognostication record isn't flawless, so that gives me comfort). But I suspect this book will launch a conversation. Or rather, multiple conversations."

– **THOMAS JAY OORD**, from the Foreword, Author of
The Uncontrolling Love of God and *God Can't*

"Gabriel Gordon's thought-provoking book *God Speaks* is a fascinating and profound exploration into the hermeneutical adventure of biblical inspiration. How do we understand inspiration in light of a stark reality where God's powerful Trinitarian love is uncontrolling and therefore cannot instantly download absolute truth into the human mind? If you are passionate about understanding the biblical text and want to find out, I highly recommend you read Gabriel's book!"

– **MARK KARRIS**, Author of *Divine Echoes* and *Religious Refugees*

"In *God Speaks*, Gabriel Gordon offers a worthy exploration of important ideas related to essential kenosis, the nature of inspiration, the Word of God, and participatory revelation with creativity and a light touch of humor. Drawing from both contemporary and early

Christian theologians, Gordon argues well for a participatory theology that values humanity's interpretive role in our relationship with God and scripture and sees the text as a place where Christians can still encounter the living Word—Jesus the Christ."

– **SHERI KLING**, Author of *A Process Spirituality*

"How does relational theology shape our understanding of the 'word' of God? In this exciting project, Gordon revisits and reimagines our notion of the 'word' in a Christologically-oriented fashion and grounded primarily in Thomas Oord's notion of essential kenosis. If God is essentially loving and uncontrolling, then when God speaks, God invites humans to participate, respond, and enter into a loving relationship with God. Interpretation, therefore, becomes an open and uncontrolled play between God and humanity. Drawing on the richness of the long tradition of Christian theologies, particularly the early Christian writings, this book offers a fresh theological proposal that moves us away from a mechanic, rigid, and controlled model to a dynamic, relational, and participatory model of a theology of the word."

– **DR. EKAPUTRA TUPAMAHU**, Assistant Professor
of New Testament, Portland Seminary

"This book provides a relational account of the inspiration of scripture wherein humans genuinely participate with God in the production of scripture. The approach is Christ-centered and makes great use of the Bible and church tradition, particularly the church fathers."

– **JOHN SANDERS**, Emeritus Professor of Religious Studies, Hendrix
College; Author of *Embracing Prodigals* and *The God Who Risks*

"In *God Speaks,* Gabriel Gordon has given us a magisterial work on how to better understand the inspiration of scripture. Exhibiting a deep engagement with both patristic literature and contemporary scholarship, God Speaks points us to a way of interpreting scripture that is beholden to neither modern liberalism nor fundamentalism, but in keeping with a Christocentric hermeneutic that is at once ancient and contemporary. This is an illuminating book!"

– **BRIAN ZAHND**, Pastor of Word of Life Church in St. Joseph,
Missouri; Author of *Sinners In the Hands of A Loving God*

"Gabriel Gordon challenges deeply-held beliefs about the nature of Scripture by applying the innovative approach to divine providence pioneered by Thomas Jay Oord called Essential Kenosis. By beginning with a God who is uncontrolling love, as Oord does, Gordon is able to construct an approach to biblical inspiration that will no doubt frustrate Fundamentalists, but will likely encourage and (dare I say) inspire seekers and skeptics alike. *God Speaks* is an honest and scholarly exploration of important questions faithful followers of Christ will likely wrestle with in light of our postmodern world. And Gordon does this by inviting us into the story of how he's grappled with these questions, modeling for readers a faith that embraces both critical thinking and the path laid before us throughout the Christian tradition. Whether or not you end up agreeing with Gordon by the time you finish reading, you will be better for it."

– **REV. T. C. MOORE**, Lead Pastor of Roots Covenant Church (St. Paul, MN)

"It's remarkable how this is at many times memoir mixed with doctrine. More importantly I found myself feeling comforted that God still speaks today. In our culture of 'get in this boat or else' this book is a permission slip to venture into listening to our hearts as we tune into the divine. You're gonna love this."

– **SETH PRICE**, Host of the "Can I Say This At Church?" Podcast

"In *God Speaks,* we get a historical and theological tour of biblical inspiration along with an invitation to think about it through the lens of relational theology—specifically 'essential kenosis.' This book is worth reading (for the research alone!) no matter your view. Whether or not you end up agreeing with all of Gabriel Gordon's arguments, one will be hard-pressed to ignore them. For those who are convinced that God is love and who want to honor the sacred scriptures, I highly recommend considering this creative and thoughtful exploration of biblical inspiration. It will get you thinking!"

– **KURT WILLEMS**, Pastor and Author of *Echoing Hope: How the Humanity of Jesus Redeems Our Pain* (EchoingHope.com)

GOD SPEAKS

A PARTICIPATORY THEOLOGY
OF BIBLICAL INSPIRATION

GABRIEL GORDON

FOREWORD BY THOMAS JAY OORD

Copyright © 2021 by Quoir.

Cover design and layout by Rafael Polendo (polendo.net)
Cover images by Nejron Photo (shutterstock.com)

First Edition

Unless otherwise noted, all scripture quotations are taken from the New Revised Standard Version of the Bible, copyright © 1989 by the National Council of the Churches of Christ in the U.S.A. Used by permission. All rights reserved.

ISBN 978-1-938480-86-7

This volume is printed on acid free paper and meets ANSI Z39.48 standards.

Printed in the United States of America

 QUOIR

Published by Quoir
Oak Glen, California
www.quoir.com

DEDICATION

To my loving wife, friend and songbird, Hannah.
Your faith and kindness inspire me every day.
Your bright eyes give me hope on the darkest days.

ACKNOWLEDGEMENTS

No authors simply write a book by themselves. They are assisted at various stages by a whole host of people. I am deeply indebted to a number of friends who have either looked at portions of my manuscript at various stages or, in a few instances, the whole book.

The feedback of Steve Reichenbach, Hannah Tines, Charlie Tines, and Braden Norwood was helpful in clarifying aspects of the book. Thanks to Jason Price, a former professor of mine, who looked at chapter 3 and gave me feedback that strengthened it. I also want to thank David Young, who took a look at some of the arguments in chapter 4. His expertise was helpful in affirming some of my own arguments and observations. I'd also like to recognize my friend Sandi Brisolara, who also gave helpful feedback.

I am sincerely grateful to Adam D'Achille, who was at my beck and call whenever I needed a sentence, paragraph or chapter checked by a friend with a theological eye. He spent much of his own time and effort to make sure I had any necessary feedback. We also spent a significant amount of time on the phone discussing the rewriting of particular chapters. In many ways, he was my co-editor. Much of the strength and readability of the book will be his doing.

Thanks to Grandma for being a listening ear when I needed to make sure a sentence, concept, or paragraph made sense to the grandmas of the world. I also would like to thank the faculty, students, and my own professors at Portland Seminary. This diverse group of people has been a huge inspiration to my own faith and has served to shape and grow my theological thinking. Special thanks to Quoir Publishing and Rafael for taking a chance on me. I don't take it for granted.

I also want to give a special recognition to Thomas Jay Oord, whose work was integral to the writing of my own book and who gave constructive developmental feedback on the completed first draft.

And of course, to my wife and best friend Hannah Gordon, without your continual encouragement there is a likely chance I may never have finished the book, especially in the rewriting process when I wanted to bang my head against the wall just about every other paragraph I rewrote. To you, I dedicate this book.

Lastly, special thanks to my editor Suzanne who worked tirelessly to make this book readable to the normal reader and to those who care about things like the difference between "too" and "to." She has made literally thousands of corrections to the fourth draft. While my ideas may be good, without proper language to mediate those ideas, they end up being incomprehensible. This book is as good as it may be because of her effort. I am entirely grateful to all of you.

To the extent that there are errors or the book is found unreadable, the responsibility rests solely on me alone. To the extent that the book is any good, I have them to thank.

CONTENTS

*Patristics; the Word of God and Inspiration; and New Testament
Usage of the Phrases "Word of God" and Scripture*

FOREWORD

Gabriel Gordon takes the Bible seriously. So do I.

We are like many who find in the pages of sacred writ profound truths and insights about God. We also find inspiration and information about how we might live well, now and after our bodies die. The Bible is a source to which we turn often when searching for answers to the biggest questions of life.

But Gabriel and I also know the Bible has problems. Some of those problems are internal; others have to do with how we make sense of it. In fact, Gabriel begins this book by listing some of the most important obstacles we face when trying to make sense of the Bible.

Some encounter these problems and assume they must choose one of two options. Either they must regard the whole Bible as exactly what God wanted, as inerrant in all that it says, and as a document we can interpret flawlessly through a plain reading (with the aid of the Holy Spirit, of course). Or the Bible is just another book, no better than others, no more inspired nor trustworthy.

There's a third way. Making sense of that way involves more than exploring the history of how Christians have understood the Bible, although that's important. That third way involves some *theological* claims.

To make sense of the Bible—in all its diversity, ambiguities, and insights—we must enquire about the nature of the God who purportedly inspired it. What *kind* of God should we think is revealed in scripture and reveals today?

One option is to think God exists but is uninvolved, aloof, and twiddling his thumbs on Mars. Any revelation we might think God provides is merely just the best of human insights, unaided by the divine. If this is true, the Bible is no more divinely inspired than the Harry Potter series. That distant and uninvolved God is not in the revealing business.

Another option starts with the idea God can and does control. This view says God has the ability to guarantee crystal clear, inerrant, and unambiguous revelation. Some who think God has that kind of power claim the Bible *is* free from any errors, inconsistencies, and or conflict with science and commonsense. In their view, the Bible is *exactly* as God intended it.

Others think God has controlling power and *could* provide a perfectly clear revelation, but God has voluntarily chosen another course. God allowed the writers of the Bible to make errors, to be ambiguous, to make mistakes about God's nature, and more or less muddle along. But to this view we must ask, would a loving God who could provide an error-free text allow errors in a message vital for our salvation?

Imagine you asked someone to write a message essential to saving the lives of others. As the person wrote, you noticed major errors that distorted the message. Instead of correcting the writer and making the message clear, you left in the mistakes knowing many would misinterpret it. Would that be loving?

Fortunately, we have a third option called "Essential Kenosis" theology. Gabriel Gordon explains this theological alternative in these pages. I've long thought a full-length book ought to be written on the implications of Essential Kenosis for understanding the Bible. And now thanks to Gabriel, we have it!

Not only does Gabriel explain implications Essential Kenosis has for understanding the Bible, he gives his readers a gift: he writes in a conversational way. This book is insightful *and* accessible.

I'm not great at prognostication (but according to the Bible, God prognostication record isn't flawless, so that gives me comfort). But I suspect this book will launch a conversation. Or rather, multiple conversations.

For people like Gabriel and me who take the Bible seriously, this book could be the game-changer they need. It could be the prod that prompts readers to see God as a loving and uncontrolling Spirit revealed powerfully in the Bible and who continues to reveal today.

May this book be God's teaching tool for you!

– Thomas Jay Oord
1/20/2021

INTRODUCTION

Where did it all begin? I remember in my sophomore year of college at Oklahoma Baptist University someone asked me to preach at this tiny Southern Baptist church in Duncan, Oklahoma. It would be my first time preaching, as I didn't get very many opportunities to do so as an anthropology and cross-cultural ministry major, which apparently wasn't considered a good pool from which to draw preachers.

I think it had something to do with our tendency to walk around barefoot. Hippies apparently don't make good preachers. Suffice it to say, I was both excited and very nervous. Growing up, all I knew of the faith was the Protestant fundamentalism that I had been reared in, and up to this point it had made sense to me. However, something had shifted during my second year at OBU. My views of the Bible were changing. Or maybe it would be more accurate to say that they had loosened. What you're about to read in this book can be traced back to this moment, to this year, and this opportunity to preach.

For whatever reason, I was considering preaching without using the Bible. I can't remember exactly why, but what I do remember was my conversation about this with my roommate Garrett, who despite our disagreements is still a brother and a friend to this day. Both of us looking back on the moment would readily admit we weren't the most mature at eighteen and nineteen, but then again, what teenager is! I'm not exactly sure how the conversation initially got started, but at some point, he asked on which biblical passage I was planning to preach. I told him a bit hesitantly that I was thinking of not using the Bible at all.

As you can well imagine, this sparked a heated debate between two young passionate men. The ensuing conversation centered on two questions: Was the Bible necessary for salvation and was it necessary to live the Christian life after salvation began? These seemed like pretty important questions back then, and they still do.

At the time, Garrett answered yes to both questions; I answered no. I said if Abraham did not need the scriptures to know God initially, nor did he need them to walk in relationship with God, then how could something be necessary that wasn't yet accessible to so many before who faithfully sought God?—unless we are saying that Abraham and countless others who never had a Bible simply did not know God. Of course, I wasn't saying the scriptures were useless or that we should throw them away. Nonetheless, this is the moment that eventually led to the writing of the book you now hold in your hands.

After this, I continued to think about the place of the Bible in the Church's life, biblical inspiration, what or who the Word of God is, and a lot more. That summer I did an internship in my home city of Seattle (technically, I'm from the suburb of Renton). After a day of fasting, one of the few times I've ever fasted in my life, I heard God ask me a question, "If you lost everything in your life—a future family, your spiritual gifts, a roof over your head, your college education, your brothers and sisters in Christ, *and the Bible*—would I be enough?" It stung because I knew the answer was no.

The Bible had become an idol for me—is still an idol for many others—and I couldn't possibly have lived without it at that point in my life. A few weeks later entering my junior year of college, I was reading a book by John Eldredge on prayer, and I heard the Holy Spirit say, "Put down the book and ask me what I want to say to you." So, I put down the book and asked. God spoke *I Am Enough.* God answered in the affirmative, as I was unable to do during my conversation with Garrett that past summer. While I felt God was not yet enough for me and the need to supplement my faith with the Bible, the Spirit was slowly persuading me that this was an idol I no longer needed. This would prove to be an integral moment in my journey with the Word.

The next big epiphany came later that summer. I was mulling over the concept of revelation and how that related to the Bible. It began to dawn on me that revelation is inerrant since it comes from an inerrant and infallible God. But since humans are fallible and errant, once the revelation encounters the mind of a human being and is received by it, what we have received and responded to is no longer the revelation itself—but a *human interpretation of what we have encountered.* This was foundational for much of my later thinking, especially as I found other theologians who had further developed this concept.

During my last year of college, I spent a wonderful four months fall semester with a local church in Oklahoma City participating in a church planting internship. I still have fond memories of my friends from that season of my life. Since I was establishing myself there at this time, I moved into a discipleship community house that was part of the church. There were regular Bible studies, worship nights, and opportunities for bonding with my fundamentalist roommates.

One fateful night, we were reading Acts 17:11, and I saw something I had never seen before. The author of Acts was speaking about scripture and the Word of God as two different things. Through this, I only fell deeper down the rabbit hole. I began to see this theme throughout the New Testament—whenever the Word of God was used it was rarely, if ever, speaking about scripture. I concluded that the Bible was not only inerrant, but also not the Word of God.

Having grown up being taught that Christianity was founded on the Bible as the inerrant Word of God, I spent a good portion of this season worrying that I had become a heretic, and I fretted extensively about losing my salvation. At this point, I knew little church history. I didn't know C. S. Lewis thought the same thing or that Martin Luther, the founder of the Protestant Reformation, believed that Jesus—not the Bible—was the Word of God. I was unaware that Karl Barth believed that Christ himself, not the Bible, was revelation.

I didn't realize the faith tradition that Jesus alone was the Word of God dated back to the second century and, as I pointed out above, was also in the New Testament itself. So really, it went back to the very first Christians. I had yet to learn that there was an entire branch of Christianity, the Eastern Orthodox Church, that to this day doesn't believe the Bible is the Word of God. My intuition about the New Testament was right—I just didn't know it yet. And so, I hid my deep, dark heresy until one day I mustered up the courage to talk to my anthropology professor.

I poured out my heart to him, explaining that I no longer believed the Bible was the inerrant Word of God. I'm paraphrasing, but he responded by saying, "Gabe, you're not a heretic, you're just not evangelical anymore." I sighed with stone cold relief. Those words of affirmation gave me the courage to keep exploring Christianity, to mine the depths of the Christian tradition. Eventually I graduated, and having sensed a call from God to seek unity in the church, I went to work at a summer camp in Colorado considered both *fundamentalist* [1] and *evangelical* [2]. It didn't hurt that one of my best friends from college was going to be working there either.

That summer was simultaneously one of the best and worst summers of my young life. Within the first few days of training, one of the head honchos came up from the headquarters in Texas to go over their statement of faith. Lo-and-behold, they believed the Bible was the inerrant Word of God and even claimed every Christian believed this, which I would later learn was simply not true. I spent the next couple of days in a panic, wrestling over what to do. Would I stay and hide what I thought or would I lay my cards on the table and have to leave for the summer?

[1]   There are five main pillars of fundamentalism: the inerrancy of the Bible, penal substitutionary atonement, the virgin birth of Jesus, the bodily resurrection of Jesus, and the historical accuracy of the miracles performed by Jesus. The last three of these pillars are held by all historic Orthodox Christians, and therefore these beliefs do not make fundamentalism distinct as a tradition. Neither does the second pillar, since penal substitutionary atonement is historically a broadly Protestant doctrine. Therefore, in my view, the one doctrine that is new to the fundamentalist movement, and therefore that distinguishes them as a distinct tradition, is a belief in scripture's inerrancy. I would therefore broadly define someone as a fundamentalist as someone that subscribes to inerrancy.

[2]   While there are different definitions of an evangelical, David Bebbington's definition is seen as sort of the standard to which others must respond. And I think he has the most accurate definition. There are four central tenets to the definition of an evangelical. The four pillars of evangelicalism are biblicism, conversionism, activism, and crucicentrism. Biblicism is the idea that Bible has some kind of authority. Conversionism is the idea that one must be converted. Activism is the idea that Christians must be active in social justice and evangelism. Crucicentrism is the idea that the faith is centrally focused on the cross.

It was a difficult decision, especially given that I didn't have a car to drive back to Oklahoma. After several days of feeling conflicted, I heard the Lord speak to me in my cabin, "If they want to get to you, they have to go through me." My arrogant tribalism quickly reared its head, and I thought to myself, "Yes! God is on my side." Then, God spoke it again, like a nice red-hot slap to the face, "But if you want to get to them, you also have to go through me." God doesn't play sides with God's children. It was an important lesson for me to learn. These were and still are my brothers and sisters in the faith. I took this as a sign that I should stay, and it has continued to shape my ministry to this day.

Fast forward a few months after I moved to Seattle, I had started to read guys like Peter Enns and Thomas Jay Oord. Their writings about scripture and God not only resonated with me, but also deeply shaped my thinking. Through Peter Enns, I found several other theologians and biblical scholars that led me further down this road and closer to the writing of this book. One of the key scholars whose work I have drawn on here, Benjamin Sommer, I found through Peter Enns.

Eventually, I started to read the church fathers, who further affirmed many of my intuitions. Now in my third year of seminary, these influences, experiences, and pivotal moments in my story coalesced to form the book you now hold in your hands. I want the book you're holding to be radical—but radical in the sense of going back to our roots. It's not meant to be an apology for why I believe what I believe, nor is it meant as a jaded attack on those with whom I disagree. I am deeply indebted to those who have shaped my thoughts, but also to those who passed the faith onto me, as well as those who hold many of the convictions I reject.

Throughout my life, I've had a lot of questions about who God is because of my own experiences. As a child, I was abused by my mother and sexually molested by her boyfriend. As if that wasn't enough, my missionary grandfather left my grandmother for a Thai prostitute. The two disparate viewpoints I heard to explain why evil and suffering happens in the world were that God controls all things, or alternatively, that God could prevent evil but chooses not to. These simply did not line up with who I knew Jesus to be in my own life and as I saw him described in the gospel accounts.

Oord's theology that "God is Uncontrolling Love" spoke to my profound dissatisfaction with the prevailing answers I had been previously offered and echoed my deep intuition that something else was going on. When my views of the Bible loosened and changed, everything kind of came together in a sort of glorious harmony. I have thought a lot about Oord's theology, and the Bible since that conversation with Garrett. What you're about to read is an exploration of Thomas Oord's theology and its implications for biblical inspiration: If God cannot control free creatures, because that ability falls outside of God's nature, then how did the biblical authors interact with God's revelation and what did their experiences produce as the biblical text? If God really is *Uncontrolling Love*, then how did our Bible come to us and how do we use it today?

Oord's theology has radical implications for a lot of things, but especially for biblical inspiration. Good theology always does, and it is always practical. But beyond that, as in all things, I hope that this book will help you become more faithful to our one and only Lord Jesus Christ.

In the end, I went to preach at that church. Perhaps to your surprise, I did use scripture and wasn't booed out. For a time, however, I needed scripture to be taken out of my hands because it was an idol in my life. But through time and God's patient guiding hand, Jesus became the center, foundation, and sole authority in my life—and that process is still ongoing. With Jesus in the center, I got back scripture. But this time, it was not as an idol stealing the throne of my King but as a humble servant to the King—animated by the Spirit— holding my hand and guiding me to my Lord and dear friend. As Paul once wrote, "Every knee shall bow and tongue confess that Jesus Christ is Lord to the glory of God the Father." While the Bible doesn't have any knees, at least that I'm aware of, it too shall bend its pages to the Lordship of Christ and confess that Jesus alone is King.

CHAPTER ONE

SIX PROBLEMS WITH POPULAR VIEWS OF INSPIRATION

Why this book? How does this work contribute to current conversations and the problems inherent in popular notions of inspiration at large? If there aren't any issues, and the topics at hand have been adequately addressed, then this book is simply not needed. However, I would like to suggest that, indeed, there are tremendous problems with our popular notions of inspiration.

Furthermore, I find many attempts to address them helpful in part but not in whole. While I will address some of these issues, my book is not primarily a deconstructive argument for these problems, as others have satisfactorily discussed the deconstructive aspect of many of them. My aim is rather more constructive. The time for the jaded former fundamentalist who's always deconstructing, always tearing down, is over. It's time to build something.

My primary goal for this book is to explore the implications of essential kenosis and how they shape the doctrine of inspiration, making it less susceptible to the problems found in popular dogmas of inspiration. It is also an aim of mine to provide a more holistic and interdisciplinary account of inspiration. Too many are coming to the table with only one perspective on the topic. I would like to approach it from multiple disciplines and perspectives. Although I'll explain the particular problems in what follows, it may be helpful to note that many of the dilemmas I will address share the perspective that biblical inspiration and authorship are synonymous—which, as I will argue, ultimately presupposes a God who can control.

1. PROBLEM OF EVIL

One of the biggest problems within popular notions of inspiration is the underlying depiction of God that creates what we call the "problem of evil." We can explain the basic problem as this: If God is all good (*omnibenevolent*[3]) and all powerful (*omnipotent*[4]) why is there evil, suffering and pain in the world? Common notions of inspiration presuppose a God who either causes evil or allows it. The church has supplied a few different answers; however, I do not intend to recount all the ways philosophers and theologians have tackled the problem of evil. What I want to highlight is that the theologies behind popular notions of inspiration are the same theologies of God that are subject to the problem of evil and fail to give adequate solutions to this problem.

We can explain the first answer given for the problem of evil in this way: *since there's evil, suffering, and pain in the world, God cannot exist*, at least not God as traditionally defined. As Lex Luthor says in the terrible movie[5], *Batman vs Superman*,[6] "If God is all powerful, He cannot be all good, and if He is all good, He cannot be all powerful." This answer is dependent on how you define, "all-good" and "all-powerful." The one who gives this first answer seems to define "all-powerful" *as the ability for God to do anything and everything*. This

---

3   Omnibenevolent means that God is all good.

4   Omnipotent means that God is all powerful.

5   #Nerd Alert: The whole DC franchise has unfortunately tried to play catch up with the Marvel Cinematic Universe. Whereas Marvel spent over a decade developing their storyline, which is part of the reason it's so good, DC has tried to mush the same amount of storyline into a couple of years, making their movies terrible—which if you ask me is a travesty because I love Superman and Batman.

6   *Batman v Superman: Dawn of Justice* (Warner Bros, 2016).

is a definition of God's power not held by all of Christianity.[7] To be sure, there are streams within Christianity that affirm this definition, but not all Christians do. And it is unnecessary to do so. If God's power means that God can do all things, and we agree on what "all good" means, then the first answer is self-evident. God cannot exist. While definitions of what is "good" may of course differ, here they seem to mean the prevention of suffering, pain, and evil in the world.

The second answer given *is to deny that God is all good*. While some of my more extreme reformed brothers and sisters will verbally affirm that God is all good, in practice their theology denies this supposition. Rather, they favor a theology that centers itself on a doctrine defining power—or the more commonly used term in reformed circles, "sovereignty"—as the ability for God to do anything. Said another way, "For those whose theology of divine sovereignty and providence is shaped by the Augustinian-Calvinist tradition, everything that transpires within creation—including every specific thing done by Satan and demons—is divinely ordained [caused] and thus is ultimately attributable to God's all-encompassing sovereign will."[8] In this type of thinking, really what matters to God is God, God's glory, and what God wills for reality. Goodness, for the sake of goodness, is not really what's on God's mind, so to speak.

An example of this is in the 1646 Westminster Confession, a document many Presbyterian churches must avow. It reads: "God, the great Creator of all things, doth uphold, direct, dispose, and govern all creatures, actions, and things, from the greatest even to the least, by his most wise and holy providence, according to his infallible foreknowledge, and the free and immutable counsel of his own will, to the praise of the glory of his wisdom, power, justice, goodness, and

---

7   In much of Christian philosophy, there is agreement that God is only able to do that which is logical. In this sense, God can do all that which is logically possible but unable to accomplish that which is impossible. Two examples will suffice: God cannot make a married bachelor, and God cannot make a square circle. I flesh this out a bit more in chapter 2.

8   Walter Wink et al., *Spiritual Warfare: Four Views*, ed. James K. Beilby and Paul Rhodes Eddy (Grand Rapids, MI: Baker Academic, 2012), 22-23.

mercy."[9] This view sees God as a God who controls all things, as the cause and author of both good and evil. Every little thing from the falling of a feather, the birth of a newborn baby, the kindness of a stranger, to the Holocaust is caused and willed by God. From this perspective there is nothing, and I mean nothing, that does not come ultimately from the hand of God.

Yet if God causes all things, both good and evil, it becomes hard—if not impossible—to distinguish between the two. If I kidnap my neighbor's baby and dash its head against the rocks of the nearby river and then go feed our local houseless population, who's to say which action overrides. One is evil and the other good. Since both events are caused and willed by God, this completely blurs our common definitions of "good" and thus implicitly rejects such goodness. What I want you to see here is that one solution to the problem of evil is to deny that God is all good, either explicitly or implicitly, as many of our neo-Calvinists brothers and sisters do.

The third response to the problem of evil *is to deny that God is all powerful.* Again, this depends on how one defines "all powerful." But if one just simply denies omnipotence, one may get around the problem of evil. The logic is such that if God is not all-powerful, even if all-loving, He cannot prevent genuine evil, pain, and suffering in the world and is therefore not morally culpable for either causing it or allowing what he could have otherwise prevented. However, if you choose to go this route, you deny what most Christians have avowed throughout history and are left with a pretty weak god. If I was a betting man, I'd place a fairly large bet that I'll have the same accusation leveled against me, but we'll get to why that's not accurate in a moment.

The problem with each of these "answers," at least for someone that finds themselves in the stream of historic Orthodox Christianity, is that it denies the God revealed in Christ and witnessed too by the

---

9   G. I. Williamson, *The Westminster Confession of Faith for Study Classes* (Phillipsburg, NJ: Presbyterian and Reformed Publishing CO., 1964), Pg. 46.

ancient church. The God in *traditional Christianity*[10] is both all-powerful and all-good. However, these need not be rivals as they are in our modern renditions of the problem of evil. There's another option. In his book, *God Can't*, Thomas Jay Oord says the following regarding these options.

> "[Many] think we must choose between a God who controls and a God who can't do anything ... There's a third option. The God of Uncontrolling love is the most powerful and loving person in the universe! I use the biblical word "almighty" to describe this God's power. By this, I don't mean God has all the power. And by "almighty," I don't mean God can coerce ... God is almighty as 1) the source of might for all creation (all-mighty), 2) the one who exerts mighty influence upon everyone and everything (all-mighty), and 3) the one mightier than all others (all-mighty). This might is all-ways expressed as Uncontrolling love. In other words, our loving God is almighty without being able to control. Like a good parent with an appropriate amount of influence, an Uncontrolling God is neither feeble nor oppressive, neither inept nor domineering, neither anemic nor manipulative. God's love is supremely active and powerful! God heals, protects, redeems, saves, empowers, inspires, calls, creates, guides, sanctifies, persuades, transforms, and more—in loving relationship with creation. God does those activities without controlling others."[11]

Besides Oord's amiable definition, I would add that God can do all things which accord with God's nature. In other words, God can only act as God. All-powerful means that God can do all things that are within God's nature, and that God is not limited from being fully God. Yet, if it's not in God's nature, God cannot do it—for a perfect God need not do anything that falls outside God's perfection. Indeed,

---

10 What I am calling traditional or historic Orthodox Christianity is a religion that more or less has historically affirmed the creeds (Apostles, Nicene and so forth), specifically the four doctrines of the *Trinity*, the *full humanity* and *full deity of Jesus*, his *bodily resurrection*, and *virgin birth*.

11 Thomas Jay Oord, *God Can't: How to Believe in God and Love after Tragedy, Abuse, or Other Evils* (Grasmere, ID: SacraSage Press, 2019), 182-183.

for God to have the ability to act outside of God's perfect being would be a blemish on God's perfection.

Goodness, wisdom, and love are not mere attributes of the Creator, rather the Creator is goodness and love itself—it is God's very essence and being. God cannot be the author of evil, for no evil exists in God. For God to take part in evil would mean God is ceasing to be God, which God cannot do. From this definition, to truly deny that God is all-powerful would be to state *that God cannot act as God*. Through understanding "all-powerful" this way, we see that perhaps the Augustinian-Calvinist so-called affirmation of God's omnipotence, as discussed above, is actually a denial that God is all-powerful for it says God can act unlike God.

If there are things that exist outside of God's nature, and God can only act according to God's nature, then there are some things God cannot do. For example, if God is all good and evil outside of God's nature, then, God cannot do what is evil. If we further say that it is evil to control or be coercive, then God cannot control or coerce. We then can say that God cannot control creatures that commit evil. And therefore, God is all-powerful and all-good while not being culpable for preventing evil. All that is to say there are more nuanced ways to answer the problem of evil.

Now that we have laid out the basic options in addressing the problem of evil, we can briefly discuss why this is problematic for popular notions of inspiration. The prevailing views of biblical inspiration equate authorship and inspiration. This view presupposes and is based upon a definition of God's power as being literally able to do anything and everything, as well as control. Those who hold this view of inspiration generally agree on the way "all-powerful" and "all-good" gets defined. But they reject one of the primary responses to evil, turning away from God, by affirming His existence. The Church needs a doctrine of inspiration that does not suffer from the problem of evil.

For a theology of inspiration that accepts God's ability to control—actually requires a controlling God—also grants that either God is the author of evil in the world or could control evil but chooses not to and is therefore culpable for tragedies such as the Holocaust, rape, police brutality, child abuse, economic poverty, and so forth.

Said another way, the same theology behind popular notions of inspiration is the same underlying problematic theology that cannot stand up to the problem of evil. According to this theology, God controls the biblical authors in order to ensure that what they write is God's own Word. Otherwise, how could it be God's Word without some level of control? But if God can control creatures, why does God not prevent tremendous evils?

While no theology may adequately solve the problem of evil, some are more helpful than others. The finitude of humanity means we can never fully answer these questions with certainty. However, essential kenosis seems to be our best answer yet to the problem of evil. Theologies of inspiration that require a controlling God thus are inadequate for dealing with the problem of evil and thus cannot remain adequate as doctrines of inspiration.

2. INERRANCY

Despite concerns from fundamentalists[12] that there is an erosion of *inerrancy*[13] in American culture, there seem to be various strongholds in the country. In the "Bible Belt," where I currently live, the belief that scripture is without error feels like the reigning doctrine. Those who deny inerrancy appear to be in the minority. While there seems to be a movement away from inerrancy, the sentiment of many

---

12 A further definition of what a fundamentalist is would probably be helpful. There are five main pillars of fundamentalism: the inerrancy of the Bible, penal substitutionary atonement, the virgin birth of Jesus, the bodily resurrection of Jesus, and the historical accuracy of the miracles performed by Jesus. The last three of these pillars are held by all historic Orthodox Christians, and therefore these beliefs do not make fundamentalism distinct as a tradition. Neither does the second pillar, since penal substitutionary atonement is historically a broadly Protestant doctrine. Therefore, in my view, the one doctrine that is new to the fundamentalist movement, and therefore that distinguishes them as a distinct tradition is a belief in scripture's inerrancy. I would therefore define someone as a fundamentalist as someone that subscribes to inerrancy.

13 I will define this in greater detail in just a bit but suffice it to say that inerrancy is the belief that the Bible is God's Word and therefore is without any errors.

fundamentalists seems to be exaggerated, at least in certain regions of the country. From the perspective of someone that doesn't affirm this doctrine and is currently working on this book in a coffee shop five minutes down the road from a Word of Faith, fundamentalist mega-church and Oral Roberts University, while sitting a few chairs down from a man who works for Trinity Broadcasting Network, it does not feel that inerrancy is losing ground.[14] Rather, it feels as if I'm drowning in the Pacific Ocean of inerrancy!

Whether the doctrine of inerrancy is being eroded away as fast as its proponents seem to think it is, there still remains the necessity of addressing the doctrine and the inherent problems wedded to its DNA. So, what is the doctrine of inerrancy? While there is a spectrum of interpretations regarding how this doctrine gets defined, the most common definition follows: Because the Bible is the Word of God—ultimately authored by the Holy Spirit (where the fundamentalist term "inspired" originates)—and there is no error or falsehood in God, there is accordingly no error or falsehood in God's Word.

I think it's important to note that this logic is sound. If the Bible is the Word of God in any genuine sense—that is, if God is actually somehow its ultimate author, and God is perfect and does not lie—then the Bible is inerrant. If the humans who wrote and recorded the Bible were merely vessels that recorded exactly what the Holy Spirit wanted them to, then there should be no errors in the Bible. The problem I think isn't in the formula but in the underlying presupposition that the Bible is the Word of God. It is true that God is perfect and that God's Word is perfect, but the Divine Word is always Jesus, the second person of the Trinity. (We'll come back to this later.)

Inerrancy and its presupposition that the Bible is the Word of God get fleshed-out in various degrees by different people and different institutions. To the original fundamentalists, as laid out in the second volume of *The Fundamentals*, a collection of essays written by several prominent fundamentalists published in 1917, the Bible is inspired. This, of course, is not really debated among the different

---

14 Not that TBN and the Word of Faith (prosperity gospel) movement is representative of all of fundamentalism, they certainly fall within that tradition.

branches of Christianity. What is disputed is the *definition* of inspiration. Specifically, fundamentalists believe the Bible to be "verbally inspired."[15] As stated by Evangelist L.W. Munhall, "The doctrine of verbal inspiration is simply this: The original writings came through the penmen direct from God."[16] Hence, this is why they believe it to be the Word of God.

The logic is as such: All scripture is inspired, or more literally, God-breathed. The Greek word for scripture is *graphe*, meaning writings. Since it means writings that are composed of words, it follows that Paul is speaking of verbal inspiration, or so the thinking goes. As understood by the fundamentalist, God himself is a witness to this verbal inspiration of scripture, and this view of inspiration has been the view for all of Christian history. As another facet of inspiration, they believe that God gave the very words to the authors in a particular time in history, and thus the biblical text is also historical. Since the text was given in a historical context, it must be interpreted historically. In this way, the concepts of verbal inspiration, inerrancy, and a literal historical interpretation are all intertwined.

We should note that there is a tension within the fundamentalist's thinking on the matter of authorship. While on the one hand, they affirm it involved human authors. On the other hand, they seem to minimize—if not completely obliterate—the human side of things. As Reverend James M. Gray wrote, "In the scriptures we are dealing not so much with different human authors as with one Divine Author."[17] It would be unfair to suggest that fundamentalists themselves completely deny any sort of human involvement in the writing of scripture, yet the tension remains with little explanation.

---

15   R. A. Torrey et al., eds., *The Fundamentals: A Testimony to the Truth*, vol. 2 (Grand Rapids, Michigan: Baker Book House, 1917), 45.

16   Ibid., 2:45.

17   Ibid., 2:35.

Although God uses them as "instruments"[18] and "uses their powers as He will to express His mind by them,"[19] Gray later claims "the freedom of the human writers."[20] But what Gray gives with one hand, he takes back with the other by stating the authors' minds are "controlled [by the] Holy Spirit."[21] There is clearly a desire to save the dignity of the writers from becoming "mere machines."[22] Whether they have accomplished the goal of said desire is another matter entirely.

As we will see, lest any room be left for error, during the receiving of the Word by human beings, God remains all-controlling. In the case of *Balaam*[23], he is "compelled to speak against his will."[24] Considering all this, God is therefore the Bible's author—and since God cannot lie—it is without error. We should note that inspiration, however, is not a doctrine extended to cover manuscripts and translations of the Bible but only the *original autographs*[25]. *However, if inerrancy is only extended to the original autographs, since we do not have them, it leaves us with the conclusion that we do not have an inerrant Bible.* This is something that seems to escape most inerrantists.

Said another way, since we have none of the so-called inerrant autographs, we don't have an inerrant bible because they're lost to

18   Torrey et al., *Fundamentals*, 2:45.

19   Ibid.

20   Ibid.

21   Ibid.

22   Ibid.

23   Balaam is the gentile prophet that was hired by the Moabites to curse the Israelites entering into the promised land of Israel and yet blessed them instead. His story starts in the biblical book of Numbers 22.

24   Torrey et al., *Fundamentals*, 2:25.

25   An original autograph is the actual piece of parchment or scroll that, say for example, the apostle Paul used to write his letter to the Corinthians. There are absolutely no original autographs that have survived to this day. All we have are copies of copies. That doesn't necessarily mean we don't have a good idea of what the original autographs actually said. Sometimes we do. There are scholars who devote their lives to the task of discerning what the original autographs said. This is what is called textual criticism.

the past, probably forever. One of the primary goals of such a doctrine of scripture is that if one believes the Word and submits to its requirements, "it will impart spiritual life and save the soul."[26] (This is something I think only Christ can do.) If one does not have a Bible that is the inerrant Word of God, then one cannot attain spiritual life and be saved. The stakes, therefore, seem high to have such a view of scripture. For as we don't have any original autographs, the logic would suggest we really don't have God's Word and therefore cannot be saved.

Some would claim a complete inerrancy that assumes the Bible is both a scientific and historical piece of literature, and therefore when it speaks on all matters—whether historical, scientific, or theological—it cannot be in error. This view, which seems to be the view of the original fundamentalists, is tied to a literal, historical interpretation of the text. Although many fundamentalists today are more likely to seriously take genre into account.[27] From this perspective, Genesis 1 should be considered historically accurate and scientifically sound, and therefore not only proclaims that the Earth was created in six days but also does so inerrantly, prompting us to accept this at face value, thereby rejecting biological evolution. (We should note that it wasn't until the Scopes Monkey Trial that evolution was viewed as a major issue for fundamentalists.)

The former is probably one of the most popular renditions of inerrancy; however it is the least sophisticated version. A much more nuanced variety will also claim that the Bible does not err in historical, scientific, and theological claims. Yet it adds the important caveat that we cannot impose our modern scientific and historical models on the ancient genres that make up scripture. In this model, Genesis 1 is not addressing modern scientific schemes of the origin of species or

26 Torrey et al., *Fundamentals*, 2:57.

27 John Walton, an Old Testament scholar at Wheaton Seminary, as well as Craig Keener, a New Testament scholar at Asbury Theological Seminary, are two examples of Christians whom I would identify as fundamentalists since they affirm inerrancy and yet take genre much more seriously than many other fundamentalists.

the universe but is speaking to an *ancient Near Eastern*[28] audience in their own ancient cosmological genres.

Therefore, it is not in error because it doesn't speak to the question of the origin of species. From this perspective, biological evolution and a fourteen billion-year-old universe are not in tension with the biblical narrative because the Bible is speaking to concerns and questions that would have applied to its audience, not ours. Expecting otherwise would be like reading a romance novel and anticipating the kind of action found in an adventure novel or watching a drama and expecting it to be a comedy. As John Walton likes to say, and I'm paraphrasing, the Bible was not written to us, but it was written for us. In other words, we can't expect it to speak to our genres. We need to read the biblical texts in their own ancient Near Eastern context and genres.

The next major rendition of inerrancy is sometimes called limited inerrancy. (Some would call this infallibility; I however would not since, in my mind, infallibility has less to do with whether a particular issue in scripture is true or untrue and more to do with the idea that scripture will not fail to accomplish its goal.[29]) It also assumes taking the biblical account in its own ancient terms according to its own genres, while going a step further by admitting that the biblical text can have errors regarding historical or scientific issues—though

---

28 Essentially the ancient Near East is what we would today typically call the Middle East.

29 However, even if one agrees on this, we still have a number of questions regarding the concept of infallibility. While many who would affirm infallibility would say the goal of scripture is God's goal, this in my mind often presupposes that God placed that goal into the biblical text itself since he is assumed to be its ultimate author. I, however, reject God's authorship of scripture as we will see throughout this book. So, whose goal is it? I do think we can say it's God's goal, but then we must address where and how that goal is placed. If God is not the author, then maybe the goal is placed upon the text from outside by God after its human production rather than into the text itself through God's writing. In other words, the goal is placed into its interpretation of the text rather than into the writing itself. That is to say the scripture is infallible and will accomplish its goal—which is to witness to Christ—when it is read through Christocentric hermeneutics. If it is not read Christocentrically, then it's not being read as Christian scripture, therefore has no goal that must be accomplished; in this sense, it becomes fallible. It is therefore only infallible when read Christocentrically.

always speaking truth without error when communicating theological and doctrinal subjects. All of these renditions of inerrancy share the assumption that inspiration and authorship are synonymous. According to these schemes, God is in some way the ultimate author of scripture.

Now that we've discussed what inerrancy is, we can glimpse some of its inherent problems. The first one is that the doctrine of inerrancy is a theology that implicitly, if not explicitly, condones and may even celebrate violence. It is no coincidence that some of the strongest supporters of violence are adherents to the doctrine of inerrancy. If the Bible is the very inerrant Word of God, then it follows that genocide is at times a good thing in the eyes of God. Since the Bible seems to teach that God in times past has commanded genocide and various other types of violence.[30] When this is paired with the historical teaching that God does not change,[31] it means that what was considered good for God to do at one time is considered good for all times.

Said another way, since God has seen fit to command genocide and violence in the past, it must also be a good thing today and tomorrow. God does not change and thus what is moral or immoral does not change. This does not mean that God *will command genocide*, only that it is always morally acceptable in the eyes of God. Therefore, an inerrant view of the Bible condones genocide. This is the kind of logic that could—and indeed would—support the claim that Hitler was only carrying out the work he was commanded to do by the God who doesn't change, and having commanded genocide in the past, has sought fit to command it today in the modern world. I personally do not know any adherents to inerrancy that would make such a claim, but the logic is there.

The doctrine of inerrancy paired with a historically literal interpretative method is thus one of the most dangerous and utterly un-Christ-like threats to the world and church today. Let me be clear

---

30 See the book of Judges in the Bible.

31 The term for this is the immutability of God. This is something the church has historically affirmed: God does not change. I happen to agree with this doctrine. I just believe that God is uncontrolling Love and Goodness and will never depart from being such.

in stating that if your theology—and the implications of your theology—don't line up with the ways of Jesus, then it cannot, in fact, be a Christian doctrine. For, by definition, in order for something to be "Christian," it must be Christocentric. That is, it must line up with who Jesus is and what he himself taught.

The very method to determine whether a doctrine is Christian is to ask if it places Jesus in the center. Or as Barth put it, "I had to learn that Christian doctrine, if it is to merit its name, and if it is to build up the Christian church in the world as it needs to be built up, has to be exclusively and consistently the doctrine of Jesus Christ. Jesus Christ is the living Word of God spoken to us men."[32] Our theology, in order to merit the name "Christian" must be founded and centered on Christ alone. To the extent it deviates from Jesus, it deviates from being an acceptable Christian doctrine.

If Jesus taught non-violence[33](I believe this is pretty impossible to argue against, and the only reason to oppose this stance would be to uphold the theological unity of scripture, thus its inerrancy), then any theology, such as inerrancy, that allows for genocide as a moral good is not a "Christian" doctrine. Only if we see Jesus and scripture as equal, do we need to reconcile the two: the violence of the Old Testament and Jesus' non-violence. However, only God has equality with God—Jesus being God. This is where we encounter another way

---

[32] Mark Galli, *Karl Barth: An Introductory Biography for Evangelicals* (Grand Rapids, MI: Eerdmans Publishing Co., 2017), 109.

[33] Of course, I realize I'm making a huge claim for some, without actually substantiating it. If I'm honest, upon seeing someone else doing this, I would immediately call them out for it. So, you'll have to accept my apology. However, the point I want you to consider here: if you believe violence is consistent with the Christian faith, *why do you believe that it is acceptable for a follower of Jesus?* Is it because Jesus taught violence? Or is it largely because the Old Testament teaches violence? In order to uphold the idea that all scripture teaches the same thing—and is thus without error or contradiction—Jesus must therefore have taught the moral goodness of violence? If you held the possibility that scripture was not God's word—but Jesus is the Word of God—the contradictions of different teachings throughout scripture become non-problematic. If approaching it through this lens, would you actually see Jesus teaching violence? I could, of course, make the case of why the gospel passages that people use to justify violence actually don't teach violence, but I think this gets more to the heart of the issue.

in which inerrancy is problematic: the implication that scripture and God are equals.

Matthew Barrett, a Southern Baptist professor at Midwestern Baptist Theological Seminary, claims the equality of scripture to God in this way when he wrote, "It is clear that for Jesus, *God and Scripture can be spoken of synonymously*, demonstrating that Scripture *is* the very Word of God. We should not attempt to drive a wedge between the two."[34] (Emphasis mine.) He seems to say, whether consciously or not, that scripture and God are one. The conclusion we can draw from this is that scripture is equal to Christ because scripture is itself God—an utterly idolatrous conclusion. It therefore stands that the need to reconcile Jesus and scripture presupposes that scripture has such equality with God because scripture is God. Since there can be no contradictions or disunity in God, there must be none between God and scripture. Hence, when a fundamentalist says the Bible has spoken, it is the equivalent to saying that God has spoken. They are one and the same, so much so that to drive a wedge between them is to divide God.

Furthermore, inerrancy cannot be a Christian doctrine because it is not rooted in God.[35] Conversely, this doctrine [inerrancy] is actually rooted in the Bible. As it is God that we worship, not scripture, Christian doctrine must first of all be rooted in God. The doctrine of inspiration, for the fundamentalist, is intrinsically tied to the doctrine of inerrancy. One may argue that inerrancy is rooted in God, but without the certainty provided by their particular view of inspiration, the fundamentalist is left no basis for their doctrine of God.

Said another way, their belief in God is founded on whether scripture is the inerrant Word of God. Scripture, according to the original fundamentalists—just as we saw above from Matthew Barrett—is

---

34 Matthew Barrett, *God's Word Alone: The Authority of Scripture* (Grand Rapids, MI: Zondervan, 2016), 243-244.

35 As Christians, we have always affirmed that Christ is the second member of this triune God. In this way, I can say that Christian doctrine must be rooted in God and Christ since Christ is the second person of the triune God.

seen as being "a living organism equal with God,"[36] whose "witness of God Himself,"[37] is the "the foundation of our faith"[38] and is the ultimate authority, bedrock, and arbitrator of all doctrine. The doctrine of God then must come from scripture, and as a result, for all practical reasons, is secondary to scripture.

Although it is important to note from the fundamentalist's point of view, scripture's identification with God would not so much place the doctrine of God in a secondary position—rather, theoretically, it essentially places them on equal par; but as I've already shown, this would make scripture God. And since the Bible is clearly not God, such a doctrine in practice places God in a subjugated position to scripture.

The next trouble with rooting a doctrine about the Bible in the Bible is that it's circular reasoning. It would be like saying, "The Bible teaches me I should view the Bible in this way." There's no outside source to verify any such claims that it may or may not make. It's like when your mom asks you to clean your room, and when you ask why, she says, "Because I told you to." There's no external evidence to suggest that you should actually clean your room! Even Jesus in John 5 provides numerous outside sources to back up his own claims.

The following problem with this is that it places the Bible as the one and only ultimate authority,[39] which explicitly denies the authority of God. It does no good for the adherent to claim that this is not so due to the Bible being God's Word, for this returns to circular reasoning. One may simply ask: If God came to you right in this moment and contradicted some passage of scripture, whom or what would you believe? Would you believe God or the Bible? The inerrantist would

---

36 Torrey et al., *Fundamentals*, 2:50.

37 Torrey et al., *Fundamentals*, 2:46.

38 Ibid., 2:47.

39 We should also note that the Bible doesn't actually teach that the Bible has authority. Matthew 28:19, for instance, says that Jesus has all authority. Of course, God can mediate God's authority through the Bible or the Church but that's not the same thing as either of those actually having their own authority.

most likely claim "all experiences must be measured against the Word of God, i.e., the Bible; therefore, I know that the Bible is right and that God could not have spoken to me something that would contradict his Word." The inerrantist is inevitably left with one consistent conclusion concerning their doctrine: *The Bible decides who God is and what God says.* In subjecting God to the Bible, this leaves the doctrine utterly outside the bounds of what we can consider Christian.

For our purposes here, besides the issues already broached about inerrancy (inevitably, we are left to conclude that scripture is God, and yet God is subject to scripture, thereby denying the authority of God), there is one more glaring issue I want to quickly point out. According to inerrantists themselves, as we saw earlier, their doctrine of verbal inspiration and its entailment of inerrancy require God to be at some level controlling and coercive, which of course has huge implications.

One of those issues, as we saw from our section on the problem of evil, is if God can control human minds in order to produce God's inerrant Word, then why does God not control humans that commit evil actions (such as Hitler's systematic annihilation of the Jews) in order to prevent said evil acts? In addition, the idea of God taking over the biblical writer's mind to use as an instrument or pen seems more akin to demonic possession, as I'll discuss later. This control, presupposed in the process of verbal inspiration, also produces the scriptures as God's Word. As we just discussed, and will elaborate more later, this would make scripture equal to God—and therefore God—since only God is God's equal. Considering all of this, the doctrine of inerrancy seems to be outside the limits of acceptable orthodoxy.

3. APPARENT ATTRIBUTIONS OF SCRIPTURE

One of the foundational proposals of *historical criticism*[40] is that the Torah was written by multiple scribes who lived hundreds of years

---

40 Historical criticism is a modern, historical way of studying the Bible. Historical criticism explores the origins of ancient texts in order to better understand them in their own historical and social contexts.

after the time Moses himself would have lived. Out of the many critiques of modern biblical scholarship[41] produced by the fundamentalists was their argument against the *documentary hypothesis*[42] found in the *Fundamentals: A Testimony to the Truth.*

The gist of the argument is as such: Moses is the attributed author of the Torah. Therefore, if these supposed non-mosaic authors actually wrote the Torah while attributing its authorship to Moses, they would be lying about who wrote the first five books of the Bible. There are inherent problems in this argument which I will address shortly. What I want to highlight at the moment is that this same criticism could be leveled against their assertion that scripture is written by God. *This is because the scriptures seem to attribute authorship to humans. According to their own logic, if God really wrote it, God would be guilty of lying.*

Paul claims sole ownership of his words when he specifies in 1 Corinthians 7:12, "To the rest *I say-I and not the Lord…*" Paul's claiming of authorship and attribution for this text has been observed by more brilliant minds than mine. C. S. Lewis (twentieth century) and Origen (2nd-3rd centuries) both observed this. In his letter to Lee Turner, Lewis wrote:

> "Our ancestors, I take it, believed that the Holy Spirit either just replaced the minds of the authors (like the supposed 'control' in automatic writing) or at least dictated to them as to secretaries. Scripture itself refutes these ideas. St. Paul distinguishes between what 'the Lord' says and what he says 'of himself'-yet both are 'Scripture.' Similarly the passages in which the prophets describe Theophonies and their own reactions to them would be absurd if they were not writing for themselves."[43] (Emphasis mine.)

---

[41] I am using the term "modern biblical scholarship" as another way of saying historical criticism.

[42] The documentary hypothesis is what biblical scholars call the theory that the Torah was not written by Moses but instead consisted of multiple sources, scribes, editors, and compilers.

[43] C. S. Lewis, *The C.S. Lewis Bible: New Revised Standard Version* (New York, NY: HarperCollins, 2010), 1247.

Seventeen centuries earlier, Origen made the same comment,

"The things which are spoken through a prophet are not always to be taken as spoken by God. And even though through Moses God spoke many things, nevertheless Moses commanded other things by his own authority [the bill of divorce is given as an example]. ... And Paul also shows things in his letters, when he says concerning some things: 'The Lord says and not I,' and concerning others, 'These things moreover I say, not the Lord' (1Cor. 7) (Kalin, "Argument from Inspiration," 103-4)."[44]

For both Lewis and Origen, Paul's statement is a clear indicator that, at least sometimes, Paul attributes his own authorship to his letters. Indeed, for both these theologians and biblical commentators, the prophets were plainly writing for themselves. It's also clear from Origen's quote that there are other clear instances in which a prophet is speaking for themselves. His example of Moses giving the certificate of divorce is poignant since Jesus had made this point long before.

Looking at the 1 Corinthians text, we might take the preceding verses of 10-11 to be Paul's claim that this particular command *is God writing through him.* Yet when analyzed, not only can we see that it's still Paul writing for himself but also that he's not claiming anything to the contrary. In verse 10-11 Paul writes, "To the married I give this command-not I but the Lord-that the wife should not separate from her husband (but if she does separate, let her remain unmarried or else be reconciled to her husband), and the husband should not divorce his wife."[45] In writing, "not I but the Lord," it might appear at first glance as if Paul is claiming God's authorship. Yet, as we will see below, he's not claiming verbal inspiration at this moment or even that God is using him as a personal pen or secretary even.

What he is saying is that he is passing on a command that Jesus, the Lord, spoke during his earthly ministry. In Luke 16:18, Jesus said,

---

44   Craig D. Allert, *A High View of Scripture? The Authority of the Bible and the Formation of the New Testament Canon* (Grand Rapids, MI: Baker Academic, 2007), 183.

45   Lewis, *C.S. Lewis Bible.*

"Anyone who divorces his wife and marries another commits adultery, and whoever marries a woman divorced from her husband commits adultery."[46] And in Matthew 19:9 "Whoever divorces his wife, except for unchastity, and marries another commits adultery."[47] So, Paul isn't claiming here that he's writing God's Word as a secretary. Nor is he claiming that God is writing God's Word through him [Paul] as a controlled instrument. Rather, Paul is pulling from the same oral tradition of the story of Jesus that all Christians including the gospel writers had access to.

Said another way, Paul was aware of what Jesus had taught orally during his ministry, and he is pointing this fact out. Paul is not conveying his own teaching on marriage, but Jesus' teaching. It would be like if my priest, Father Everett, had taught our church that they really shouldn't eat their own boogers, and I am speaking to a group of friends who are also aware of that message. Thus, I would explain that they should listen to this wise teaching—not because I taught it but because Everett taught it—since he's obviously a reputable authority in these sorts of things.

The author of 2 Peter 3:15-16 also seems to attribute the authorship of Paul's letters to Paul himself.[48] "So also our beloved brother *Paul wrote* to you according to the wisdom given him, speaking of this as he does in all his letters." (Emphasis mine.) While the author of 2 Peter claims Paul was aided, there is no sign he thinks someone else was writing alongside him or even controlling his mental faculties. Paul is presented here as the sole author. Michael Lodahl writing about this passage says, "While I think we should assume this wisdom to be divine wisdom, it is clearly also the case that a very human Paul

---

46   Ibid.

47   Ibid.

48   The majority or mainstream view in New Testament scholarship is that 2 Peter was not written by Peter the apostle but was probably written by someone else writing in his name around 125 C.E.

wrote the letters."[49] So while Paul is writing for himself, he does so according to wisdom. But what exactly does that mean?

Lodahl points out that the "wisdom given to him" is "Christ crucified ... the power of God and the wisdom of God" (1 Cor 1:23, 24) or, as it says in verse 30, that God "is the source of your life in Christ Jesus who became for us wisdom from God." So wisdom, at least as Paul understood it, is both the gospel message and Jesus the one who is the embodiment of that message. If the author of 2 Peter also shares this understanding of wisdom, then he is not claiming that God is writing through Paul but that Paul was writing according to the gospel message—that is according to Christ crucified, the wisdom that was given to him.

As an example of this, we could say of my writing that "Gabe wrote his book according to his years under the tutelage of Bobo the Clown." This statement is not saying that Bobo the Clown directly helped me write my book only that it was through my years of learning under Bobo, and according to all his clown principles, that I wrote my book. Disregarding my terrible clown analogies, it's clear that whoever wrote 2 Peter attributed the authorship of Paul's letters to Paul himself rather than co-authored by Paul and God.

We also read about Jesus attributing human authorship to at least some of scripture. In the text mentioned earlier, Jesus even attributes the laws about divorce to Moses, not God.

> "Some Pharisees came to him, and to test him they asked, 'Is it lawful for a man to divorce his wife for any cause?' He answered, 'Have you not read that the one who made them at the beginning 'made them male and female,' and said, 'For this reason a man shall leave his father and mother and be joined to his wife, and the two shall become one flesh'?[50] So they are no longer two, but one flesh.

---

49 Richard P. Thompson and Thomas Jay Oord, *Rethinking the Bible: Inerrancy, Preaching, Inspiration, Authority, Formation, Archaeology, Postmodernism, and More* (Nampa, ID: SacraSage Press, 2018), 79.

50 While some would assume that verse 5 is an affirmation on Jesus' part that scripture is the Word of God, I think that's a shallow reading of that text. Even if we grant that Jesus believed in a historical Adam and Eve, a literal six-day creation and so forth and

Therefore, what God has joined together, let no one separate.' They said to him, *'Why then did Moses command* us to give a certificate of dismissal and to divorce her?' He said to them, 'It was because you were so hard-hearted *that Moses allowed* you to divorce your wives, but from the beginning it was not so'"[51] (Emphasis mine.) (Matthew 19:3-8).

In this text, we observe that Jesus attributes the divorce law to Moses rather than to God.[52] Even the Pharisees attribute these divorce laws to Moses when they said that Moses taught us. However, if one goes back to Deuteronomy 24:1-4, these commands are being presented as ultimately coming from Yahweh. One might think Deuteronomy 24:14 contradicts my claim that scripture attributes its authorship to human sources rather than God. However, even if this were the case that this scripture was presenting God as the author of these texts, for my claim to hold true, the scriptures need not wholly attribute scripture's authorship to humans. If there's even one place where there's a

was thus assuming the historicity of this account in Genesis that he was referencing, which I am not necessarily convinced of, it does not mean that his reference in verse 5 to "and said" is in and of itself a statement that the text is the Word of God. Even if God spoke those two words "and said," the author who recorded them into the Genesis account would be the ultimate author of those words, since nothing is without interpretation. Unless we assume the author was being controlled by God and that God through the author recorded his own words that he spoke in the beginning, "and said," (some couple of thousands of years before) and that this author of Genesis was now being controlled and used by God to record this previously spoken set of words; these recorded words in Genesis, "For this reason a man shall leave his father and mother and be joined to his wife, and the two shall become one flesh" would not be that of God's Words but would be the interpreted version of those words by the author of Genesis 1-2. Whatever our conclusion regarding this, Jesus clearly attributes the Torah's divorce laws to Moses rather than God, which is problematic for those who think Jesus believes the Bible was the Word of God.

51 Lewis, *C.S. Lewis Bible.*

52 I suppose the argument could be made that Jesus meant God when he stated that Moses gave those laws, which is to say it was through Moses that God gave these commands concerning divorce. However, in light of Jesus' use of scripture in other places and his blatant contradictions of certain passages from the Torah, I think that unlikely. For evidence argued to substantiate that Jesus contradicted parts of the Torah see section 5 of this chapter and chapter 4.

clear attribution of the scripture's composition to human authorship and God is actually the author, then God seems to be lying.

So, this same critique of historical criticism by the fundamentalists, as I have shown, can also be made of their view that God is the ultimate author. In addition, I also want to show another underlying issue. The same basic thinking underpinning the critique of the documentary hypothesis is also held by non-fundamentalists and non-Christians. They consider the Torah's attribution of its authorship to Moses as religious fraud. However as Sommer points out, this logic fundamentally "misunderstands the nature of authorship and *pseudepigraphy*[53] in the ancient world."[54] This is poignant for all who share this thinking, fundamentalists or not.

This is an inherently modern way of conceptualizing authorship. In fact, the reason both fundamentalists Christians and many non-Christians understand such attribution of authorship as a lie is because they are superimposing our modern Western conceptions of authorship onto the ancient biblical texts. Today modern Westerners see originality as the highest good and therefore strive to create their own unique voice as distinct from their predecessors. As a result, we tend to see pseudepigraphy as the author's intention to be untruthful. But, in its own historical and cultural context, they understood it as an act of humility,[55] whereas we try to minimize the indebtedness we have to our predecessors.

In contrast, authors from the medieval and ancient world viewed their own compositions as valuable only if they stood on the shoulders of those who preceded them. As modern people in the West, we are enculturated as hyper-individualists and thus value the gifts of the individual. But ancient people found value in being part of the collective communal tradition. Something we could certainly learn from.

---

53   This is the attribution of authorship by an author to someone who isn't the true author of a work.

54   Benjamin D. Sommer, *Revelation and Authority: Sinai in Jewish Scripture and Tradition* (New Haven and London: Yale University Press, 2015), 139.

55   This is why the author of 2 Timothy, for instance, isn't lying when he or she attributed the letter to Paul's authorship.

These literary composers understood sincerely that any of their writings that were worth merit were built off of insights they had mined from those who went before them. Their cultural notion was based on and seen as a posture of humility. In this understanding, to take credit for a piece of writing would be a kind of theft—not acknowledging their indebtedness to those who had enabled them to come to their conclusions. From this perspective, it would be far more honest to attribute the writing to the experienced people who are responsible for any value that it may have.

Now, of course, many of the names of the older sages seen as predecessors and truly responsible for the work were unknown; in any case, being able to ascribe all the many names to one work would be quite impractical, therefore one such figure was sufficient for this purpose. In the world of ancient Israel—particularly in connection with their legal traditions—that figure was Moses.

While the scribes were not necessarily unaware that they had created a new law, or that it had departed from a previous older law, the ancients involved were convinced that the qualities of their new or revised law ultimately came from forebears greater than themselves to whom their origin was tied. This was their way of avoiding pride: by refusing to take credit and by acknowledging Moses as, in a deeper sense, the author of what was meritorious in the text. "To attribute a teaching to Moses, then, was to attribute it to a sage in the Mosaic tradition."[56] Judging this conception of authorship by modern standards will not only lead one to misunderstand it, but it is extremely *ethnocentric* and arrogant.[57]

The concept of what an author is today versus what it was in premodern times is radically different. For an ancient to say that God composed scripture is a claim said within the framework of an ancient understanding of authorship, not a modern, individualist one. When

---

56 Sommer, *Revelation and Authority*, 140.

57 I am deeply indebted to Benjamin Sommer for this last section on authorship and pseudepigraphy in the ancient near east. It was through his book that I learned about this. (Sommer, *Revelation and Authority*.) Ethnocentric means to place one's own ethnic group and culture as inherently superior to others.

we make claims of God's composition of scripture, we do so from a present day standpoint, reflecting our understanding of authorship. To say that God, as an individual, wrote scripture is probably not what the ancients had in mind when they claimed God's composition.

4. THE GENERALITY OF INSPIRATION

We find a further complication for popular notions of inspiration in how the *church fathers*[58] understood the concept and its extent. This is important since popular notions of inspiration only account for how God speaks to us through the Bible. A sufficient account of inspiration will also provide room for God to speak to all of creation. For a God who only speaks through the Bible is a God whose voice is unheard in most of creation. Therefore, any notion of inspiration that cannot account for how all of creation (anything outside of God) receives God's communication is inadequate. The church fathers, as we will see, have much broader categories concerning what can be inspired by God, contrary to popular notions of inspiration, which view the Bible as revelation and inspiration as authorship. This narrow view does not account for the extent to which the concept of inspiration was applied by the church fathers. Modern accounts of inspiration are largely ignorant of the church fathers in general, let alone in how they conceived of inspiration. The broad ways in which the church fathers understood inspiration would seem to indicate that it was seen as something more akin to influence by God rather than coercive authorship. It would make little sense to call some of the things they called inspired, if by inspiration they meant authorship.[59] While this might not have been explicitly stated by the church fathers, it seems to be the logical outcome of their thinking.

The extensiveness of which the church fathers apply the concept of inspiration is problematic for popular notions of inspiration

---

58 Depending on whom you are asking, the term church fathers is referring to Christians that lived either from the second to the fourth centuries or the second to the eighth centuries. It is more or less interchangeable with the term "patristic."

59 At least modern authorship

because its proponents equate it with authorship. If inspiration and authorship are really the same thing, then granting the church fathers believed this, they also believed there were many other things outside of scripture which were authored by God—and therefore the Word of God. If one *does not* equate authorship and inspiration, the broad use of the concept of God-breathed by the ancient church is unproblematic. However, if the church fathers *did not equate inspiration with authorship*, their broad use of the concept is troublesome for popular notions of inspiration, which see inspiration and authorship as synonymous, since it would show a discontinuity between modern renditions of inspiration and the way it was understood in the early church.[60]

Unless we want to completely discredit the church fathers in what they have to say about the scriptures, this problem will not go away. To my way of thinking to disparage the *patristic*[61] Christians would be devastating, as it would be the equivalent to a tree ripping out its own root system. Much of the foundational elements of Christianity—given by Christ to his first followers who faithfully continued the movement throughout the first century—were developed, fleshed-out, and held fast by the patristic era Christians. While Christ is our foundation, they were the skeleton, and even the walls, of the house built on that foundation. Without those beams and that plaster, those inside would be without adequate shelter—subjected to the elements—and would have died from exposure. We are forever indebted to the church fathers and would do well to seek their wisdom.

Among the items that the church fathers cited as inspired were several texts considered scripture at the time: writings from philosophers such as Plato along with texts from various authors claiming

---

60   This is so because the church fathers, who were closer in proximity to the very first Christians in the first century, are likely to have views less developed and more like the first Christians than say Christians from the last 150 or so years. This is not necessarily so, but it does make it more likely.

61   Depending on whom you are asking, the term patristic is referring to Christians that lived either from the second to the fourth centuries or the second to the eighth centuries. It is more or less interchangeable with the phrase "church fathers."

themselves to be inspired such as Clement of Rome, members of ecumenical councils, bishops and so forth. (This refers to texts found outside our current list of twenty-seven New Testament books and those outside the Protestant canon of the Old Testament, but found within the Catholic and Orthodox Old Testament lists.)

From the following sample it is clear the ancient church did not limit inspiration to the books we consider canon.[62] For most of these examples, I am indebted to Craig D. Allert from whom I first learned of them.[63]

THE PATRISTICS AND INSPIRATION

I cite examples from oldest to newest.

Clement of Rome (Lived 35-97,101 AD)

From his letter 1 Clement (96 AD)
Early on in his letter (47.3) Clement states, "How truly the things he [Paul] said about himself and Cephas and Apollos were inspired by the Spirit!"[64] Then later (63.2) goes on to say *that he himself wrote the letter through the Holy Spirit:* "So you will afford us great joy and happiness if you will lay to heart what *we have written through the Holy Spirit.*"[65] Another translation says it this way, "Yes, you will make us exceedingly happy if you prove obedient *to what we, prompted by the Holy Spirit, have written.*"[66] (Emphasis mine.)

---

62 Although to speak of a biblical canon is a bit of a misnomer, since in reality there has never been an ecumenical council that declared a canon officially closed. We talk about a closed canon, but in reality, it has never been closed.

63 Allert, *High View of Scripture*, 185-188.

64 Andrew Louth, ed., *Early Christian Writings: The Apostolic Fathers*, trans. Maxwell Staniforth (London, England: Penguin Books, 1968), 42.

65 Ibid., 49.

66 Cyril C. Richardson et al., *Early Christian Fathers* (New York City, NY: Simon & Schuster, 1996), 73.

Here, we have Clement of Rome writing around the same time that the Gospel according to John was written, sometime in the 90s, claiming either he[67] wrote his letter to the Corinthian church "through the Holy Spirit" or that he was "prompted by the Holy Spirit" to write such a letter. The first translation seems a bit harder for me to account for. It could mean that—like the oracle at Delphi—he wrote in a sort of trance, being possessed by the Spirit. But since that kind of thinking was more pagan than Jewish, I find it a less likely option.

If we take the first translation as the more accurate one, and yet reject the possibility that they meant it in the sort of way pagans thought of inspiration, then we could see it in a more participatory fashion. That is to say Clement and the other senders of the letter were interacting with God through the Spirit and thus what they wrote was in agreement with what the Spirit willed. This need not imply God's authorship, and yet it possibly accounts for the first translation.

If, however, we receive the second translation as more in harmony with the intent of its author, this more readily aligns with a view of inspiration akin to a sort of influence. One can be prompted to write something and yet, from that prompting, freely write of one's own accord within one's own free mind. What is thus produced is one's own. However, either of these translations is problematic if one affirms that scripture alone is inspired, and there exists a closed canon of scripture. This would be less problematic for popular notions of inspiration if this was a solitary case of someone claiming writing (which was outside of scripture) as inspired, and the claimant was a fringe character. However, the truth is that Clement is far from the only one to claim inspiration of some sort for his writing outside of scripture, and he is far from being a fringe character. He was the bishop of Rome and is known for being an orthodox mainstream figure.

---

67 Technically, he says "we" not "he," implying a collective sender to the church at Corinth.

Clement of Alexandria (Lived 150-215 AD)

From his work Exhortation to the Heathen
6 (ANF 2:191): Clement of Alexandria states that some philosophers, Plato as an example, proclaim that the only true God is God, and these philosophers who have spoken "are recorded by God's Inspiration."[68]

Here we have what one might find quite odd: Clement of Alexandria, a teacher, claiming that at least some Greek philosophers spoke according to the inspiration of God. This assertion goes a step further than Clement of Rome had since he, as a visible Christian, only claims inspiration for his own Christian writing. However, Clement of Alexandria's statement isn't that far of a stretch because Plato and the other Greek philosophers lived before Christ's Incarnation, as all the prophets had lived before the sojourn of Christ.

Where it might seem like a stretch to us is the fact that he claims such inspiration for a pagan. In their own context, this was probably much less radical since many of them believed that the Son of God—the Word—had always been present among humans even before he took on flesh. Regardless of what Clement meant by inspiration in the previous quote, it is obviously a much broader expression of the concept than popular theories allow. Within *Exhortation to Heaven,* Clement pushes the boundaries even further. He writes (6.17 ANF 2:517), "Besides the thoughts of virtuous men are produced through inspiration of God."[69]

With this next quote from Clement, we see the category of inspiration expanded further to include even the thoughts of people with virtue! So not only does Clement of Alexandria state that pagan Greek philosophers were inspired by God, but that any thoughts of virtuous human beings are also produced through God's inspiration. This goes well beyond relegating of inspiration to the scriptures alone. With this in mind, would it make sense for Clement to believe inspiration and authorship are synonymous?

68 Allert, *High View of Scripture,* 185.

69 Ibid.,185.

Do we really think that he believed the thoughts of people with virtue or the writings of the Greek philosophers were the Word of God—that they were composed directly by God? Maybe, but given that the early church believed Jesus alone to be the Word of God, as we will see in the next section, I find that unlikely. The more feasible explanation is to presume Clement didn't see authorship and inspiration as identical.

Cyprian of Carthage (Lived 200-258 AD)

From his book Exhortation to Martyrdom
Preface 1 (ANF 5:496): Here Cyprian describes his writing as "instructed by the aid of divine inspiration."[70]

The wording of this seems less likely to imply authorship or control on the part of God. I think it's more likely that what's being described here is participatory in nature. In the sense that Cyprian is encountering the divine nature, reflecting on what he's learning from God, and writing from this experience of his own accord. In this sense, he is being aided by inspiration from God. However, we might interpret what he means here; he exemplifies the fact (as we have continually seen) that inspiration for the ancient church was not a notion restricted to what they considered scripture. If one's account of inspiration is limited to what is "canonical" scripture, then they must contend with the discontinuity between their view and that of the ancient church. If the early church's perspective on this has anything to say to us it's that our particular concept of inspiration as authorship doesn't fit into an inspiration that is as broad as the early church contended, and therefore maybe our notions of inspiration are also too narrow.

Gregory of Nyssa (Died in 385 AD)

In his work Apologia in Hexaemeron
PG 44:61-62: Gregory praises his brother Basil's commentary on Genesis 1 as an "inspired [*theopneuston*] exposition ... [admired] no

---

70   Ibid., 186.

less than the words composed by Moses himself."[71] Gregory goes so far to say, concerning his brother's analysis, that it might even exceed Moses' work on Genesis 1 in its intricacy, greatness, structure and beauty. Talk about high praise!

This passage from Gregory of Nyssa is particularly important since he uses the exact word that is found in 2 Timothy 3:16. What we should be noticing here is twofold: firstly, Gregory is drawing a comparison between his brother and Moses regarding *the same level* of inspiration in their writings on Genesis 1; secondly, the words of Genesis 1 are composed by Moses, not God. Said another way, inspiration here is not synonymous with God's authorship, and it's not limited to the scriptures.

Cyril of Scythopolis (6th AD)

From Vita Sabae
16: Here Cyril reports a group of anchorites accordingly: "By the grace of God his company reached seventy persons, all inspired (theopneustos), all Christ-bearers" (cited in Kalin, "Argument from Inspiration," 172).[72]

Last, we have Cyril of Scythopolis of the sixth century claiming that a group of seventy anchorites are all inspired. While it's possible that some of the other quotes we've examined could be interpreted as understanding inspiration as authorship, this last one certainly cannot. The phrasing of this sentence doesn't imply that what the people are writing in particular moments are inspired or even that specific decisions that they are making are inspired. It very broadly, as we have seen as the theme of all these passages, applies inspiration to these seventy persons in general.

Therefore, to say that Cyril could have had our conception of inspiration as authorship in mind here makes little sense. Are all these seventy persons thought to be authored by God? For many today, to claim that the Bible is inspired is to claim it as the Word of God. In

---

71   Ibid., 187-188.

72   Ibid., 186.

this passage, would it make sense for Cyril—had he that same conception of inspiration in mind—to call them the Word of God? I don't think so. It doesn't seem like Cyril is trying to claim that these seventy anchorites are the Word of God. It's almost absurd to think that he could mean this. So, inspiration for Cyril here must mean something else. Said another way, this kind of thinking is incompatible with Cyril's statement and therefore can't be the ideology supporting it.

5. GREG BOYD AND THE WORD OF GOD

Up to this point, we have discussed four discrepancies with popular notions of inspiration: the problem of evil, inerrancy, apparent attributions of scripture, and the generality of inspiration. Here, we turn our attention to the fifth issue found among popular notions of inspiration. Each of the previously examined problems are deeply related and connected to this issue—calling the Bible, the Word of God. We'll refer to the work of Greg Boyd to address this issue head on. In *Cross Vision: How the Crucifixion of Jesus Makes Sense of Old Testament Violence,* Boyd comments on violence in the Hebrew Bible, or in his own words, "How do macabre portraits of God, such as the portrait of Yahweh commanding Israelites to mercilessly engage in genocide, reflect and point to the nonviolent, self-sacrificial, enemy-embracing love of God that is supremely revealed on the cross?"[73] This is of course a tremendous problem for common views of biblical inspiration, issues which Boyd does a superb job imparting. If God is the inspirer of scripture, why does the Old Testament depiction of God appear much more violent than the God depicted in the New Testament?

The number of books that have come out on this topic alone in the last few years could fill a library. We need not write another one here. Instead, I want to look at two specific points in Boyd's book, which is one of the best treatments I have found on the topic of Old Testament

---

[73] Gregory A. Boyd, *Cross Vision: How the Crucifixion of Jesus Makes Sense of Old Testament Violence* (Minneapolis: Fortress Press, 2018), 46-47.

violence. Expanding on Boyd's *Cross Vision*, I aim to help develop a more consistent theological approach to the topic of inspiration.

There are two main issues I find problematic in Boyd's proposal. We will deal with the first issue here in this section, and we'll deal with the second one in the next and last section of chapter 1. The first is his assumption that the Bible is the lowercase word of God. I think this is inherently problematic for various reasons that I will address momentarily. Suffice it to say for now that trying to reject the Old Testament depictions of God as inconsistent with Christ as the Revelation of God, while still trying to affirm the Bible as the word of God is in the words of my best friend Colt, "Like forcing a puzzle piece into a spot that doesn't fit."[74]

The second problem is his stance on God's accommodations for the limited cultural perspective of the ancient Hebrews. While I don't think this is in and of itself an issue, his approach and underlying presuppositions are what I want to address. According to Boyd, God *allows* the ancient Hebrews to misunderstand him. Which begs the question: if God is *allowing* the ancient Hebrews who wrote the Bible to misunderstand him to be a warrior god that commands genocide, doesn't that presuppose God has the ability to share a more accurate view of himself so that the ancient Israelites don't slaughter their enemies? His approach seems to presuppose implicitly that God has the ability to control, which we will explore in more detail shortly.

THE BIBLE IS GOD'S WORD-AUTHORSHIP AND INSPIRATION SEEN AS SYNONYMOUS

Ultimately, I find popular notions of inspiration and revelation that render scripture as the Word of God in any sense[75] to be problematic

---

74 This quote comes out of a personal conversation with Colt Meyer.

75 I say in "any sense" because there is a distinction made in some circles between the lowercase word of God and the uppercase Word of God. I find this distinction untenable and ultimately idolatrous. While it may be a matter of semantics, I prefer we just restrict the concept of "The Word of God" to refer to the logos, the second person of the Trinity. It does not make sense to say there are two "words."

for multiple reasons, some of which we will discuss here. Greg Boyd's own affirmation of these issues makes his approach to the biblical text and its nature a brilliant case study and jumping-off point, as he has incorporated some of the more nuanced views on the subject. I think the same issues that underlie calling the Bible "the Word of God" found among *fundamentalists* are also problematic for his own more nuanced *evangelical* perspective.[76] As such, I won't distinguish between the nuances found among fundamentalists and evangelicals in addressing what I find problematic behind their belief that the bible is the W/word of God.

Right out of the gate, Boyd tackles the issue at hand, which he addresses in *Cross Vision*. "Christians have always affirmed that Jesus Christ, and especially Jesus Christ crucified, is the full and complete revelation of God. From him we learn that God's nature is love-the kind of self-sacrificial love that led God to become a human and to offer himself up for us when we were yet enemies. *But what are we to think when we find Yahweh acting in surprisingly sub-Christlike ways in the OT?*"[77] Surely, he is referring to *ways* such as commanding the Hebrews to slaughter men, women, and even infants! He rightly points out that this is not the self-sacrificial love revealed by Jesus.

At this point in his text, I'm fully on board with what he's saying. But a moment later, he offers one option (a choice he rejects) is to dismiss these violent passages of scripture. While I would not

---

76   It's important to note here that while all fundamentalists are evangelicals not all evangelicals are fundamentalists. Fundamentalism has unfortunately co-opted the word *evangelical* for itself to the extent that the culture at large thinks "fundamentalism" when they hear the term *evangelical*. As far as I'm aware, Greg Boyd would be classified as an evangelical, while he would not fit into the fundamentalist category. For a definition of each of these terms see the glossary.

77   Boyd, *Cross Vision*, xi.

advocate straight-out rejecting these texts[78] (I'm not a *Marcionite*[79]), his own reason for refusing to dismiss these texts is highly untenable. He says that in rejecting these violent texts we solve "our dilemma, *but it conflicts with the fact that Jesus repeatedly endorsed the OT as the inspired word of God.*"[80] I think if this is true, then we cannot reject anything in scripture,[81] even if Christ's revelation doesn't line up with what's in scripture. Indeed, if scripture is God's W/word in any intrinsic sense—that is in its essence, its *ontological*[82] being—then we should expect it not to conflict with God's Revelation, who is the person of Jesus.

---

78 Depending on how one defines "reject," I may or may not be on-board with rejecting certain passages. If one means that these passages, in their original historical meanings given by the author and shaped by its context, do not line up with the Word of God [Jesus Christ], then yes, we must "reject" certain passages as out of character with the very nature of Christ and therefore God. That is of course if one is interpreting these passages in a historical sense, in its original meaning. If one interprets these passages by an allegorical method, one may be able to accept them as in line with the full revelation of God, who is Christ. However, if by the term "reject," one means that these passages cannot be scripture, then one lacks the imagination capable of seeing all things as a possible vehicle for the Word [Christ] of God. This I heartily reject. For scripture need not be perfect or even accurate wholesale regarding the nature of God to be used by God to speak accurately. Our God does not lack the imagination or power to do so since the Creator is present in all things.

79 Maricon was a heretic, who believed the God revealed in Jesus was a different God than Yahweh—whom he thought was an evil god but not the creator God; he thus rejected the Old Testament as Christian scripture. It's also important to note that Christians were not oblivious to the wildly different depictions of God found between the Old and New Testaments. Their answer, more or less, was to read the Old Testament allegorically. As a result, they did not see the Old Testament as literally teaching that Yahweh was hungry for violence. To read it in such literal terms seemed nonsensical to them. Maricon, however, did read it literally, and this is what led him to believe that Yahweh was a different God than the one revealed in Jesus. It was thus his way of reading scripture that ultimately set Maricon apart from the mainstream orthodox church.

80 Boyd, *Cross Vision*, xi.

81 At least what I mean by rejection as described in footnote 37

82 Ontology is essentially an academic term for nature. Specifically, it is a branch in the philosophy of metaphysics that investigates the nature of being. So, when I use the word "ontology" or "ontological," I use it to refer to the inherent nature of something, its essence, what it is that makes it that thing.

The fact that we do see conflict, as Boyd admits, would lead us to believe it is not God's word, which is one reason that fundamentalists are so adamant about their claim that Jesus' teachings do not conflict with the Old Testament. Furthermore, his claim that Jesus believed the Bible to be the word of God doesn't match the witness of the gospel accounts. A full account of each time Jesus refers to the word of God and whether he understands it to be synonymous with scripture would overwhelm at this moment.

Instead, a full account of this and each time the word of God and scripture is mentioned in the New Testament will be addressed in the appendix at the back of this book. It will suffice for now to address a few examples, including the examples Boyd supplies. Preceding this, I will present a logical argument for why the Bible cannot be the word of God. Then, we will look at two other passages in the New Testament that are used to support the view that the Bible is the word of God. Next, we will examine a few instances in the New Testament in which the authors use the phrase "the word of God."

Lastly, before looking at the gospel accounts that Boyd's references, we will view a few passages from the early church describing who the word of God is. Overall, this will allow us to build a framework on which to situate ourselves in a contextual perspective on the topic. Only from a big picture of what the ancient church understood the Word of God to be can we properly contextualize the particular uses of this phrase. It's like looking at a two-story tall rubber ducky up close; you can't really see it for what it is until you step back and get the big picture.

So now we consider Boyd's viewpoint on Jesus being the full revelation of God and having "superior authority to the Old Testament."[83] Amen. If Boyd believes that Jesus understood the Bible to be God's word and that therefore Christians should believe it is God's word, we end up with a serious issue. How can Jesus have a superior authority to the Old Testament (which I agree with) *if the Old Testament is the word of God, and Jesus is a member of that Divine Godhead?* Said in

---

[83] Boyd, *Cross Vision.*

another way, if the Bible is God's word and Jesus is God, the *Bible is therefore Jesus' word. How then can Jesus have a superior authority to his own word??* This naturally leads to the intuition that a person's word is never separate from themselves. It is preposterous to claim that we have greater authority than our own word.

When someone gives us their "word" on a matter and then breaks that "word," we naturally find ourselves upset. We hold that person, or at least we should, accountable for not being consistent with their "word." This is because we inherently intuit that a person's word should be consistent with that individual's character. If a person who is known for lying and generally having an untrustworthy character gives us their "word," we will expect them to break it because this is what is most consistent with their character. In this way, their "word" (or the actual intent behind their word) is consistent with who they are. The outer facade of their "word" said one thing, but the real meaning and intention behind their ill-given word was one of deceit.

My point being, we expect someone's word or the actual intention behind their word to be consistent with their character, to be—in a sense—a part of who they are. Jesus once said, "But what comes out of the mouth proceeds from the heart, and this is what defiles."[84] When he said this, he described that which comes out of the mouth as connected to the heart, the center of our will, intention, and character. Said another way, one's "word" or authority cannot be separated from the one who has spoken the "word." It comes from their inner being and is therefore a part of themselves. If this is the case with a human being, how much more so with God's word?

Karl Barth, a twentieth century Swiss Reformed Theologian, understood this when he wrote, "What God speaks is never known or true anywhere in abstraction from God Himself. It is known and true in and through the fact that He Himself says it, that He is present in person in and with what is said by Him."[85] Said another way, God's

---

84   Lewis, *C.S. Lewis Bible*, Mt 15:18.

85   Karl Barth and Geoffrey William Bromiley, *Church Dogmatics: The Doctrine of the Word of God*, ed. Thomas F. Torrance, trans. Geoffrey William Bromiley, vol. 1 (Peabody, MA: Hendrickson Publishers, 1975), 137.

Word is never separate from God's self. If the scriptures are therefore the Word of God—the Creator's very speech—*then scripture ends up being eternal* since God can never say something which God has not already said. That which God speaks, God speaks eternally. For God, who is *immutable*,[86] speaking something new would mean a change in God. (Whatever God does, God must do in some sense eternally, otherwise God changes).[87]

In addition, *scripture would hold full equality* with God, as the one who spoke forth the word. Since one's word is never separate from oneself. If this were the case, scripture being the Word of God, we would thus not expect it to conflict with Christ, whom we testify to be God incarnated into human flesh. There is another problem to the equating of scripture and God's Word that I must explicitly point out. If what I have said above is true concerning scripture holding both the qualities of eternity and full equality with God (since God's Word is never separate from God's self), then scripture is God, somehow a part of the Godhead—whether scripture be conflated with the Holy Spirit, Jesus, or as a fourth member of the Godhead.

For only God is eternal, if scripture be his Word it must also be eternal. Therefore, it would be God. Scripture however is not God and cannot be eternal, therefore it is not God's Word. *The true Word of God is Christ*, the eternal Son of God who holds full equality with God because He is God—the eternal Word—which the Father has spoken eternally. Said another way, since God's Word is never separate from God's-Self, God's Word must therefore be a member of the triune God. The ancient church has testified that this member is Jesus Christ, the son of God.

---

86   Immutable is the classical term that means God does not change.

87   For some, a God who changes is unproblematic. In my mind, however, if God is Perfect Love then any change in God would be a move away from Perfect Love. Thus, we would have a God who could one day be the kind of father Jesus describes that sends rain on the just and unjust, that is a God who loves indiscriminately and the next day a God who kills, steals, and destroys indiscriminately. Logically this could be the case, but I don't understand why anyone would prefer a God who can change if that God is already Perfect Love.

2 PETER 1:19-21

Now, we move onto addressing two passages that are often used to support the doctrine that states the Bible is the Word of God. The first one is 2 Peter 1:19-21, a passage commonly referenced to support defining inspiration as authorship.

> *"So we have the prophetic message more fully confirmed.* You will do well to be attentive to this as to a lamp shining in a dark place, until the day dawns and the morning star rises in your hearts. First of all, you must understand this, that *no prophecy of scripture is a matter of one's own interpretation, because no prophecy ever came by human will, but men and women moved by the Holy Spirit spoke from God."*[88] (Emphasis mine.)

Even if one were to grant that this passage defines inspiration as authorship, it is a logical fallacy *to assume* it is true. It may or may not be correct. It is not simply correct because the passage is in scripture, nor is it merely incorrect because it's in scripture.[89] While it's

---

88 Lewis, C.S. Lewis Bible.

89 When it comes to scripture, much like many things in life, it's not all or nothing. Too often people react and immediately put themselves in one of two different camps, two different extremes. They either think scripture must be correct on everything it addresses, or it must always be false and inaccurate in what it addresses. I think this is extremely unhelpful when reading scripture or doing much else in life. We see this approach adopted by both those who would tend to label themselves or be labeled by others as conservatives and progressives. Conservatives tend to accept popular notions of inspiration, and therefore if the Bible teaches something, they must affirm it. Progressives, on the other hand, often after rejecting popular notions of inspirations have a tendency (note I'm generalizing, there are probably exceptions to this) to reject something often *because it is taught in scripture. The assumption behind both these groups* is that if popular notions of inspiration are true (e.g., that inspiration is equated with authorship—therefore, the Bible is the Word of God) then that which is taught in scripture is true because it's taught in scripture. And if popular notions of inspiration are not true (e.g., the Bible is not the Word of God and is not inerrant) then what is taught in scripture is false. As an example, homosexuality is often a case in point. For those who hold the conservative position, but share the same assumption with the progressives, homosexuality is a sin because scripture teaches it. The progressive, who while sharing the same assumption rejects the popular notion of inspiration, holds that homosexuality is therefore not a sin. Of course, there are some on the progressive side that would argue that scripture does in fact *not teach* that homosexuality is a sin (some interesting points for sure). My point being that from my approach to

important to ask what the biblical authors were actually saying about the inspiration and nature of scripture, to assume their perspective is legitimate based upon a prior commitment to the text's infallibility is circular reasoning.

However, I'm not so quick to grant that this passage supports defining inspiration as authorship. The first verse in this passage mentions the "prophetic message." A common interpretation of this phrase equates "prophetic message" with scripture, but the previous three verses to this text—vitally important for understanding what this "prophetic message" is exactly—would suggest otherwise:

> "For we did not follow cleverly devised myths when we made known to you the power and coming of our Lord Jesus Christ, but we had been eyewitnesses of his majesty. *For he received honor and glory from God the Father when that voice was conveyed to him by the Majestic Glory, saying, "This is my Son, my Beloved, with whom I am well pleased." We ourselves heard this voice come from heaven, while we were with him on the holy mountain."*[90]

The author of 2 Peter writes that Peter, James, and John heard this voice up on the mountain while they were with Jesus. The verses mentioning the "prophetic message" proceed directly from this discussion of the voice heard on the mount of transfiguration. This leads us to conclude that the "prophetic message" here is not the scriptures but is the experience of the transfiguration when Christ's glory was revealed and the Father spoke!

Craig Allert[91] concurs about the meaning of these passages and adds that this text is about the Father's prophecy on the Mount of

---

inspiration and the nature of scripture one is not in such a position *regarding any teaching* within scripture. They may or may not reject it (whatever topic is being addressed), but it must be decided on its own merit—not based off a prior assumption that it must be true or not true simply because it's found in the Bible.

90   Lewis, *C.S. Lewis Bible.*

91   "The immediate context gives us a sense of what this reference to prophecy is. In verse 16, Peter claims to have firsthand experience of the power and coming of Jesus: 'We were eyewitnesses of His majesty.' That the resurrection is in view here is apparent from the reference in verses 17-18 to the transfiguration, where God confirms

Transfiguration concerning the resurrection. Based on reading the passage in context, it becomes clear that the prophetic message referenced in 2 Peter is directly related to the disciples' witness of the transfiguration and voice of the Father. Therefore, the prophetic message in view here is not scripture, but a particular moment that happened in the life and ministry of Jesus. The readers of 2 Peter can thus trust the prophetic word since the apostles saw this with their own eyes. This is the emphasis and point of the passage.

Furthermore, while verse 20 does say that "*no prophecy of* scripture is a matter of one's own interpretation," it does not say that *scripture is prophecy*. There's no justification for interpreting this verse to be a claim that the whole Bible is prophecy and is thus God's Word. As Craig Allert again writes about this passage he says, "The context is prophecy; it is not an extended account on the inspiration of the entire Bible."[92] Even if we agree that prophecy in general (which is not what this passage is about) finds its source in God and that prophets do and have spoken things from God, what is spoken by the human mediators isn't necessarily God's Word.

Those receiving prophecy must interpret what is spoken. A level of control over those mediating that Word would be required in order for it to remain uninterpreted, and thus God's Word. (We will discuss this at a much greater length later.) But again, if we presuppose God can control free creatures like this, and even seemingly possess them, then we run into other issues such as the problem of evil we discussed earlier.

2 TIMOTHY 3:16

Our next passage is another one often used to argue that inspiration means authorship. Or rather, when readers come to this passage, they often carry the presupposition that inspiration means authorship and

---

his honor and glory by uttering the words of the prophecy, '*This is My beloved Son, with whom I am well-pleased.*'" Allert, *High View of Scripture,*157.

92 Ibid., 157.

thus unwarily superimpose this meaning onto the text. In my experience, the text is rarely engaged with to find out what it actually says but is instead used to reinforce what people already believe about the Bible. Said another way, there's very little argument involved concerning this particular interpretation of the text. Most readers merely assume it says what they think it says.

The passage I'm referring to is the famous 2 Timothy 3:16-17 passage. What I want to do here is try to show that the text isn't actually saying what we[93] think it's saying. Instead, we're merely taking our own theology and uncritically assuming that the scripture agrees with us! This isn't a respectful way of handling the scriptures.

One thing that may surprise readers is that the text itself is not primarily concerned with the origin of scripture but with its usefulness or function as scripture—something that should surprise us if the text was actually a claim that scripture is God's Word. It's also interesting to note that the author of this letter makes his appeal in 15-17, after he has made his appeals to tradition. Thus, we see here that the author's concern for right doctrine and practice does not lie alone or even primarily in scripture.

Said another way, according to the author of 2 Timothy, sources for right behavior and teaching do not rest solely in scripture but may be found in both scripture and tradition. The major concern in the overall passage is to preserve sound teaching and right behavior, rather than trying to explain the nature of scripture. I should also note here that the phrase "all scripture" isn't a reference to the twenty-seven books found in our New Testament. To make such a claim is an anachronism since the New Testament, as we know it, did not become canon until roughly the fifth century.[94] The author of 2 Timothy therefore could not have meant our New Testament.

---

93 By "we," I mean those who hold to popular notions of biblical inspiration.

94 See Warren Carter's book, *The Seven Events that Shaped the New Testament*, or Craig Allert's book, *A High View of Scripture*, for further reading. In reality, while by the fifth century these twenty-seven books were mostly accepted by the universal church, there was never an official closing of the biblical canon, either for the New Testament or Old Testament—even to this day.

In addition, this phrase also cannot be a reference to a closed Old Testament canon, since there wasn't one in the first century when this letter was written. What they considered a part of the Hebrew scriptures during the time this text was written was still fluid. Regarding Judaism, the Old Testament canon did not become closed until the early second century,[95] but the books contained therein diverged from what Christians included in their scripture. The Christian version of the Old Testament would have been what many Jews, including Jewish followers of Jesus, read in the first century. This is the Greek translation of the Hebrew Bible called the Septuagint, and it includes many books that Protestants do not consider scripture but that the Eastern Orthodox and Roman Catholics do.

Furthermore, 2 Timothy 3:16 says all scripture is God-breathed or inspired, depending on the translation. It does not say, "All scripture is the Word of God." We read this into the text. Said another way, *we see what we want to see.* The phrase God-breathed may in fact mean scripture is God's Word, but one cannot just assume it since the text doesn't actually say this.[96] We must first do the hard work of interpretation to determine its meaning. However, there are issues that complicate unearthing exactly what this phrase means. One problem with determining the meaning of "God-breathed," *theopneustos* in Greek, is that this word is only used once in all the New Testament.

95　Here I'm also assuming a lot of background information. For more on this see Craig Allert's book, *A High View of Scripture.* Essentially, we need to understand that canon and scripture were not synonymous at this time. Since canonization had not happened yet, scripture was just scripture, and there was a consensus on what was and what was not scripture. That consensus, if you will, was what the canonization process was about, which took place much later and even continued into the Protestant Reformation. There the Protestants refined what was considered scripture up until that point by the church and many Jews of Jesus' day and before. The books that Protestants would later call the Apocrypha were removed from what they now considered canonized scripture. At the time of Jesus, none of the Old Testament scriptures had yet been officially canonized because not everyone agreed on what all was and was not scripture. The Sadducees for instance, a very prominent group of Jews in Jesus' day, didn't include the prophets or Psalms but only the Torah.

96　And even if it did say this, we would still have to ask what was meant by that. "The Word of God" could be taken in different sense.

We're thus not able to compare it to other usages in the New Testament or even the surrounding Greek culture and literature (since the word seems to have been invented by the author of 2 Timothy) to help make its meaning clear. This is unfortunate because the key to determining the meaning of a word is its use. This is because words have no meaning apart from the meaning we give them. When I hear a new, unfamiliar word, I ask for it to be used in a sentence, and this helps me determine and understand its meaning.

But since we have only one occurrence of *theopneustos* in the entire New Testament, it becomes unbearably hard to discern what it means. While the word is a compound of *theos* (God) and *pneo* (to breathe/ blow), we cannot assume its *etymology*[97] determines its meaning. "If etymology indeed determined meaning, then the very act of calling someone "nice" would actually be an insult because the Latin root for the English word "nice" (nescius) actually means ignorant."[98] No one that calls someone nice today believes themselves to be insulting that person for at least two reasons. The first is that, as I have said, we base the meaning of a word upon its use. The second reason is that most of us don't even know the etymology of the word "nice"! Words and their meanings are constantly changing. The point being the etymology of a word does not determine the meaning of that word since words and their meanings change.

While 2 Timothy certainly assumes that scripture is inspired by God, it does not define what that means. As we have seen, defining exactly what this means is difficult and becomes more so when one sees how the term was later used by Christians in the second, third, and fourth centuries. We have already discussed the broadness of the term's use.

This begs the question: If the word *theopneustos* was probably created by the author of 2 Timothy in the late first century and its first use outside of the New Testament was by Christians of the second, third, and

---

97 This is the study of the origin of words, their use, and their historical development and how they have been used throughout their existence.

98 Allert, *High View of Scripture*, 153-154.

fourth centuries—whose use of the word was certainly broader than ours—why should we understand it as more than a general, undefined statement about God's influence on scripture? Why define it as saying something so specific, such as the Word of God? Particularly since we don't have anyone in the first few centuries of Christianity using the term in that way, it doesn't make sense for us to do it.

Moreover, the term "God-breathed" seems metaphorical—that is the author does not mean God literally breathes out scripture since God is Spirit and doesn't physically have breath. I think it's plausible that the author is alluding to the story in Genesis 2:7 of the creation of Adam. "Then the Lord God formed man from the dust of the ground and breathed into his nostrils the breath of life; and the man became a living being."[99] Here the Lord forms the man out of the dust of the earth and only after he is initially formed, when God later breathes into him, does he become a living being. In other words, in this story, God's creation of Adam is a separate act from God's breathing into Adam. The breathing happens after the initial creation, and it is this breathing that brings Adam to life. Of course, in the story both are carried out by God, but they are two separate acts.

If indeed the author of 2 Timothy is alluding to the Genesis story, they need not fully adhere to every aspect of the narrative in order to allude to it using their own metaphor. Rather, the author could be saying that while scripture is created by something other than God, i.e., humans, they are brought to life through God's breathing when read and interpreted. This certainly seems to jive better with how the patristics in the Eastern church understood inspiration.

Inspiration for them was not located in the text itself but in the interpretation of the text. In truth, one would be hard-pressed to find a separation between the ancient church's view of inspiration and their *hermeneutic*.[100] Through studying the *exegetical*[101] methods of the first Christians, one recognizes that their practice of interpreting

---

99 Lewis, *C.S. Lewis Bible*, Gn 2:7.

100 Hermeneutic is the art of interpretation.

101 Exegesis simply means interpretation.

scripture is what Richard Hays calls a "figural exegesis"[102] or "reading backwards"[103]—a sort of figurative rereading of the Hebrew Bible in light of the Christ event. One can see how this understanding of God-breathed meshes well with the patristic understanding of scripture's interpretation. It is the new meaning of scripture created by and read through the lens of Christ that is brought to birth by the inspiration of the Holy Spirit.

Said another way, this understanding of 2 Timothy 3:16 that I'm proposing fits better with how the first Christians understood inspiration—as located in scripture's interpretation—and with their creative, allegorical methods of interpretation. If "God's breathing" is in the text's interpretation, as the early Christians believed, we might expect to see creative, figurative rereading's of the Old Testament in light of the Christ event that do not match up with the historical, contextual, original meaning of the scriptures. Simply put, if this is true, then we should expect to see the early Christians reading scripture allegorically or spiritually. But if inspiration is located in the historical text and its meaning, as it has tended to be seen in the West, then we should be surprised to see the first followers of Jesus straying so far from the original meaning of the text.

Adam Hamilton helpfully explains this view of the text when he writes concerning the author of 2 Timothy 3:16:

> "Was he suggesting that God breathes upon the human words of scripture thereby animating them, making them "living and active"? The words come alive in the moment when God, by the Spirit, uses these human words to speak to us … To clarify this parallel to Genesis 2, we might say that in the view of Genesis 2,
>
> 1. God forms the man.
> 2. God breathes into him.
> 3. He becomes a living being.

102 Richard Hays, "Figural Exegesis and the Retrospective Re-Cognition of Israel's Story," *Bulletin for Biblical Research* 29, no. 1 (2019): 32-33, https://doi.org/10.5325/bullbiblrese.29.1.0032.

103 Ibid., 35.

In the case of the scriptures,

1. Authors write scriptures.
2. God breathes on them.
3. The words come to life."[104]

If we may say it another way, Hamilton is suggesting that one way of understanding what this passage could mean is by saying that the scriptures are written by humans and breathed on by God, thus sort of animating them. I would say it this way: the very human scriptures, when read by those seeking God, are taken up by the power of the Holy Spirit and used to bring the one who is the Word of Life to us through the interpretation of the text.

Lastly the early Christians, including those who wrote the New Testament, almost exclusively use the phrase "Word of God" to denote either Jesus or the gospel message, of whom Jesus is both the one who proclaims the message and its content. If the first Christians understood Jesus as the Word and not the Bible, then it is unlikely that 2 Timothy 3:16 would have been understood by those early Christians to be a declaration that the Bible is the Word of God. Below is a small sampling of the church fathers' and New Testament authors' use of the phrase "Word of God." For a larger sample, please reference the appendix.

2 TIMOTHY (80-100 AD)

Once again, we can see that in 2 Timothy 4:2, "the Word" mentioned here is not a reference to scripture but the gospel message.

"In the presence of God and of Christ Jesus, who is to judge the living and the dead, and in view of his appearing and his kingdom, I solemnly urge you: *proclaim [kerusso] the word [Logos]*; be persistent

104 Adam Hamilton, *Making Sense of the Bible: Rediscovering the Power of Scripture Today* (New York, NY: Harper One, 2014).

whether the time is favorable or unfavorable; convince, rebuke, and encourage, with the utmost patience in teaching."[105]

This passage is often used as a support for encouraging young pastors to preach scripture, but given the words used here, it is quite unlikely that this passage is referring to the Bible. The word "preach," *kerusso* in Greek, means just that: to preach, proclaim, or witness, and it's a word used in connection with the gospel message. The fact that they use it in connection with the "Word," *logos* in Greek, means that the "Word" being spoken of here is not the scriptures but the spoken message of Jesus. This is confirmed by New Testament scholar N.T. Wright when he writes:

> "Timothy must 'announce the *word*'; as usual, 'the word' here doesn't just mean 'the bible'...'The word' regularly refers to the Christian *message*, the announcement of Jesus as Lord...focused on telling what happened to Jesus, ramming home the point that, through his *resurrection*, he is now installed as king and Lord."[106]

Said another way, the term "Word" here in this passage is often assumed to be regarding the Bible, but in reality, the focus of this text is about preaching the story of Jesus, not scripture. Of course, scripture can be utilized to do just that, but the fact remains that the author of 2 Timothy isn't exhorting the reader to preach the Bible but to preach Christ crucified and resurrected. In other words, the goal for this writer isn't that the preacher would point people to scripture, but that the preacher would point them to Jesus. He or she may use scripture to do that, but the object to which our attention is meant to be drawn is always Jesus and not the text. This distinction is night and day. For Christ calls us to follow him, not the text. This is what the "Word" is referencing. We cannot simply presuppose that when we come across the "Word" in the text, it is synonymous with the scriptures.

---

105 Lewis, *C.S. Lewis Bible.*

106 N. T. Wright, *Paul for Everyone: The Pastoral Letters: 1 and 2 Timothy, and Titus (The New Testament for Everyone)* 2nd ed. (Louisville, KY: Westminster John Knox, 2004).

THE BOOK OF ACTS (85-95 AD)

In addition, we see a distinction being made in the book of Acts. The author does not use the terms "Word" and "scripture" synonymously. In 17:11 the author writes, "These Jews were more receptive than those in Thessalonica, for they welcomed *the word* [*logos*] very eagerly and examined *the scriptures* [*graphe*] every day to see whether these things were so."[107] Not only does the author present the Word and scripture as two different entities but the term used for each one is different in both the original Greek and our English translations. What this tells us is, at least in some instances, the biblical writers do not equate the Word of God with the scriptures.

THE GOSPEL ACCORDING TO JOHN (90-100 AD)

In the rather classically well-known prologue found in 1 John, it says, "In the beginning was the Word, and the Word was with God, *and the Word was God.*"[108] (Emphasis mine.) John could not be clearer that the "Word" here is God, Jesus Christ. This is extremely significant because by the second temple period the Torah had come to be identified as the Word of God. What John is purposely doing, and would have been understood as doing, is claiming that Jesus rather than the Torah is the Word of God.

FIRST EPISTLE OF JOHN (AROUND 100 AD)[109]

We get a further distinction in 1 John 5: 7-8; the NRSV reads, "There are three that testify: the spirit and the water and the blood, and these three agree."[110] A few other ancient manuscripts of this passage read, "There are three that testify in heaven, *the Father, the Word, and the*

---

107 Lewis, *C.S. Lewis Bible.*

108 Ibid., Jn 1:1.

109 While dating this letter is allusive, a date around 100 CE is plausible.

110 Lewis, *C.S. Lewis Bible*, 1 Jn 5:7-8.

Holy Spirit, and these three are one. And there are three that testify on earth."[111] (Emphasis mine.) These ancient manuscripts show us that the Trinitarian formula (Father, Son, and Holy Spirit) could exchange the term *Son* for the term *Word* as perfectly interchangeable since the Son is the Word, and the Word is the Son. They were not saying that the Bible is the second person of the Trinity.

JUSTIN MARTYR (100-160 AD)

In his work, *First and Second Apologies,* Martyr writes: "Now the Word of God is His Son, as we have before said."[112]

It is significant that Justin Martyr does not write, "as I have said before," insinuating that this is an opinion of his own. Instead, he writes that "we" have said this before, implying that he believes other Christians affirm this statement. In effect, Justin seems to be saying that it is widely acknowledged in the church that the Word of God is the Son. As an interesting case study of compare and contrast, we should note that most fundamentalist definitions concerning the Word of God read something like, "Now the Word of God is the Bible, as we have said before." As one delves further into the ancient church, there is an obvious discontinuity in how the Word of God is defined.

IRENAEUS (115-202 AD)

In *Against Heresies,* Irenaeus writes, "For He did Himself truly bring in salvation: *since He is Himself the Word of God, Himself the Only-begotten of the Father, Christ Jesus our Lord*"[113] and "but following the only

---

111 Michael David Coogan et al., eds., *The New Oxford Annotated Bible: New Revised Standard Version with the Apocrypha: an Ecumenical Study Bible* (New York, NY: Oxford University Press, 2018).

112 Justin Martyr, *The First and Second Apologies* (Middletown, DE: Beloved Publishing LLC, 2015), 52.

113 John R. Willis, ed., *The Teachings of the Church Fathers* (San Francisco, CA: Ignatius Press, 2002), 305.

true and steadfast Teacher, *the word of God, our Lord Jesus Christ.*"[114] The point for us to take note of is that Irenaeus does not mince words here—in no uncertain terms does he allow for anything else to be classified as the Word of God. For Irenaeus, it is Christ himself that brings salvation because he is the Word of God. And he is the only true and worthy teacher because he is the Word of God. Here, as in many other passages from Irenaeus, the author clearly defines Christ, rather than the Bible, as the Word of God.

ATHANASIUS (298-373 AD)

From his work On The Incarnation
In the fourth century, Athanasius commented on the text of Hebrews 4:12 as if it was making a reference to Jesus, not the Bible. There he wrote, "For *the Son of God 'is living and active'* (Hebrews 4.12), works daily, and affects the salvation of all."[115] In modern fundamentalist circles, this passage is about the Bible. Yet, Athanasius did not think so, and for good reason. When read in the surrounding context with verse 13 in mind, it clearly is about a "him," and since the Bible does not have a biological sex,[116] we should be alerted that this passage is about something or someone else.

> "Indeed, the word [Logos] of God is living and active, sharper than any two-edged sword, piercing until it divides soul from spirit, joints from marrow; it is able to *judge the thoughts and intentions of the heart,* And *before him* no creature is hidden, but all are naked

---

114 Ibid., 305.

115 Athanasius and John Behr, *On the Incarnation* (Yonkers, NY: St Vladimir's Seminary Press, 2011), 82.

116 I use the word "sex" here because it is the correct terminology. The term "gender," far from being synonymous, denotes a cultural construct that is entirely subjective. "Sex" however is based off one's chromosomes, whether they have a pair of XX chromosomes or XY and thus is much more biologically objective and is the correct terminology when referring whether someone is a male or female. Of course, from what I understand, those who are intersex, having both pairs of female and male genitalia, still have either an XX or XY pair of chromosomes, but this is a biological abnormality.

and laid bare *to the eyes of the one to whom we must render an account* [Logos]."[117]

We see also that the "Word" in verse 12 is a judge in addition to being "him," someone to whom we "must render an account." Who is the great judge if not Christ!? Moreover, since Christ Jesus was fully human, and his sex was biologically male, we should conclude that this passage is referring to him. So, besides this passage from Athanasius being another example of the ancient church's belief that Jesus is the Word of God, it also shows us our clear blind spots that cause us to misinterpret the text.

AUGUSTINE OF HIPPO (354-430 AD)

In his work, On the Gospel of St. John
Here Augustine commenting on John 17:19 writes:

> "'That they also may be sanctified in the truth' (Jn. 17:19). And what else is this but in me, in accordance with the fact that *the truth is that Word in the beginning which is God*? In whom also the Son of man was Himself sanctified from the beginning of His creation, when the Word was made flesh, for the Word and the man became one person. Then accordingly He sanctified Himself in Himself, that is, Himself the man in Himself the Word; for the Word and the man is one Christ, who sanctifies the manhood in the Word."[118] (Emphasis mine.)

John 17:17-19 is often read in fundamentalist and evangelical circles as if Jesus is praying for his disciples to be sanctified in the Bible. What Jesus actually requests from the Father in his prayer is that his followers would be sanctified in God's truth, which is the Word of God. Augustine rightly points out that this truth and word that Jesus refers to is Jesus himself. When read in the context of John's gospel, this could not be any clearer.

---

[117] Lewis, *C.S. Lewis Bible.*

[118] Willis, *Teachings of the Church Fathers*, 333.

It is notable that only the Holy Spirit and Jesus are given the titles of truth. In John 1:17, the author contrasts the Torah (since by that time Torah had come to be identified with the Truth) and Jesus by saying that truth came through Jesus alone. While in John 14:6, Jesus explicitly calls himself the Truth rather than the Torah. We also know from the Prologue that John defines Jesus as the Word of God. So, when Augustine says that the truth, who is God's Word, mentioned in chapter seventeen is Jesus himself, he has every reason to think this.

MAXIMUS THE CONFESSOR (580-662 AD)

From his work On the Cosmic Mystery of Jesus Christ

> "This, in his love of humanity, the only-begotten Son and Logos [Word] of God became perfect man."[119]

> "For this reason, the Logos [Word] of God, who is fully divine by nature, became fully human."[120]

Lastly, with Maximus the Confessor in the seventh century, we have yet another witness to Jesus being understood to be the Word of God rather than the Bible. For Maximus, the Word of God is the very same only begotten Son of God who became a human being while fully retaining his divinity. It is nothing more and nothing less.

Considering all that I have said, 2 Timothy 3:16, 2 Peter 1:19-21 and the other New Testament passages that we have attended to seem to be more problematic for popular notions of inspiration than they might have first appeared to be, particularly in light of the fact that the early Church did not understand the Bible to be the Word of God. Time and time again when reading the church fathers and New Testament authors, we find that they understood the Word of God to be Jesus Christ rather than the scriptures.

119 Maximus, *On the Cosmic Mystery of Jesus Christ*, trans. Paul M. Blowers and Robert Louis Wilken (Crestwood, NY: St. Vladimir's Seminary Press, 2003), 110.

120 Ibid., 133-134.

THE GOSPELS

We will end this part of the discussion by examining passages of the gospels Greg Boyd uses to support his claim that Jesus believes the Bible to be the Word of God. For the sake of brevity, we will examine only the texts that Boyd mentions in the footnote to his claim: Matthew 15:4, 21:42, 22:29, 22:31, and 26:54. I've bolded the passages which I think present a more difficult challenge to my claim. I've also included surrounding verses to these passages when I found it relevant to understanding the text.

Matthew 15:1-9 says:

"Then Pharisees and scribes came to Jesus from Jerusalem and said, 'Why do your disciples break the tradition of the elders? For they do not wash their hands before they eat.' He answered them, "And why do you break the commandment of God for the sake of your tradition? *For God said, 'Honor your father and your mother,' and 'Whoever speaks evil of father or mother must surely die.'* But you say that whoever tells father or mother, 'Whatever support you might have had from me is given to God,' 'then that person need not honor the father.' *So, for the sake of your tradition, you make void the word of God. You hypocrites!* Isaiah prophesied rightly about you when he said: 'This people honors me with their lips, but their hearts are far from me; in vain do they worship me, teaching human precepts as doctrines.'""[121]

While this passage may seem on the surface to support Boyd's point, when one looks more closely, it appears that Jesus is actually playing devil's advocate. The context here is that Jesus is being confronted by the Pharisees because his disciples are not following the "tradition of the elders," what would eventually become known in Rabbinic Judaism as Oral Law.

Jesus plainly admits that his disciples are not following the tradition of the elders and then poses a question. Now, here is the important sticking point. The question he asks either reveals his own thoughts

121 Lewis, C.S. Lewis Bible.

and beliefs or those of his opponents. The question we need to ask is this: Is Jesus pointing out their hypocrisy based upon shared standards between the Pharisees and himself or is he pointing out their hypocrisy based upon their own theology rather than his? I find it more plausible he is doing the latter. Said another way, I think he is saying, "You believe the Bible to be the Word of God, and yet you forsake it for your tradition. Can't you see how inconsistent this is?"

It seems he is using their own theology against them. Jesus cites the Torah saying, *"For God said, 'Honor your father and your mother,' and, 'Whoever speaks evil of father or mother must surely die.'"* This verse seems to be a home run. Here it is, Jesus declaring that this passage of the Torah was spoken by God. But not so fast! Jesus, as portrayed in the book of Matthew and the other three gospels, consistently endorses the promotion of life and consistently rejects violence and killing. If Jesus isn't playing devil's advocate here and actually believes in the theology presented in the verse above, then Jesus endorses killing a child as punishment for speaking evil against a father or mother. This is something Boyd would surely reject.

Let's look at some of these passages in which Jesus rejects violence and promotes life. In chapter five of the book of Matthew, the famous Sermon on the Mount, Jesus says a few things that would lead us to conclude that he does not believe it is good for a father and mother to kill a son or daughter who has dishonored them, nor that God commanded this. In verse 9 Jesus says, "Blessed are the peacemakers, for they will be called children of God." It's important to note that this concept of peace does not merely refer to a lack of violence— although it certainly includes that—but to a mutual interconnectedness of right relationships to God, yourself, others, and all of creation. Violence, of course, breaks these relationships. Jesus, in declaring that it is the peacemakers who are blessed (those who live in mutually interconnected right relationships) excludes the possibility of killing one's offspring because it would permanently break right relationships within a family.

A few verses later, in 38-48, Jesus rejects the notion of *lex talionis* (eye-for-eye, tooth-for-tooth) and then commands his followers to love their enemies. Indeed, the reason he gives for issuing such an unbelievable command is so they may better reflect a God who loves his enemies and does not practice eye-for-eye retaliatory violence. In Jesus' view, God makes his sun to rise on the wicked and the righteous alike and sends rain on both!

God loves everybody—including those who hate God and those who love God—and if we want to be perfect, we should also be like God. This God that Jesus is depicting doesn't sound like a God who would command the killing of anybody. In fact, with Jesus' condemnation of killing the enemy (you can't love your enemy and kill them at the same time), *there's no one else to kill—for to kill someone is to categorize them as your enemy.* Everyone is to be loved; therefore, no one should be killed. When you love your enemy, they cease to be your enemy. This leads to right relationships.

Considering all this, is it plausible that Jesus really believed that God commanded parents to kill their children for speaking evil against them? In light of Jesus' promotion of life and rejection of violence, does it make sense that Jesus would believe that the Old Testament scriptures are the Word of God? I think not.

Furthermore, in the Sermon on the Mount, Jesus forbids the swearing of oaths and goes so far as to say they are "from the evil one." We know that swearing oaths are not only permitted in the Torah but are depicted as condoned and given by God.[122] If the Torah teaches that the giving of oaths is not only acceptable but good, and Jesus believes the making of oaths is from the evil one, then how can Jesus believe the Torah is the Word of God? He even has the audacity to correct Moses about the commands concerning divorce in verses 31-33. Would someone who really believed the Bible was the Word of God say such things? Surely not! If someone were to make these same claims in some of our churches today, they would be thrown out!

Considering all that I have shown, I find it unlikely that Jesus *is not* playing devil's advocate. It seems that his strategy involves not his own theology but that of his opponents used against them, showing that according to their own beliefs, they are hypocritical. It seems

---

[122] See Leviticus 19:12, Numbers 30:2, and Deuteronomy 23:21.

Jesus cannot argue that his disciples are following the tradition of the elders, for they clearly are not, but the Pharisees supposedly are. So, Jesus pulls a fast one on the Pharisees by pointing out how they are breaking their own laws and are inconsistent in their own theology. Jesus having no ground to stand on to confront them about their tradition of the elders or the Law—as neither he nor his disciples observe them—instead shows that the Pharisees have little ground to stand on themselves since it is the customs and laws of the Torah that they break. How are they to condemn him for not following the traditions or Law when they themselves do not?

Therefore, in verse 6 when Jesus says, "So, for the sake of your tradition, you make void the word of God," he's not actually saying, "I believe the Bible is the Word of God." Rather he's saying, "*You* believe the Bible is the Word of God, and yet according to your own practices you make void that Word of God. Therefore, you are hypocrites who don't even live up to your own standards!"

The next passage Boyd uses to support his claim is Matthew 21:42. It reads: "Jesus said to them, 'Have you never read in the scriptures: "The stone that the builders rejected has become the cornerstone; this was the Lord's doing, and it is amazing in our eyes"?'"[123] Boyd's case with this particular verse as support for Jesus' belief in the Bible as the Word of God is lacking. The verse he is talking about is from the Psalms, of which Jesus claims is about himself. He is the cornerstone the builders rejected. The mention of "the Lord's doing" is not about the origins of the scriptures but of the cornerstone and his rejection.

Next is *Matthew 22:29-32* in which Jesus said,

> "You are wrong, because you know neither the scriptures nor the power of God. For in the resurrection, they neither marry nor are given in marriage, but are like angels in heaven. And as for the resurrection of the dead, have you not read *what was said to you by God*, 'I am the God of Abraham, the God of Isaac, and the God of Jacob'? He is God not of the dead, but of the living."[124]

---

123 Lewis, *C.S. Lewis Bible*.

124 Ibid.

It's interesting to note here that Jesus distinguishes between the scriptures and the power of God. While Jesus certainly holds up the scriptures as a touchstone for theological reflection, he does not assert that they have any power, which is odd if Jesus believed the Bible was the Word of God.

If he believed the scriptures were the Word of God, we should expect him to make such claims to power or, at the very least, not to distinguish between God's power and scripture. Jesus could again, as we saw earlier, be using their own theology against them rather than asserting what he believes. The fact that he says that it was "to you" rather than "to us" that God said these things would seem to point in that direction.

But even if he is not, in the account Jesus references from the book of Exodus, Yahweh is revealing himself to Moses in the burning bush. Here in the narrative, God said *to Moses*, "I am the God of Abraham, the God of Isaac, and the God of Jacob." Neither the text itself nor Jesus is claiming that God wrote those words down in the Torah. Jesus could merely be affirming that Yahweh really did say this to Moses. As far as we know, Yahweh spoke these words to Moses and then later someone wrote them down, which is not the same as claiming that God was writing the biblical account.

Lastly, Boyd cites Matthew 26:54 to support his claim, which reads, "But how then would the scriptures be fulfilled, which say it must happen in this way?"[125] Again, Boyd's case here is weak. Nothing about this text presupposes or makes the claim that God is the author of scripture. He may argue that the idea behind the text, namely, that the scriptures must be fulfilled, presupposes this because it is God's word, and therefore, must be fulfilled.

As the prophet Isaiah said concerning God's Word in 55:11, "So shall my word be that goes out from my mouth; it shall not return to me empty, but it shall accomplish that which I purpose, and succeed in the thing for which I sent it."[126] When one takes into account

[125] Ibid.

[126] Ibid.

the interpretative methods of the early church, one quickly realizes that many of the fulfilment prophecies in the Old Testament asserted by the New Testament authors are creative, figurative rereading's in light of Christ. The ancient church interpreted scripture allegorically through the lens of Jesus. They were not primarily concerned with the historical context or authorial intention behind the text. The idea that the scriptures must be fulfilled was rooted in this allegorical/spiritual style of interpretation rather than a historical one.

The original meanings of many Old Testament passages rarely align with the second Christocentric meanings given by the New Testament authors. For our purposes, this means that for Jesus to say the scriptures must be fulfilled does not presuppose that God wrote the scriptures and therefore that they must be fulfilled since they are his word. Rather, it presupposes *Second Temple hermeneutics*.[127] What is fulfilled is thus not the historical meaning of the text—the text itself—but the new meaning given to and superimposed upon the old text by the Holy Spirit. In other words, it's the Christocentric meaning of the text that is fulfilled not the historical meaning. For these reasons, this text cannot be used to support the view that Jesus believes the Bible to be God's Word.

In light of all this, we can see that there are clear difficulties underlying popular notions of inspiration (including Boyd's much more nuanced view of inspiration) that believe the Bible to be the W/word

---

127 The Second Temple period is the time between the rebuilding of the second temple in 520-515 B.C.E. (after the destruction of the first temple) and the destruction of the second temple by the Romans in 70 C.E. During this period, a creative type of interpretation began to flourish. This method of reading the Bible was rooted in the present moment. Since the readers of scripture by this time were removed from the original writings of these texts, for a few hundred years it became paramount to read scripture according to one's own situation. The question for the reader became "what does this mean to us and for our situation?" They were not really concerned about the author's intention or what these texts would have meant to the original audience since that was a moot point for people living in a time so far removed and in new post-exilic scenarios. Furthermore, since they had no scholars who were dedicated to discovering the original meanings and social contexts of the texts they were reading, it would have been an impossibility to have such a concern. Second Temple hermeneutics is therefore the creative reading of the text that developed during the Second Temple period.

of God. Included among those reasons outlined above is the case that neither Jesus, the New Testament authors, nor the patristic Christians believed the Bible was the Word of God. Furthermore, as stated, the case that Jesus claimed a superior authority to the scriptures makes little sense if they are his own word. Lastly, since God's W/word is never separate from God's self, when one claims the Bible as God's W/word, they give to it the attributes of God's eternalness and God's full equality, which would make the Bible, God. Now it's time to turn our attention to what I see as another problematic notion in Boyd's otherwise fantastic book and our sixth and last problem for popular notions of biblical inspiration.

6. GRANTING ACCOMMODATION THEORY: ALLOWING OUR MISUNDERSTANDINGS

Boyd's primary point in *Cross Vision* is that through the cross Christ not only reveals what God is like but also what God has always been like. This is a pretty good point by my account. If you remember from earlier, I said that Boyd wrote *Cross Vision* to address the dilemma we find between the widely different ways God is portrayed between the Old and New Testaments. The former often characterizes God as a violent, hungry, tribal war deity who kills and also requests his followers kill men, women, and children; whereas, the latter frequently characterizes God as loving, charitable, and forgiving.

Obviously, this presents a huge issue for many popular renditions of inspiration which assert the *theological unity of scripture.*[128] While

---

128 The theological unity of scripture is a doctrine that asserts because God inspired scripture (often understood to mean God is the author of scripture), all of scripture's theology is consistent. In this sense, what scripture teaches in one area cannot contradict what scripture teaches in another. For example: If the Old Testament teaches that God commands genocide, then the New Testament cannot teach something that is contrary. This is why often many Christians do not affirm that Jesus taught non-violence, because it would contradict other parts of the Old Testament. So, while this is the modern fundamentalist understanding of the doctrine of the theological unity of scripture, it's important to note that the early church also believed in a sort of theological unity of scripture. The main difference of how such theological unity was obtained was through the use of a Christocentric allegorical interpretation of the

my point here isn't particularly to answer this dilemma, I want to show why his specific way of answering this issue doesn't go far enough.

Boyd accounts for these discrepancies through the revelation of God crucified on the cross. While his argument is hard to summarize in such a short amount of time, we can boil it down. First, he says that we are to interpret all scripture through the lens of Jesus. Secondly, because of the revelation of the cross whenever we see God being depicted as a violent warrior deity in the Old Testament, we should recognize that something else is occurring. He explains what is going on beneath the surface—just as on the cross Christ takes on the sin, violence, and the ugliness of the world, so too does God in the Old Testament shoulder the sinful thinking and conceptions of the ancient Israelites.

In this sense, the cross serves as a kind of mirror that reflects not God's character but ours. Essentially, this is what emerges from the biblical authors in their depiction of God. In this way the biblical authors display their own ancient Near Eastern views of God rather than what God is actually like. Boyd explains:

> "God out of his love, is humbly stooping to bear the sin of his people, thereby taking on an ugly appearance that reflects this sin. This is how I propose we interpret all portraits of God in the Bible that on the surface reflect a character that is inconsistent with the cruciform character of God revealed on the cross, including especially the OT's violent depictions of God."[129]

An example he uses is Jeremiah 13:14 which reads, "And I will dash them one against another, parents and children together, says the Lord. I will not pity or spare or have compassion when I destroy them."[130] To Boyd, if we trust the God who is fully revealed on the

---

Bible. In other words, while the historical meaning wasn't always simply dismissed, it wasn't the main meaning to be found in the biblical text. The primary meaning was the allegorical meaning that spoke about Jesus. When read in this way, all of the scriptures spoke about Jesus and therefore were unified theologically.

129 Boyd, *Cross Vision*, 53.

130 Lewis, *C.S. Lewis Bible*.

Cross, then it follows that we, in light of Jesus, realize that God would never do such a thing as repress his love and mercy in order to dash families to death.

Because of this, we must view this ugly depiction of God on a surface level as a reflection of the prophet's own sinful, culturally conditioned ideas of God while also revealing a God that stoops down to bear Jeremiah's sinful depictions and meet him where he is in his understanding of God. This is where, from Boyd's perspective, the revelation peeks through. We call this the accommodation view (which isn't novel to Boyd, but hundreds of years old), and to an extent, I actually hold to it myself. According to the accommodation theory, what we see in at least some of the Bible isn't what God is like, rather God is meeting us in our culturally conditioned interpretation of God. God meets us in our own playing field, so to speak, rather than expecting us to come up to his level—which of course as finite creatures, we cannot do.

The problem, in my estimation, is that Boyd has a hole in his particular rendition of the accommodation theory. He once again states his view,

> "I hold that God has always revealed his true character and will as much as possible while stooping to accommodate the fallen and culturally conditioned state of his people as much as necessary. In his love, *God was willing to allow* his people to think of him along the lines of a ANE [ancient Near Eastern] warrior deity, to the degree this was necessary, in order to progressively influence them to the point where they eventually would be capable of receiving the truth that he is actually radically unlike these violent ANE deities."[131] (Emphasis mine.)

The problem is not the accommodation theory, per se. I could almost affirm his above statement if it wasn't for one little phrase, *"God was willing to allow."* Stated differently, God allowed the ancient Israelites to misunderstand him. If God *allowed* them to think in unhealthy ways about him, it begs the question, could he have done

131 Boyd, *Cross Vision*, 73-74.

otherwise and why did he let his people think he was a moral monster if he could have done otherwise? Allowing the Hebrew people to commit genocide,[132] stone a man for picking up sticks on the Sabbath,[133] and so forth when God could have done otherwise seems fairly evil, at least passively so.[134]

If my friend's daughter believes that her dad wants her to kill their cat and my friend knows about this misunderstanding—*granted that he's not out of his mind*—since he can correct her wrong idea, he certainly will do so. He will not allow her to remain misinformed on the issue. Otherwise, the cat's life is at stake!

If God is love and can indeed *prevent* misconceptions about himself that would otherwise create pain and evil in the world, then it seems that God, like my friend, would correct our misunderstandings and those of the ancient Hebrews. In the book of Numbers, we find the story of the man stoned to death for picking up sticks on the Sabbath. This same text asserts that it was God who commanded the death penalty. Both Boyd and I concur that this story does not accurately depict the will and nature of God. Boyd, however, believes that God *allowed* the Hebrews *to think* that he wanted them to kill the man. This implies that God could have done otherwise. It would be like my friend allowing his daughter to think he wanted her to kill the cat—to the point that she actually kills the cat! Boyd's accommodation theory makes God culpable for passively allowing all the evil acts that have taken place because of misunderstandings about the nature of God.

---

132 This assumes one believes the biblical accounts of the Exodus and conquest narratives are historically accurate. While it is a complicated subject, the evidence suggests that the biblical accounts are not entirely historically accurate. For further reading on the topic, see William G. Dever's book, *Who Were the Early Israelites and Where Did They Come From?*

133 See Numbers 15:32-36.

134 Here, I am distinguishing between active evil and passive evil. Active evil is when someone acts in an evil way. Passive evil is when someone has the ability to prevent the active evil of someone or something and chooses to remain passive. In this sense, the person—by refusing to prevent active evil—has, in remaining passive, committed passive evil themselves.

However, the solution to this isn't to reject accommodation theories all together, thus affirming the Hebrew people always had a correct view of God. If we are to be faithful to Christ by acknowledging him as the full revelation of God, then we cannot affirm depictions of God which allow for violence. Rather, we should subscribe to what I'm calling a *necessary accommodation theory*[135]: one that states that God cannot coerce free creatures and therefore must *accommodate* himself to their time and place in history, as well as to their intellectual limits. God *must be* incarnational, always meeting us where we are in our interpretations of God, no matter how accurate or inaccurate they may be. But far from God being unable to do anything about our misconceptions, Yahweh is always influencing and using persuasion overtime to slowly correct our misunderstandings without hindering our freedom.

If I may again quote Boyd with my own edits, considering a necessary rendition of the accommodation theory I would say something like this: "I hold that God has always revealed his true character and will as much as possible while," *necessarily*, "stooping to accommodate the fallen" *nature, human intellectual limits*, "and culturally conditioned state of his people." This God must do "as much as necessary." "In his love, God" *cannot override the human freedom or intellectual and cultural limits of* "his people" *who* "think of him along the lines of a ANE [ancient Near Eastern] warrior deity, to the degree this was necessary, in order to progressively influence them to the point where they eventually would be capable of receiving the truth that he is actually radically unlike these violent ANE deities."[136]

Of course, people like my friend's daughter must cooperate with God in order to understand God, and she—like people in general—could refuse to change their minds. But there's also a level of human finitude that filters and limits how we see God. So, while there's certainly merit to Boyd's view of accommodation, I propose that his theory of God *allowing* the ancient Hebrews *to think* he was a violent

---

135 This would be the essential kenosis version of the accommodation theory.

136 Boyd, *Cross Vision*, 73-74.

tribal warrior deity ultimately falls prey to the problem of evil. If God allows, then God could do otherwise and is therefore morally culpable for any evil that humans have committed based on misconceptions of God. He would also be guilty of committing passive evil. This is not the God revealed in Christ. Essential kenosis can do better.

So far, we have examined six problems behind popular notions of inspiration. While I have tried to elucidate those pitfalls, I hope it is also clear that I in no way deny the full inspiration of scripture. Bad definitions are just that, bad definitions. There's no need for us to throw the baby out with the bath water. We just need to have a better theology of God and inspiration. Now that I have presented what doesn't work, it's time to move onto fleshing-out a solution, one that better accounts for the problems we have discussed with popular notions of inspiration and one that provides a better theology of God and by extension scripture. We now move on to what I have been hinting at throughout this chapter, essential kenosis.

CHAPTER TWO

ESSENTIAL KENOSIS: A BETTER THEOLOGICAL SOLUTION

There is no other theology that I can think of that has more of an impact on how we define biblical inspiration and the nature of scripture than that of essential kenosis. When we think about the very nature of God, it reshapes our theological notions. If we think God is trinitarian, then we will be inclined to emphasize community, relationship, and love. If we understand the Trinity to be hierarchical, we will tend to emphasize hierarchy in our own relationships and leadership structures. If we think God is by nature a wrathful God, then we will be inclined to create theologies of appeasement towards that God. If we believe that God controls everything, then we might be inclined towards a *stenographer* or *dictation*[137] view of the inspiration of scripture. Suffice it to say, our view of who and what God is and why God acts in certain ways affects all of our subsequent theologies and doctrines. Our doctrine of God is thus our starting point.[138]

---

137 The stenographer or dictated theory of inspiration states that what was written down was written down exactly how God wanted it to be since God was using the authors as direct writing utensils.

138 Those coming from a conservative evangelical/fundamentalist background will most likely disagree with this as our starting point. For them, the starting point must always be the Bible. From this theological standpoint, God must be interpreted according

Before we jump in, I should make a couple of clarifying points: in this upcoming chapter, rather than exhaustively arguing for essential kenosis, I will spend little time defining it. Since the goal of my book is not to argue for essential kenosis, but to flesh out its implications for the nature of scripture and its inspiration, I will therefore refrain from going into a full-fledged apology. Thomas Jay Oord, the premier theologian of essential kenosis, has adequately argued for it in at least three of his books.[139] I point the reader to these books for a more thorough argument. Here it will be sufficient to merely give the reader enough explanation to grasp the theology of essential kenosis in order that they may follow my argument in the rest of the book.

The layout of this chapter will be as follows: I'll define essential kenosis, trace some of its historical precedence in the church tradition, then address some possible criticisms and why they are problematic, thus presenting further reasons for accepting essential kenosis.

DEFINING ESSENTIAL KENOSIS

The doctrine of essential kenosis presupposes that God, as John Wesley was so fond to emphasize, is Love. At first appearance, this does not seem to be a controversial statement. After all, it's in the Bible and has been affirmed throughout Church tradition.[140] As 1 John 4:16 says, "God is love."[141] But, when one digs deeper, as we will do with essential kenosis, there may be nuances to this declara-

---

to the Bible. However, I believe interpreting God according to the Bible rather than interpreting the Bible according to God as fully revealed in Christ is placing the Bible as a higher authority than God.

139 See Oord's *The Nature of Love: A Theology, The Uncontrolling Love of God: An Open and Relational Account of Providence*, and *God Can't: How to Believe in God and Love after Tragedy, Abuse, and Other Evils*. This last book is a more accessible read while the first and second are a bit more technical read.

140 Just because it's in the Bible does not mean that we should automatically affirm or deny something. My point here is that for fundamentalists whose theological starting point is the Bible this point is not controversial because this statement is in the Bible. Of course, it's also not controversial for a lot of other types of Jesus followers as well.

141 Lewis, C.S. Lewis Bible.

tion found, depending on one's theological background. Those who hold God to be, in some sense on some level, a wrathful God will want to make God's wrath a quality inherent to God's very nature. Some in the Church, particularly those in the Reformed-Augustinian tradition, believe that God is sovereign and that this is God's primary attribute. By "sovereign," they typically mean (but not always) that God controls all things. Yet for the proponent of essential kenosis, as I will mention further on, love is God's very essence rather than merely an attribute among other various characteristics of equal standing. God's love is not an attribute—*it is God*—to such an extent that you could replace the term God with Love and you would be saying the same thing.

Because of this, it will be important for us to define how I am using the term love. In Thomas Oord's book, *The Nature of Love: A Theology*, he states, "Love is to act intentionally, in sympathetic/empathetic response to God and others, to promote overall well-being."[142] Oord and I would both agree that this excludes control and coercion. So, while this is a basic definition of love, we need to take a step further to acknowledge that love is inherently uncontrolling.

Besides being a theology rooted in the faith statement that God is Love, and the claim that love is uncontrolling, it's also a form of *kenosis theology,* hence the name *essential kenosis*. Therefore, to understand what EK is, we need to give a brief description of what kenosis theology is and where it comes from. To do this, let's look at the book of Philippians. There we see the noun form of this word translated in the NRSV as "emptied himself," used in that famous hymn that Paul recites in chapter 2:6-11:

> "Who, though he was in the form of God,
>   did not regard equality with God
>   as something to be exploited,
> but ***emptied himself*** [ekenosen = kenosis],
>   taking the form of a slave,

142 Thomas Jay Oord, *The Nature of Love: A Theology* (St. Louis, MO: Chalice Press, 2010), 17.

being born in human likeness.
And being found in human form,
    he humbled himself
    and became obedient to the point of death—
    even death on a cross.
Therefore God also highly exalted him
    and gave him the name
    that is above every name,
so that at the name of Jesus
    every knee should bend,
    in heaven and on earth and under the earth,
and every tongue should confess
    that Jesus Christ is Lord,
    to the glory of God the Father."[143]

While related forms of this word kenosis (as a verb and as a noun) appear in the New Testament, for kenosis theologians, this is often the go-to passage. The questions theologians ask regarding this concept are: What does it mean for God in Christ to empty himself? Is this phrase about the incarnation of Christ—to indicate that God in becoming human gave up some of his divine qualities? Or is the kenosis in this hymn about the divine nature itself—what God has always been like? Or could it be both? While I would probably make the case it's about both, contemporary kenosis discussion has centered on the second question. In other words, it is in Christ that we see God revealed as the one who empties himself, the one who places the needs of others above his own. As Jesus once put it, the Son of Man came not to be served but to serve, and to give his life as a ransom for many.[144]

In writing about this contemporary discussion, Oord suggests, "Following the lead of some biblical scholars, many theologians now read *kenōsis* primarily in light of phrases such as 'taking the form of a

---

143 Lewis, *C.S. Lewis Bible.*

144 Ibid., Mt 20:28.

slave,' 'humbled himself' and 'death on a cross.'"[145] The term *kenōsis* is
followed by these phrases, and they all shed light on the upside-down,
kingdom-minded power that seeks the service of others, as Jesus so
taught and exemplified. The hymn in Philippians is alluding back to
how Jesus interacted with others, not as a lord above them but as a
humble king among the people as one of them. This suggests a type
of power that is persuasive rather than coercive, that makes itself vul-
nerable rather than standing on the outside far from the possibility of
being hurt.

All of this Godly non-coercive power so displayed throughout
Jesus' life culminates on the cross where he says, "Father, forgive them;
for they do not know what they are doing."[146] If kenosis is a description of how God acts, the next question naturally becomes is this
self-emptying of God voluntary or is it an inherent quality of God,
a non-voluntary self-giving? For many, the answer is a voluntary self-
giving. For Thomas Oord and I, and many others, it is inherently who
God is, therefore not something God chooses to do but must do. Just
as God must be God. Here we have why Oord has added the word
"essential" to his own kenosis theology: All of this "indicates that self-
giving and others-empowering come from God's essence. Loving others is who God is and what God does. Essential Kenosis says God
cannot withdraw, override or fail to provide freedom, agency, and
existence to creation. God's love always empowers, never overpowers,
and is inherently uncontrolling."[147]

Said another way the self-emptying character and attitude revealed
and lived by Christ is not only what God is like but what God must
be like. The kenotic theology revealed in Christ's life and harkened
back to in the hymn from Philippians is for essential kenosis not a
voluntary act. God's kenotic nature is essential to who God is. Oord
has also written regarding God's nature, "It is impossible for God to

145 Thomas Jay Oord, *The Uncontrolling Love of God: An Open and Relational Account of
    Providence* (Downers Grove, IL: InterVarsity Press, 2015), 155.

146 Lewis, *C.S. Lewis Bible*, Lk 23:34.

147 Oord, *God Can't*, 28.

be unloving because being so would require God to be other than divine."[148] This is to say, that love is so essential to who God is that if God ceased to act in love, God would cease to exist, which God cannot do. In this way, kenotic theology is essential.

HISTORICAL PRECEDENCE

Despite the seeming radicalism, we see the seeds of this thinking establishing a precedent in the Christian tradition. Jacob Arminius said something similar: "God is not freely good; that is, he is not good by the mode of liberty, but by that of natural necessity ... if God be freely good, he can be or can be made not good."[149] What he's saying is that God does not choose to be good—God simply is good with no choice to be otherwise. Arminius even went so far as to say that the idea that God was freely good was utterly blasphemous.

John Wesley, an Anglican and founder of the Methodist movement also shared similar views, "Were human liberty taken away, men would be as incapable of virtue as stones. Therefore (with reverence be it spoken) the Almighty himself cannot do this thing. He cannot thus contradict himself or undo what he has done."[150] Thus, according to Wesley, God has given humans the freedom to choose the good or the bad, and God cannot retract this gift. Furthermore, God cannot do what is contrary to who God is. In this way, both Arminius and Wesley saw God as unable to contradict God's own nature or act outside of that nature.

Curiously enough, Justin Martyr also made the claim that God has given humans the freedom to choose virtue or vice.[151] Although, he

---

148 Oord, *Uncontrolling Love of God*, 161.

149 Jacob Arminius, "It is the Summit of Blasphemy to Say That God Is Freely Good," in *The Works of James Arminius*, trans. James Nichols (1828; repr., Grand Rapids: Baker Books, 1991), 2:33-34.

150 John Wesley, "On Divine Providence," Sermon 67, *The Works of John Wesley*, vol. 2 (Nashville: Abingdon Press, 1985), paragraph 15.

151 Justin Martyr, *The First and Second Apologies*. (Middletown, DE: Beloved Publishing LLC, 2015), 34-35.

did not explicitly make the connection, as Wesley or Oord has, that God could not take this freedom away. However, he does seem to suggest that, to his way of thinking, were humans to be without this freedom would be ridiculous and boil down to moral relativism. Since for Justin God is the one who has given this freedom, it is possible to infer that he could have believed something similar to Wesley and Oord. I hardly think it possible that Justin would believe God capable of doing something ridiculous because, as with the other apologists of his time, he believed God rationally coherent.

We also see the seeds of this idea, if not clear precedence, about sixteen centuries before Wesley in the letter to Diognetus.[152] Here the author writes, echoing the same kind of kenotic power we saw in the Philippians hymn, regarding the sending of Christ.

> "And was his coming, as a man might suppose, in power, in terror, and in dread? Not so, it was in gentleness and humility. As a king sending his royal son, so sent He him; as God He sent him; as Man to men He sent him; and that because He was fain to save us by persuasion, and not by compulsion—for *there is no compulsion found with God*. His mission was no pursuit or hounding of us, it was an invitation to us; it was in love."[153] (Emphasis mine.)

It is clear here that according to Diognetus, love is not compatible with compulsion. Although I think it suspect and possibly anachronistic to claim that the author of this epistle had a full-fledged theology of essential kenosis, it is nevertheless clear that there are seeds of this theology found here. If what the author of Diognetus has said is true, the logic follows that if God is Love, then love is inherently non-compulsory. Love never forces itself upon the other. We would never call a spouse loving who forced themselves upon their partner. In the same way, we should not assume that God forces God's-Self upon God's creatures.

---

152 This was most likely written between 120-200 C.E.

153 Louth, *Early Christian Writings*, 146.

As touched on briefly above, some Christians view all of God's many attributes to be of equal standing, such as that God is equally a God of wrath and of love. But for those who hold to essential kenosis, God's Love is not merely one out of many attributes or qualities of the Creator but is the very ground of Being; it is logically first in God's immutable nature. It is the very essence and core of what makes God, God.

In other words, God does not merely love or contain love as one of God's characteristics, but *Love and God are one and the same.* All other qualities or attributes of the Creator flow out of God's essential nature. God is only holy because God is Love. God is only just and righteous because God is Love. God is only sovereign because God is Love. These attributes do not define God's love because God's love is logically prior. Love defines God's attributes.

UNCONTROLLING AS AN ADJECTIVE

One may still be unconvinced of adding the term "uncontrolling" to the word love, in order to describe the nature of God. Of course, I understand that this may be hard to swallow. A question and an analogy may help. When one thinks of love, do they think of a controlling person? Is the dictator of Venezuela, who is controlling, a loving person? Are controlling parents loving to their child? Is a husband or wife who controls their spouse deemed as a loving partner? The answer is, of course, no. Love, as Paul says in 1 Corinthians 13:5, "does not insist on its own way."[154] Love that forces itself on the other is not love. It is a contradiction. Many, however, will say that it's wrong for people to be as such because only God has the right to be controlling. But how can humans be held to the standard set by God if the Creator isn't held to the same standard?

This becomes immediately problematic because it makes good and evil arbitrary. This line of thinking implies that something that could be bad for humans, such as mass genocide, could, in fact, be good for

154 Lewis, *C.S. Lewis Bible.*

God to do merely because God is the one performing the action.[155] This thinking says since God is God, he can do whatever he wants. But this doesn't allow for a universal set of morals.[156] This strike me as moral relativism masked in piety. Either there are some things that are always good (for God and creatures) and some things that are always bad (for God and creatures), or there's not really such a thing as good and evil.

To quote Justin Martyr, this notion of moral relativism "is the greatest impiety and wickedness."[157] Which begs the question: where do morals and ethics come from? What makes good, good; and what makes bad, bad? I don't think it's what God says is good or bad since if God can do whatever God wants—and what's good is determined by that which God does—then there's no such thing as true evil and good. It's all relative depending on God's mood at the moment. In contrast is the theology that *God is the ultimate good,* as Gregory of Nyssa has said, and therefore is the standard for what is good. Just as, in a similar way, Christ is not true *but is The Truth* and therefore the criteria for determining what is true.

Athanasius said it this way, "For God is good, or rather the source of all goodness."[158] The good is not some law outside of God, but it also isn't something that God creates. The Good is God's very self, the ground of reality and existence. Goodness only exists because God exists. The Divine is the source and fountainhead of all Goodness. And God is the creator of all things. This could seem like I'm attributing evil as a part of God's creation. Please don't misunderstand me. Evil is uncreated; it is the absence and corruption of the Good that flows from God. It is the decay of creation and existence.

Athanasius and Maximus sum this up well when they said, "Evil is non-being, the good is being, since it has come into being from the

---

155 This line of thinking is also often guilty of interpreting God according to the Bible.

156 Determinism in the form of Neo-Calvinism also suffers from this problem.

157 Martyr, *First and Second Apologies,* 34.

158 Athanasius, *On the Incarnation,* Trans. John Behr (Yonkers, NY: St Vladimir's Seminary Press, 2011), 52.

existing God."[159] Since God is Being, Existence, Goodness itself and has "by his gracious will ... created all things visible and invisible out of non-being,"[160] all things have their existence due to the overflow of God, so all that is good in creation comes from God's creative powers. All things which are evil are an undoing of God's good creation, a distortion of God's creative imprint.

As Maximus says, "For all things, in that they came to be from God, participate proportionally in God."[161] Creation's very being, as created by God, participates in its source, which is God. Evil is the destruction and degradation of God's cosmic blueprint, a disconnection between our source of life—God—and that which God created. The further we sever the source and connection of our being, the outflowing of God's existence, we revert creation into non-being, that is, into non-existence. To the extent we reject this natural participation with God, because God is Goodness, we choose the very absence of Goodness. In rejecting participation with God, we choose to create evil—which is really the absence of life—a spiraling down into the darkness of chaotic non-existence.

CALLED TO IMITATE

Furthermore, another reason to declare that love is uncontrolling is because we are *called to imitate God*. This is also a call we see recorded by the biblical authors. The author of Ephesians 5:1 says, "*Therefore be imitators of God...*"[162] I think most people would acknowledge this as God is, in some sense, the blueprint for reality, thereby making it natural to imitate God. We also see this same call to imitate God in Matthew 5:48: "Be perfect, therefore, as your heavenly Father is

159 Ibid., 53.

160 Maximus, *On the Cosmic Mystery*, 55.

161 Ibid., 55.

162 Lewis, C.S. Lewis Bible.

perfect."[163] The concept of imitating God is scattered throughout the scriptures both explicitly, as in my examples here, and implicitly.

In addition, this concept is also found in other parts of the Christian tradition outside of the scriptures as in the letter of Diognetus which states, "And if you love Him, you will become an imitator of His goodness. Do not be surprised that a man should be an imitator of God; he can, since God has willed it so."[164] If human beings are called to imitate God and God is at some level by nature controlling, then who is to say we shouldn't also be controlling? In fact, if that's the case, then for the sake of imitating God, we should be controlling. You see why this is problematic? If God does not adhere to God's own standard, that makes God hypocritical and, as stated above, doesn't allow for universal morals. Either we follow God's example in its fullest sense or we don't. For these reasons, holding to a belief that God is controlling is problematic for the life of faith.

IS GOD LIMITED?

This is an uncomfortable depiction of God for some. It seems like we are limiting God. While in a sense we are, in quite another genuine sense, we are not. Before I explain, it will be important to point out that some biblical writers, as well as theologians throughout church history, have "limited" God. The author of Titus says, "In the hope of eternal life that God, *who cannot lie*, promised before time began."[165] The author of James writes, "*God cannot be tempted* by evil and he himself tempts no one."[166] The author of 2 Timothy states,

---

163 Ibid.

164 Louth, *Early Christian Writings*, 148.

165 *CSB Study Bible: Christian Standard Bible* (Nashville, TN: Holman Bible Publishers, 2017), Titus 1:2. The NRSV says essentially the same thing, but I prefer the stronger translation here of the CSB. NRSV translates it as "in the hope of eternal life that God, who never lies, promised before the ages began."

166 Lewis, *C.S. Lewis Bible*, Jas 1:13.

"If we are faithless, he remains faithful for *he cannot deny himself.*"[167] C. S. Lewis once said, "Not even Omnipotence can do what is self-contradictory."[168] Oord, in his book *God Can't*, writes, "God cannot oppose God's own nature."[169] C. S. Lewis made the claim that Omnipotence cannot do what is self-contradictory, and Oord echoes the author of 2 Timothy when he claims God cannot act outside of God's nature.

In these ways, God is "limited." But those are not true limitations. In fact, I want to argue that those are not limitations at all. As I mentioned in chapter 1, for God to be all powerful means God *can* act like God. Said another way, the Creator is free to be the type of God that God actually is and is in no way constrained. The revelation of Christ shows us that God's power is not defined by how humans have defined power. God's power is not the self-serving, hierarchical power so common in our world. It is not, as Cone says, a "self-interested power."[170] To say that it is one kind of power is to say that it is not another kind of power. It is a power that is not defined by what it cannot do but by what it can do.

These things, which some might wrongly assume are limitations, are things that fall outside of God's nature. The ability to be tempted, to lie, to deny one's self, or to be selfish all fall outside of God's nature. These kinds of behaviors and their underlying motivations do not represent the type of power that God has. These kinds of actions do not exist within God in the same way in which the ability to fly lies outside of a horse's nature. Horses do not have wings, and so we do not expect them to fly. Just as God is not the type of God that can commit evil, we should thereby not expect the Creator to be able to do so since it's not part of God's nature. *God cannot act out of character, so to speak, but God is unlimited within God's own nature.* Exactly as an eagle is able to fly all it wants to, since flying is a capability of the

167 Ibid., 2 Tm 2:13.

168 C.S. Lewis, *Miracles: A Preliminary Study* (New York: HarperCollins, 2001), 90.

169 Oord, *God Can't*.

170 James H. Cone, *The Cross and The Lynching Tree* (Maryknoll, NY: Orbis Books, 2019).

eagle, so too is God able to carry out all the good which the Divine desires because goodness is God's nature. But we must note that God is not constrained by an outside force, but God is bound by God's *own nature.*

Far from this being a modern perspective, as I'm sure some will contend, Gregory of Nyssa made this claim in the 4th century: *"No good has a limit in its own nature, but is limited by the presence of its opposite* ... Since then, it has not been demonstrated *that there is any limit to virtue except evil, and since the Divine does not admit of an opposite, we hold the divine nature to be unlimited and infinite."*[171] (Emphasis mine.) Said another way, Gregory's point is that God is not capable of evil because, as we have said, it lies outside of God's nature. Instead, God is unlimited in the Divine's own nature of Goodness. In this way, it is a false accusation to claim that essential kenosis limits God. Rather, to claim God can act unlike God—that he can act outside of who he is, that he is a horse who can fly—is to impose actual limits on God's power. The real irony is in saying God is completely unlimited and able to operate outside of his nature, one ends up limiting God.

OUR DEFINITIONS OF GOD

In hearing this, one may counter: Isn't this just using *our* definitions of who God is and of his characteristics? Well, of course. When we speak of God, we do so from a human—therefore limited—and tentative perspective. However, show me a theology or doctrine that isn't a human definition. All theology is a human attempt at grasping the infinite creator of the cosmos. It does not follow from this that God is not real or that our theologies are completely incorrect, but it means

---

171 Gregory and Everett Ferguson, *The Life of Moses*, trans. Abraham J. Malherbe (San Francisco, CA: HarperOne, 2006), 5. Here is the quote in whole: "*No good has a limit in its own nature, but is limited by the presence of its opposite*, as life is limited by death and light by darkness. And every good thing generally ends with all those things which are perceived to be contrary to the good ... The Divine One is himself the good (in the primary and proper sense of the word), whose very nature is goodness. This he is, and he is so named and is known by this nature. Since then, it has not been demonstrated *that there is any limit to virtue except evil, and since the Divine does not admit of an opposite, we hold the divine nature to be unlimited and infinite.*"

that human definitions are a response to our experiences of God. For those who hold that the bible is God's self-revelation, I'd like to note that even in this theology, all one is able to do is interpret the biblical text through our human definitions. Your interpretation of the biblical text as self-revelation would still be your human definition. Inerrancy of scripture, for instance, is inerrancy of the text itself, not inerrancy of the interpreter.[172]

At the end of the day, we can't escape human definitions of God. If God created us like this, as finite (limited) creatures, then it suggests that God wants us to have some humility when thinking about the mystery that is God. It's built into our hard-wiring that all theology is, at best, tentative and incomplete. We weren't meant to have the perfect intellectual comprehension of an infinite being. As Heschel put it, "The human mind is one-sided. It can never grasp all of reality at once."[173] *For God to be God, God must be beyond human comprehension.*[174]

Considering all of this, it seems best to say that love is uncontrolling. Therefore, when we make the claim that God is Love, we must define God as uncontrolling Love. In summary, those of us who hold to essential kenosis are simply taking Love to its logical conclusion. *If God is Love and love is inherently uncontrolling—and God cannot act outside of God's nature—then what follows is essential kenosis.*

Lastly, most of us seem to intuit that Love is inherently uncontrolling. When demons possess and control human beings, it is unloving. Ironically, for God to have authored the Bible through human authors, using them as mere instruments, he would have had to do something akin to demonic possession. Veselin noted in regards to the writing of the four gospels:

---

172 If we require an inerrant text to guide our life and faith and yet cannot interpret it inerrantly, then what's the point of an inerrant text?

173 Abraham Joshua Heschel, *God in Search of Man: A Philosophy of Judaism* (New York, NY: Farrar, Straus, and Giroux, 1976), 14.

174 I am indebted to my friend and former priest, Father Thomas Dahlman, for pointing this out to me.

"A great Christian Father of the fourth century, Basil the Great, stated that the Spirit does not deprive anybody of his reasoning power and freedom; only demonic possession does this. The gospels are our accounts of the **free primary response** of the disciples of Christ to what he was and to what God accomplished in him."[175]

It is in the freedom given by an uncontrolling God that the biblical authors, editors, and compilers wrote about their experiences with Divine Revelation as a free human response. In the next chapter, we'll explore the implications that essential kenosis has for our views of biblical inspiration and the nature of scripture.

---

[175] Veselin Kesich, *The Gospel Image of Christ* (Crestwood, NY: St. Vladimir's Seminary Press, 1992), 81.

CHAPTER THREE

ESSENTIAL KENOSIS AND ITS IMPLICATIONS FOR INSPIRATION

If God is best understood in terms of essential kenosis, then how does this affect our thinking about scripture and how God inspired scripture? It effectively rules out *dictation theory*[176] or what we sometimes call the *stenographers theory* of revelation.[177] This view of the Bible's inspiration says that God dictated to the authors of scripture the exact words that God wanted.[178] Not only did God dictate as one would to an assistant, but God did so in a way in which he had full control of the one scribing.

As a result, it is actually God doing the writing, and the human authors are not in control. They are merely instruments, acting as

---

176 The stenographer or dictation theory of inspiration states that what was written down was written down exactly how God wanted it to be since God was using the authors as direct writing utensils.

177 Although verbal plenary views of inspiration are different from the dictation view, functionally they produce the same product—the Inerrant Unmitigated Word of God, and therefore essential kenosis also makes this view quite impossible. (See chapter 1 on Inerrancy for a further description.)

178 The verbal plenary view of inspiration also fits this definition; the main difference is proponents of verbal plenary want to maintain that God did not override the human authors' personalities. This however does not follow logically.

pens in the hands of God. Though some may say in response, "Well essential kenosis may rule out dictation theory, but it does not rule out the possibility that the human authors of scripture could have cooperated with God and thus written God's self-communication."

Although this may seem a possibility within the theology of essential kenosis, in reality, I think we must rule this out also. Yes, humans may cooperate with God and record whatever God gives to them. However, due to our *fallibility*[179] (a result of our *finitude*[180] not necessarily our sinfulness) and our essential creaturely nature necessitating the interpretation of all things through our human faculties and various worldviews—which are themselves fallible and limited—our cooperation will always be colored by our humanity.

As Beth Jones has written, "Our access to revelation is not always straightforward. We are finite creatures, and God's revelation to us is appropriate to our limits."[181] We receive revelation according to our limited human capabilities, just as a dog might receive instructions from its human companion according to its limited abilities as a dog. The fact, as John Caputo has pointed out, that we interpret all things means there can be no such thing as coercion on a comprehensive level. Creatures may control others physically, economically, psychologically, and so forth. They may even influence and shape one's interpretation, but they can never totally control how another looks at the world. Our perspective is always ours, and no one can ever take that away. In this way, we see that the act of interpretation implies a kind of inner freedom.

This is freedom in the sense that one from the outside cannot totally control or remove our interpretations. Of course, the act itself of interpretation is not a choice freely made but is part of what makes up our nature as creatures. While we can never turn-off our

---

179 This is the ability for humans to be wrong, err, or make mistakes.

180 This finitude is to be limited to such an extent that there are things beyond our comprehension.

181 Beth Felker Jones, *Practicing Christian Doctrine: An Introduction to Thinking and Living Theologically* (Grand Rapids, MI: Baker Academic, a division of Baker Publishing Group, 2014), 32.

interpreting function, we can choose particular actions influenced by those interpretations. Though we cannot escape the act of interpretation, we can act and make certain choices within the parameters of our interpretive worldview.

From the perspective of essential kenosis, God cannot control, and therefore the interpretive nature of humans is untampered with even within an interaction between God and people. In fact, this is exactly what we see in the biblical authors: people writing from their own historical, cultural, linguistic contexts and personalities. Even God's influence, of which the biblical authors and all creatures surely experience, is something we interpret. Beth Jones elaborates:

> "Our finitude is not, for the creator God, a problem. It is part of God's good intention for us, and we have a God who can and does communicate with the finite. The fact that our knowledge of God must fit our finitude is only a problem if we rail against the sort of creatures God made us to be, if we seek knowledge that does not fit with who we are."[182]

While Jones might not agree with some of my own conclusions, her views are a good basis for our discussion.

When we call the Bible the Word of God, we reject ourselves as finite creatures, because only an infinite being could receive the words of an infinite being with no interpretation. Only an infinite being could receive the Word of an infinite being as it is. Humans, as finite creatures, receive the Word of an infinite being filtered through our finitude. What we thus receive has become not the Word of God but a finite human comprehension of that Word. What we think we have captured is only a response to the uncapturable God. To call the Bible the Word is thus to give humans a status of infinite godhood that can receive that Word in a one-to-one correlation. Thus, we would be declaring ourselves equal to God.

This "problem" only goes away if God can be seen as controlling the authors. However, I imagine if this were possible (a possibility

182 Jones, *Practicing Christian Doctrine*, 33.

essential kenosis denies), the finite instrument—the biblical author—would be crushed under the weight of an infinite hand. The human mind would melt. It would be like an infinite supply of orange juice being poured into a limited 8-ounce glass. The glass would burst under the pressure of the never-ending orange juice, under the oppression of infinity.

Considering this, it's clear that even if God could control creatures sufficiently to communicate his Word perfectly, finite beings would simply be destroyed from such an attempt. Demons could control the human mind in such a way, one might suppose. Since demons are finite creatures, the human under possession would not burst from such pressure. But that leaves only demonic control as a basis for a dictation theory of inspiration or any theory that would allow God's Word to be unmediated by human interpretation. Beyond that, even if demons were to act as a courier, bringing God's Word to humans, they too—being limited creatures—would be utterly destroyed under such infinite pressure.

Taking all of this into account, it leaves us with a human response to divine revelation. Or as Abraham Joshua Heschel says, "As a *report about revelation* the Bible itself is *a midrash* [interpretation]."[183] (Emphasis mine.) This renders the revelation received to be an interpretation, a human response to revelation. If one wishes for the divine revelation received to remain God's self-communication, God must override the essential human function of interpretation, which can only be done through coercive control. And even then, as I have briefly tried to show, a finite being would disintegrate from such infinite pressure. That leaves us with a human interpretation of God's Word rather than God's actual self-revelation.[184]

---

183 Heschel, *God in Search of Man*, 185. (This statement of Heschel's may be seen as the pinnacle of his thought on the matter, although he certainly says things that detract from the implications of this statement in other parts of his writings.)

184 I should note here that I do not distinguish between the Word of God and God's Revelation. I see both as always, the Son of God, the second person of the Trinity that we know as the crucified and risen Jesus Christ.

Benjamin Sommer, a Hebrew Bible scholar and professor at the Jewish Theological Seminary says something similar to this, "The words [the biblical text] are signposts pointing toward a transcendence that cannot be apprehended, but they are not synonymous with or written by that transcendence."[185] What Sommer is saying is that the Bible is a human witness to the incomprehensible God written by human beings. Alluding to what I have already briefly touched on, Austin Fischer, in his book *Young, Restless, and No Longer Reformed*, discusses what he calls "the Chasm of Transcendence."[186]

God being God leaves a gap, so to speak, of mystery in our comprehension of God. Fischer says that since God is the infinite being that he is and we are the limited creatures that we are, there will always be a gap in our knowledge of God. God is a mystery, not because God is irrational but because God is transrational. He is above our ability to fully wrap our minds around. This means that certainty is not possible since we cannot fully comprehend. That leaves room for doubt. It demands mystery.[187] If certainty is not possible, all we're left with is our interpretations. Such a statement means that human beings, even the biblical authors, are always grasping at the God of Transcendence.

God is not interested in nor can he give us the kind of unfiltered direct revelation that our idolatrous minds so often crave. If God was interested in this, he would have made us creatures capable of receiving such a thing. Since he has not made us those kinds of creatures, we can conclude that uninterpreted revelation is not what he intended for us. If this is all true, then we must find a better way to understand how God speaks to us.

185 Benjamin D. Sommer, "Revelation at Sinai in the Hebrew Bible and in Jewish Theology," *The Journal of Religion* 79, no. 3 (July 1999): 422-451, doi.org/10.1086/490456.

186 Austin Fischer, *Young, Restless, No Longer Reformed: Black Holes, Love, and a Journey in and out of Calvinism* (Eugene, OR: Cascade Books, 2014), 17.

187 Ibid., 17.

PROPHECY AS TRANSLATION

This brings us to Oklahoma City pastor and charismatic Calvinist Sam Storms. In his book *The Beginner's Guide to Spiritual Gifts*, Storms discusses his view of the spiritual gift of prophecy. Here, I'll quote it extensively. Storms writes:

> Prophecy is not based on a hunch, a supposition, an inference, an educated guess or even on sanctified wisdom. Prophecy is not based on personal insight, intuition or illumination. *Prophecy is the human report of a divine revelation*[188]... Prophecy is always based on a spontaneous revelation. Although rooted in revelation, prophecy is occasionally fallible. I know what you're thinking: "How can God reveal something that contains error? How can God, who is *infallible*, reveal something that is *fallible*?" The answer is simple: He can't. He doesn't. We must remember that every prophecy has three elements, only one of which is assuredly of God. *First, there is the revelation itself, the divine act of disclosure to a human recipient. The second element is the interpretation of what has been disclosed, or the attempt to ascertain its meaning.* Third, there is the *application* of that interpretation. *God is alone responsible for the revelation.* Whatever he discloses to the human mind is wholly free from error. It is as infallible as God is. It is true in all its parts, completely devoid of falsehood. Indeed, the revelation, which is the root of every genuine prophetic utterance, is as inerrant and infallible as the written Word of God itself [the Bible]. The problem is that you might misinterpret or misapply what God has disclosed. The fact that God has *spoken* perfectly doesn't mean that you *heard* perfectly.[189]

Storms does not go as far as his logic would imply. Why he doesn't extend this thinking to the biblical authors isn't clear from this work, nor is his writing entirely consistent. He maintains the possibility that a person could interpret and apply divine revelation without error;

---

[188] We will come back to this idea as this notion of "Prophecy as Translation" is found in the Jewish Tradition as well.

[189] Sam Storms, *The Beginner's Guide to Spiritual Gifts* (Bloomington, MN: Bethany House Publishers, 2012), 116-117.

although, as is clear from his thoughts above, divine revelation itself does not guarantee that the response will be without error. As I have shown earlier, human interpretation does not contain the ability for full comprehension and intellectual certitude.

However, I would shy away from using the term error as this seems to presuppose a modern epistemology. Our responses to revelation— or anything—certainly contain errors, but I think aiming for an error-less theology or interpretation of God misses the point. Our desire is to know God, something that doesn't require perfect intellectual understanding. Unless we want to say that the mentally handicapped are barred from a relationship with God because of their lack of ability to understand certain things. That would seem odd to me. I would rather say that our human response to God's revelation is always a finite *human understanding* within the conceptual framework of an infinite God.

Sam Storms' ideas are a good connecting point between essential kenosis and what I think is its natural consequence, participatory theories of revelation. This is not because he affirms these theologies (he definitely does not as far as I can tell) but because some of his theology on the gift of prophecy leads us on a trajectory towards essential kenosis and participatory theologies. His own arguments have implications of which he himself does not follow through. He seems to hold some sort of participatory theology for the gift of prophecy but does not extend this to the biblical authors and their own experiences with revelation. Sommer astutely comments on this tendency, "Thinkers sometimes do not articulate or even realize crucial implications of their own ideas."[190] Hence, this is my reasoning for engaging the ideas of many who would reject my own conclusions. Storm leads us on a trajectory that he himself would deny and does not seem to realize the implications of his own ideas.

Case in point: Storms states, *"Prophecy is the human report of a divine revelation."* This seems to correlate with the Jewish idea of prophecy as translation. This concept sees the prophet, who receives

---

revelation, as an active participant in the process of receiving divine communication by translating or interpreting the revelation received. Explaining his view of prophetic discourse, Heschel writes,

> "The prophet is not a passive recipient, a recording instrument, affected from without participation of heart and will, nor is he a person who acquires his vision by his own strength and labor. The prophet's personality is rather a unity of inspiration and experience, invasion and response...Even in the moment of the event he is, we are told, an active partner in the event. His response to what is disclosed to him turns revelation into a dialogue. In a sense, prophecy consists of a revelation of God and *a co-revelation of man*."[191]

Said another way, there is a sort of participatory dialogue happening between the prophet and God. God really is present and is revealing himself, while the prophet's response to God's divine communication really is his own human interpretative response. God speaks, and the prophet translates what is spoken into a product of his own interpreted response. This seems to fit fairly well into Storms thinking about prophecy, or at least the logical consequences of Storm's thinking.

The prophet is reporting what he or she has seen and experienced—and thus gives a *human report about divine revelation*. Storms also claims that every prophecy has three elements, one of which is interpretation, "*The second element is the interpretation of what has been disclosed, or the attempt to ascertain its meaning.*"[192] He readily admits, "that you might misinterpret or misapply what God has disclosed. The fact that God has *spoken* perfectly doesn't mean that you *heard* perfectly."[193] This seems to fit really well with the Jewish conception of prophecy as translation. Within this concept, what the prophets receive, the divine command is the *revelation* itself. That is, God reveals God's self to the prophet or human recipient. Then within the

---

[191] Heschel, *God*, 259-260. The same view is expressed in Heschel, *Prophets*, 624-625.

[192] Storms, *Beginner's Guide to Spiritual Gifts*,116.

[193] Ibid., 117.

human reception, the revelation gets fleshed-out in human language by human beings.

The difference I think between Storms' view and a full participatory view of revelation is in part by degree. He does not apply this criterion to the revelation received by the biblical authors. To him, the writing of the biblical authors is inerrant and infallible; the product thus produced is the Word of God. For Storm, there is always interpretation involved when it comes to prophecy, at least when it's not concerning the biblical authors themselves. Whereas from a full participatory perspective, particularly in tangent with essential kenosis, much more is made of interpretation than it is within Storm's thinking. It extends the fallible human reception and reporting of divine revelation to all received revelation, including any divine communication the biblical authors would have received.

According to Benjamin Sommer in his book *Revelation & Authority*,

"Already in the Rabbinic period and the Middle Ages, Jewish thinkers articulated the belief that the words of biblical prophets other than Moses were the product of the prophets themselves. The prophets received a message from God, but the formulation of that message in human language was left to the individual through whom God sent the message."[194]

This ideology of course works well with essential kenosis because from this viewpoint God cannot control or coerce. Therefore, the message received from God *must* be received through biblical authors' own interpretation, otherwise God would be guilty of overriding their human faculties and limitations. God can only do such a thing if God is coercive.[195] *The implication of essential kenosis is that God conveys a message but does not control the mind of the person receiving the message. The one who receives the message freely interprets it within their inescapable humanity.*

---

194 Sommer, *Revelation And Authority*, 102.

195 I know I'm beating a dead horse, but I need to make sure it's dead. Don't want any zombie horses running around.

Sommer does not limit this theology of a participatory theory of revelation to just the Rabbinic and medieval theologians but roots it in the Bible itself, specifically in the Pentateuch. As a historical-critical scholar, he willingly admits the multiplicity of the Torah and states that although there are participatory theories of revelation in the Torah, there are also alternative theologies that push back against them. One of the primary biblical texts that possibly promotes a participatory theory of revelation is Exodus 19. (Although here in this next section, we will also explore a few others.)

The Sinai revelatory experience as described in the Torah has different perspectives on what exactly was revealed. The E source of the Torah[196] found in Exodus 19 uses the Hebrew word transliterated as *qol* to describe what was communicated by God. Chapter 19:19 reads: "As the blast of the trumpet grew louder and louder, Moses would speak and God would answer him in thunder [*qol*]."[197] Depending on the context of the surrounding passage, we can translate "*qol*" as either voice or thunder. Both have implications for our theories of revelation. If we should translate it as *voice,* then the Sinai revelatory experience as recorded in Exodus 19 proposes that what Moses heard was actual words, and the Law or Torah is thus composed of God's actual speech. If we should translate it as *thunder,* then the E source is advocating *that God did not speak in audible words but in a sound that needed to be interpreted.* Thus, the divine revelation Moses received was necessarily being interpreted by him, and accordingly the Law is Moses' interpretation of what he heard on Mount Sinai.

There are good reasons to understand the word "*qol*" as thunder rather than voice. In the Ugaritic epic about Baal, the Canaanite storm god, there is a passage that uses the Ugaritic word "ql," which is the exact cognate of the Hebrew word "*qol*." The Ugaritic language, which is a northern Canaanite dialect, shares much of the same terminology with Hebrew and is a close linguistic relative. This helps to

---

196 The E source of the Torah is a reference to the documentary hypothesis. You can find this defined in chapter 1 or in the glossary. It will suffice to say here that the E source is one of at least four sources of which most scholars think the Torah is comprised.

197 Lewis, C.S. Lewis Bible.

clarify for us how the concept was understood in the broader context of Israel, and among its neighbors, as well as how it might have been used. In the epic of Baal it says,

> "Ba'lu emits his holy *voice* [*ql*],
> Ba'lu makes the *thunder* roll over and over again.
> His holy *voice* [*ql*] causes the earth to tremble
> At his *thunder* the mountains shake with fear."[198] (Emphasis mine.)

This passage is written in the genre of poetic parallelism, something common in the Hebrew scriptures and other Northwest Semitic languages. Poetic parallelism is a way to essentially say the same thing differently in two parallel verses. Here the first verse's usage of the word "voice" is paralleled by the use of the word "thunder" in the second verse. This also gets repeated in the third and fourth verse. Thus, the words "voice" and "thunder" here are being used synonymously. Both things are coming out of the mouth of Baal.

The same idea of voice being synonymous with thunder is also found in Psalms: 18, 19, 29, and less clearly in Psalm 77. While the whole of Psalm 18 is worth reading (as most scholars consider it to be one of the older parts of the Hebrew scriptures and in it we find an abundance of storm imagery attributed to Yahweh similar to the storm imagery that is attributed to Baal) for our purposes here, we will simply look at verse 13.

"The Lord also thundered [r'm] in the heavens, and the Most High uttered his voice [*qol*]."[199]

As we saw in the epic of Baal, we see here that in verse 13 the two terms "thundered" and "voice" are used synonymously in poetic parallelism, exactly as we find them in the Ugaritic text. In Psalm 19, we see in verse 3 the word *qol* appears once again. "There is no speech, nor are there words; their voice [*qol*] is not heard."[200] In the Jewish

---

198 William W. Hallo and K. Lawson Younger, eds., *The Context of Scripture: Canonical Compositions from the Biblical World*, vol. 1 (Leiden, Netherlands: Brill, 2003), 262.

199 Lewis, *C.S. Lewis Bible*.

200 Ibid.

Study Bible translation, *qol* in verse 3 is translated as "sound."[201] This implies firstly, that voice here can also be understood as a sound and secondly that it was not a voice with words; instead, the usage lends itself to being understood as thunder like it is in other parts of the Hebrew scriptures and in the epic of Baal.

Then once again we see the synonymous use of "thunder" and "voice" in Psalm 29:3-9.

> The voice (*qol*) of the Lord is over the waters;
>> the God of glory thunders (*ra'am*),
>> the Lord, over mighty waters.
> The voice (*qol*) of the Lord is powerful;
>> the voice (*qol*) of the Lord is full of majesty.
> The voice (*qol*) of the Lord breaks the cedars;
>> the Lord breaks the cedars of Lebanon.
> He makes Lebanon skip like a calf,
>> and Sirion like a young wild ox.
> The voice (*qol*) of the Lord flashes forth flames of fire.
> The voice (*qol*) of the Lord shakes the wilderness;
>> the Lord shakes the wilderness of Kadesh.
> The voice (*qol*) of the Lord causes the oaks to whirl,
>> and strips the forest bare;
> and in his temple all say, "Glory!"[202]

Here again we also see the use of poetic parallelism, employing different words and imagery to say the same thing, to equate the two words of "voice" and "thunder." In light of all this, it is clear that there is ample justification for translating *qol* as thunder. If *qol* is to be understood as thunder, then a participatory view of revelation is built into at least one tradition of the Torah itself. At the same time, it is impossible to know for certain if voice or thunder is intended, the resulting ambiguity of this term is suggestive of the type of revelation that necessitates interpretation on the part of the human recipient.

---

201 Marc Zvi Brettler and Michael Fishbane, *The Jewish Study Bible: Tanakh Translation*, ed. Adele Berlin (New York, NY: Oxford University Press, 2004).

202 Lewis, *C.S. Lewis Bible*.

Humans, being bound because of our sheer finitude, cannot help but swim in the waters of our humanity. It binds us to our time and place. We think within our personalities, our cultures, our experiences; and being that we are finite, we can never get outside of ourselves. The closest we can come to this is empathy, but even here are limited. We cannot truly "see" the world from another's perspective; the only way to do that would be to become that person or have a sort of intimate knowledge of everything.

Referencing Heschel's view, Sommer says, "The prophet is not merely a vehicle God uses to convey a message but also a participant who helps to shape it."[203] I cannot see us getting around this facet of life. If we cannot escape our humanity, then those who interact with God's revelation always receive that divine communication through their limited humanity and are thus actively involved in the shaping of the message. It is as if we always hear God's voice as thunder and must interpret it.

Before we end this chapter though, I'd like to expand with a few more points. While we've looked at Exodus 19, there are other portions of the Hebrew Bible, and even the New Testament, that lead us to the idea of prophecy as translation. We'll continue by first looking into 1 Kings 22, then Numbers 12, 1 Corinthians 12, John 1, 12 and Hebrews 10.

In the story found in 1 Kings 22 of the co-military campaign with King Jehoshaphat and King Ahab preparing for war against Aram, we see that some biblical authors assumed a very real, human aspect to prophecy. Ramoth-Gilead had been taken from the northern kingdom of Israel by Aram, and to secure it back, Ahab the king of Israel entreated Jehoshaphat of the southern kingdom of Judah to go into battle with him against the king of Aram. While Jehoshaphat agreed, he also insisted that they consult Yahweh through a prophet.

Ahab responded by bringing together about four hundred of his prophets. The king of Israel thus inquired, "Shall I go to battle against Ramoth-Gilead, or shall I refrain?" The prophets replied, "Go up; for

---

203 Sommer, *Revelation And Authority*, 103.

the Lord will give it into the hand of the king."[204] They all responded positively, saying that Yahweh would give the Arameans over into their hands. However, Jehoshaphat was rightly skeptical and inquired if there was not another prophet from whom they might inquire of the Lord.

Ahab responded that there was but that he hated him because he always gave him negative prophecies. Ahab gave in to the southern king's request, and they brought the prophet Micaiah, son of Imlah, before them. When asked about whether they should go into battle, he answered the way all the other prophets had, but probably sarcastically. When further pressed for what he really thought, he gave a different interpretation of the outcome of the battle: instead of success, they would utterly fail, and Ahab would be killed. Benjamin Sommer, in his article "Prophecy as Translation," points out that the standard interpretation of this passage is that the four hundred prophets were false prophets, as contrasted with Micaiah, a true prophet. We base this understanding of the passage on the lying spirits that were sent to these prophets.

Yet, as Sommer writes, it's not so simple: "What almost all commentators miss, however, is that this spirit does not actually lie to the prophets; rather, it speaks ambiguously."[205] Said another way, the word that is delivered by the "lying" spirits on behalf of Yahweh is open to interpretation. Let's look at verse 6 again, "Go up, so that the LORD will deliver into the hands of the king."[206] It's clear from this message given to the four hundred prophets that Yahweh will deliver into the hands of a king, but it's not clear who that king is. Sommer further writes, "But the wording of the oracle in v. 6, Zakovitch and Gressman note, is Delphic; it could just as well mean that God will

204 Lewis, *C.S. Lewis Bible*, 1 Kings 22:6.

205 Benjamin D. Sommer, "Prophecy as Translation: Ancient Israelite Conceptions of the Human Factor in Prophecy," *Bringing the Hidden to Light: The Process of Interpretation*, 2007, 271–90, doi.org/https://jtsa.academia.edu/BenjaminSommer.

206 Lewis, *C.S. Lewis Bible*, 1 Kgs 22:6.

deliver the Israelites into the hands of the Aramean king."[207] The point to note here is that the four hundred prophets are not what we would typically call false prophets as we see denounced in some later prophetic literature like Jeremiah or Ezekiel.

They are not frauds pretending to have received a message from Yahweh; they actually have received such a message, as it was Yahweh who sent the spirits. In this sense, they actually heard something, and it was rooted in Yahweh's own desired message. Again, it wasn't that the spirits lied so much as the message they received was given with a lot of ambiguity, and thus it was left up for the prophets to interpret. The message, presumably the same message given to Micaiah, required discernment, wisdom, and strength of character to interpret rightly, something that was lacking in the four hundred prophets who were in the king's pocketbook.

So as Sommer shows, this passage is not merely a matter of distinguishing between false and true prophets, rather the story is contrasting authentic prophets who understand God well and authentic prophets who misinterpret God. The message ultimately given by Yahweh to both Micaiah and the four hundred prophets was the same message. The difference between the two groups' interpretation of that message was not based on fraud or the inevitability that the four hundred prophets would give a bad interpretation. Rather, the differences resulted from the human interpretation of the message from both groups—contrary to a faithful interpretation of prophecy and four hundred unfaithful interpretations. This is how this story relates to the concept of prophecy as translation. Presupposed in this story is that whatever prophetic message is given by God it must be interpreted, and it can in fact be misinterpreted.

In Numbers 12, we see a distinction made between two kinds of prophecy, further explaining the idea that prophecy contains the necessary element of interpretation on the part of the non-mosaic prophet. After Miriam and Aaron complained about Moses because of his marriage to a Cushite woman and asserted that Yahweh had also spoken through themand not just Moses, the LORD summoned Miriam and Aaron out to the Tent of Meeting. In verse 6 the narrative records Yahweh saying,

> "And he said, 'Hear my words: When there are prophets among you, I the Lord make myself known to them in visions; I speak to them in dreams. Not so with my servant Moses; he is entrusted with all my house. With him I speak face to face—clearly, not in riddles; and he beholds the form of the Lord. Why then were you not afraid to speak against my servant Moses?' And the anger of the Lord was kindled against them, and he departed."[208]

Here we see that the way Yahweh usually communicates to prophets, unlike with Moses, is through dreams, visions, and in riddles. Yahweh speaks to them ambiguously, and they must interpret what his message means.

As opposed to the clear form of communication that the narrative says Moses receives, the meaning of dreams and riddles are hard to determine. Jacob Licht expounds,

> "What a dream and a riddle have in common is that their meaning is never spelled out; they need to be elucidated or interpreted in order to be understood, and of course it is possible to err when elucidating them. A normal prophet takes in God's word in a clouded fashion, a fashion that resembles a dream or a riddle. He cannot know whether his interpretation is correct, even if he receives the divine word while awake and in what seem to be clear utterances. In contrast, Moses had the great privilege to see in a way that did not resemble a riddle, and his prophecies came to him already spelled out."[209]

Here, as in 1 Kings 22 and Exodus 19, we see that receiving prophetic revelation isn't so straight forward in much of the biblical

---

[208] Lewis, *C.S. Lewis Bible.*

[209] Sommer, "Prophecy as Translation," 289.

narrative. It requires the element of human interpretation because it isn't always plain what's meant. Often it is the exact opposite of clear.

Just as in the Numbers 12 passage in which prophecy is seen in a cloudy fashion, we can see a parallel version of this notion in one of the Apostle Paul's most famous passages, 1 Corinthians 13, commonly known as the love chapter. The surrounding context of this passage is the discussion on spiritual gifts and their orderly use within the church at Corinth. The Christians there seem to have been praising their spiritual gifts over a great deal of other things. Paul sets them straight by declaring, sandwiched in between the spiritual gift chapter (12) and the chapter on prophecy (14), that Love above all else is most important. There he writes,

> "Love never ends. But as for prophecies, they will come to an end; as for tongues, they will cease; as for knowledge, it will come to an end. *For we know only in part, and we prophesy only in part; but when the complete comes, the partial will come to an end. When I was a child, I spoke like a child, I thought like a child, I reasoned like a child; when I became an adult, I put an end to childish ways. For now we see in a mirror, dimly, but then we will see face to face. Now I know only in part;* then I will know fully, even as I have been fully known."[210]

Here in the context of prophetic utterances and knowledge, Paul says that even now amongst such activity of the Spirit of God we only know in part, and our prophecies are only partial. In the ancient world of the first century, a mirror wasn't like our mirrors in the twenty-first century. They were typically made of polished bronze and didn't provide the clearest reflection of the person looking into the mirror. Thus, when Paul says that we only see in part, only know in part, only prophesy in part, and that this is like looking into a polished bronze mirror, he's clearly painting a picture for us of the distorted, unclear reflection we have in prophetic utterances.

Once more we see, this time through Paul and the New Testament, that prophecy is something that requires translation or interpretation

---

210 Lewis, *C.S. Lewis Bible.*

from the person receiving that revelation. Therefore, in the next chapter in verse 29, Paul says, "Let two or three prophets speak, and let the others weigh what is said."[211] Since prophecy must be interpreted and a prophet can wrongly interpret a message from God, having multiple prophets weigh in on what is said helps them determine the correct meaning. Otherwise, if the prophecy didn't need interpretation, there would be no need for multiple prophets to weigh in on what was said.

In John 1, the writer proclaims something that would have struck the audience as strange. He says that no one has ever seen the Father except for Jesus Christ, his son who has made him known. This would be odd considering all the instances in the scriptures in which God the Father reveals himself to prophets like Isaiah and Moses. But John says that actually no one has really seen God, not Moses, not Isaiah. According to John, the only one who has seen the Father is the Word of God who was in the beginning with God and was God. Now in these times, the Son—the only one who has known and seen the Father—has now become flesh, finite and comprehensible, and it is through him we come to know the Father.

So, just as Paul declares that we see dimly as in a blurry bronze mirror, so does John proclaim that no one before Jesus became flesh, ever really saw God face-to-face. But since God the Son has now become like us, when we look at him, we see the Father in a comprehensible manner.[212] The point being that to at least some New Testament authors, the interactions with God in the past and in the present have been ambiguous. Until Christ, we have never seen the Father as he truly is, and even now when the Spirit pours out prophetic utterances, we still only see partially.

A few chapters later in the Gospel according to John, we again encounter the thunder/voice comparison that we saw in the Old

---

211 Ibid.

212 In John 14:8-9, the evangelists write that while no one has seen the Father except the son (1:18), now the son reveals the Father to us since we can now look at the Father by looking at Jesus. "Philip said to him, 'Lord, show us the Father, and we will be satisfied.' Jesus said to him, 'Have I been with you all this time, Philip, and you still do not know me? *Whoever has seen me has seen the Father.* How can you say, 'Show us the Father'?" (my emphasis) Lewis, C.S. Lewis Bible.

Testament and the Ugaritic epic of Baal. There in 12:28-29 it reads: "'Father, glorify your name.' *Then a voice came from heaven, 'I have glorified it, and I will glorify it again.' The crowd standing there heard it and said that it was thunder. Others said, 'An angel has spoken to him.'*"[213] (Emphasis mine.) Not only does this voice and thunder similarity pop-up again, but the crowd who heard the voice/thunder had different interpretations of what they heard. Some heard the voice as thunder, others heard it as an angel speaking. Thus, we see here that God's voice/thunder not only needs to be interpreted but is automatically interpreted and (as we also see here) that interpretation can be wrong.

Lastly, we see what appears to be the concept of prophecy as translation in another New Testament passage, which of course makes sense. If the concept of prophecy as translation has shown continuity having been rooted in the scriptures of the ancient Israelites and amongst their descendants from the medieval Jewish thinkers all the way to modern Jewish scholars, we might expect to also see this concept in the New Testament, which was written by first century Jews.

Hebrew 10:1 reads, "The law [Torah] has only a shadow of the good things to come and [is] not the true form of these realities."[214] The Torah as it was given to Moses contains a shadow of things to come and is not to be identified with the "true form of these realities."[215] Said another way, the words of the Torah, the book of Moses, is not the revelation to which it points. Rather it is a reflection or, in the words of the author of Hebrews, a shadow of what it was pointing to. A shadow, as we know, isn't the thing in and of itself—it's what is cast by something else. And for the New Testament authors, that thing which is casting the shadow, which the Torah itself points to, is Christ. Jesus is the revelation of which the Torah is a response or interpretation.

213 Lewis, *C.S. Lewis Bible*.

214 Lewis, *C.S. Lewis Bible*.

215 Ibid.

However, whether some biblical authors had, or leaned towards, a theology of participatory revelation does not undermine our understanding of inspiration. Our view of inspiration could in fact be correct, which would assume the biblical authors have their own opinions rather than articulating God's. Even if the authors, editors, compilers, etc., of Exodus 19 are advocating for a theology in which actual words were given in a voice from God, a theology of essential kenosis would mean that Moses would still be bound to interpreting those actual words and voice of God through his limited human faculties, thus relegating it as a response to God's Word rather than actually being God's direct Word.

While all of which we have discussed in this chapter may be problematic for popular notions of inspiration and the nature of scripture, for essential kenosis, it's not only unproblematic but seems to be an implication of its theology. Now that we've described essential kenosis and participatory theologies of revelation as the entailment of EK, it's time to move on to explore if this way of thinking (participatory theology) fits well with the way Jesus interpreted and approached scripture and how the Christian faith has understood him.

CHAPTER FOUR

JESUS AND PARTICIPATORY THEOLOGY

In chapter 1, I described six basic problems inherent in popular notions of inspiration. In chapter 2, I briefly explained the doctrine of essential kenosis, otherwise known as the uncontrolling love of God or "God Can't" theology, and in chapter 3, I simultaneously made the case for what I believe to be the implications of essential kenosis theology while also explaining participatory revelation to the reader.

Next, what I want to do is make a reasonable case for why a participatory theology of revelation is congruent with and better explains how Jesus himself approached the scriptures. But to be clear, my goal *is not* to argue that Jesus held a participatory theology of revelation. That is another question, one that I am setting to the side at the moment. In order to do justice to that question, one would need to dedicate an entire book to its research. Rather, in this chapter, I merely want to show that Jesus' own understanding of scripture is coherent with such theologies.

Getting started, we will want to look at how Jesus interacted with the scriptures. We do that first by looking at his relationship with Torah. Then we will proceed by discussing his hermeneutic of scripture that he himself used and taught his disciples. From there, I will try to show why I think his relationship to the Torah and his hermeneutic of scripture is congruent with participatory theologies of revelation.

I think one of the best places we can look at Jesus' view of scripture is in the gospel of Matthew. There Jesus does something interesting that has boggled the minds of many. In the Sermon on the Mount, he states that he did not come to abolish the Law and the Prophets but to fulfill them, then just a few verses later rejects certain passages from that very same scripture. Let's first look at Matthew 5:17-19.

Jesus declares, *"Do not think that I have come to abolish the law or the prophets; I have come not to abolish but to fulfill. For truly I tell you, until heaven and earth pass away, not one letter, not one stroke of a letter, will pass from the law until all is accomplished. Therefore, whoever breaks one of the least of these commandments, and teaches others to do the same, will be called least in the kingdom of heaven; but whoever does them and teaches them will be called great in the kingdom of heaven."*[216]

This seems pretty straightforward. Jesus did not come to get rid of the Law and the Prophets. Yet only a few verses later he seems to contradict himself multiple times when referencing certain passages of the Torah by making the declaration, "You have heard that it is said ... But I say to you,"[217] instructing his audience to do something other than what the Torah commands.

Imagine someone coming into a fundamentalist or evangelical church building[218] today, and saying, "Hey guys, we all know about the commands of scripture, *but I actually have a greater authority,* so I'm going to tell you to disregard those commands and do something else." *This is exactly what Jesus did and how it would have come off to his*

---

216 Lewis, C.S. Lewis Bible.

217 In referencing the commands of the Torah, Jesus says, "You have heard that it is said," rather than you have read, because Israel at this time was mostly an oral culture. This was before the printing press made books readily available, and everyone and their dog had a personal copy of the scriptures. This meant that people didn't read scripture, but they heard it read in the synagogues; later, Christians for hundreds of years would hear the scriptures read during the Sunday morning Eucharist gatherings. Ibid.

218 I actually prefer using the phrase "the church's building" when discussing the building that many, but certainly not all, churches meet in because the apostrophe denotes possession. The building is not the church, and thus "the church's building" is theologically correct. However, in this sentence "church building" sounded less clunky.

listeners. No wonder his critics, and those of his disciples, claimed that they were dismissing the Torah.[219]

Continuing on, in verse 33-37 of chapter 5, Jesus adamantly argues against making oaths. This was common practice among the Hebrew people and fully endorsed by the Torah. But Jesus says in verse 37, "Let your word be 'Yes, Yes' or 'No, No'; *anything more than this comes from the evil one.*"[220] Essentially, Jesus is saying that the concept of taking oaths is from the evil one, not from God. But in Number 30:1-2 we see the concept of making oaths as coming from Yahweh, "Then Moses said to the heads of the tribes of the Israelites: '*This is what the Lord has commanded. When a man makes a vow to the Lord or swears an oath to bind himself by a pledge, he shall not break his word; he shall do according to all that proceeds out of his mouth.*'"[221] Considering what the Torah has said about making oaths, Jesus' own statement seems pretty radical.

Some fundamentalists have suggested that these commands are not prescriptive but are allowances. I would make a pretty hefty wager that the motivation behind such an attempt is a desire to maintain inerrancy by trying to harmonize the teachings of Jesus and the Torah. However, even if we grant their suggestion, Yahweh is still the one portrayed as giving the command, prescriptive or not. If one must affirm this, they cannot affirm Jesus' declaration about the origins of oaths. Since Jesus says oaths come from the evil one that would make God the evil one. This makes it unlikely that Jesus believes this command from the Torah is from God, therefore God's Word. I also find it hard to believe that God would actively encourage or endorse evil by making such allowances, especially considering what Jesus has said about making oaths. Jesus is not someone who compromises with evil.

Again, Jesus said, "*'You have heard that it was said,* "An eye for an eye and a tooth for a tooth." *But I say to you,* do not resist an evildoer.

---

219 See Matthew 12:2, John 9:16 for example.

220 Lewis, *C.S. Lewis Bible.*

221 Ibid.

But if anyone strikes you on the right cheek, turn the other also.'"[222]
Jesus could not be clearer in his contradiction of the Torah, specifically of Exodus 21:22-25:

> "When people who are fighting injure a pregnant woman so that
> there is a miscarriage, and yet no further harm follows, the one
> responsible shall be fined what the woman's husband demands,
> paying as much as the judges determine. If any harm follows, then
> you shall give life for life, eye for eye, tooth for tooth, hand for hand,
> foot for foot, burn for burn, wound for wound, stripe for stripe."[223]

The principle of an eye-for-eye is a general principle found in the Old Testament and the wider ancient Near Eastern world. So, while here there is a specific example of when one is to exchange tooth-for-tooth, it was more broadly applied than this. I should also note that this principle, while not what we would call morally good, was impressive for its time as it set a limit to the damage one could inflict upon another in revenge. However, in rejecting the tooth-for-tooth mentality, Jesus seems to distinguish between what Moses says and what God says.[224]

If Jesus is the foundation of one's faith, then his contradicting certain parts of scripture isn't the main problem found here. The primary issue for us is that he *seems* to contradict himself. People, even non-divine people such as you the reader or me, tend not to contradict themselves like this in such a short span. *Politicians do this but not normal people.* It is thus logical to ask what is going on here and to explore the possibility that he is not contradicting himself, rather maybe we are misunderstanding what he means by "Torah."

---

222 Ibid.

223 Ibid.

224 Admittedly, I see a lot of discontinuities between Jesus and much of the Jewish theology of his time. However, it is not because they are Jewish, not only would that be incredibly anti-Jewish, but it would also be absurd since Jesus is himself Jewish and has many continuities between his own theology and that of the Jewish faith; rather, I think the discontinuities can be attributed to the affirmation that God showed up in the flesh. I quite imagine if this is the case, God showing up as a human among humans, there would be some needed corrections among any culture, time, and people.

While many evangelicals and fundamentalist commentators have suggested that Jesus is not contradicting the Torah but holding people to a higher standard, I find that hard to believe when considering the evidence before us. At one level, he is of course holding us to a higher standard. The way he does so, however, is by rejecting certain parts of the Torah. It is easier to live by the principle of an eye-for-eye. It is much harder to reject this command from the Torah and to live nonviolently—to refuse to pay back evil with evil—but instead to pay back evil with good as Jesus commands us to do. But to say that Jesus is not contradicting certain commands from the Torah is to ignore the evidence.

For instance, in the book of Exodus 35:2-3, it records a command as having come from Yahweh himself that anyone found doing work on the Sabbath was to be put to death. Apparently, this included lighting a fire, as found in Exodus 35, and picking up sticks on the Sabbath, as is found in the book of Numbers. There we find a man who after being caught for picking up sticks on the Sabbath is subsequently taken before Moses. Those who found him then inquired of Moses as to what the right punishment would be. Moses, however, was unsure, so he consulted Yahweh. God answered by giving the command that the man's punishment was to be death. When compared with the stories of Jesus we have in the written gospels, the contrast is pretty stark.

The story of Jesus healing a man on the Sabbath found in Luke 6 is a case in point. Often when this story is told or read, the Pharisees are viewed through the familiar Protestant stereotype that sees them as legalists, going beyond what was written in the scriptures. The common analogy is that they drew a circle around the commands of the Torah in order to prevent people from breaking them. But as we see in the commands themselves and in the examples of those being played out in the Torah, the Pharisees—at least within the story of Jesus' healing on the Sabbath—are staunch conservatives who *uphold the law.*

In this story found in verses 6-11, Jesus enters into a synagogue on the Sabbath to teach. Among the people gathered was a man who had a withered hand. The Pharisees were also there, watching in case Jesus would heal so that they might have evidence of him breaking the

Sabbath. Jesus, despite knowing why they were there and what they were thinking, called the crippled man to come to him. Then Jesus asked, "Is it lawful to do good or to do harm on the Sabbath, to save life or to destroy it?"[225] After giving everyone the stank eye, he told the man to stretch out his hand. The man obliged, and his hand was completely restored. The Pharisees then left and began to plot what they might do to Jesus.

Now there are two possible meanings that I can see behind Jesus' question. Either way, the question seems rhetorical. He could mean that to heal and bring life on the Sabbath is how to be faithful to the law. If this is what he means, then he is judging the Pharisees for not obeying the law. Or considering that the law commands death on the Sabbath, he could be saying that to destroy life and to do harm on the Sabbath is lawful! Considering the preceding story, which we will look at momentarily, in which he argues that he can in fact break the law since he is the Lord of the Sabbath, I suppose the latter meaning is more likely. After asking this rhetorical question, he looks around at all of them, shaming them, and then breaks the law by bringing life and goodness on the Sabbath! No wonder the Pharisees were pissed!

If one is holding to the Torah and scriptures as the criteria by which to make such judgements, the Pharisees were in the right. Jesus and this man, who picked up his mat on the Sabbath (not unlike the man who picked up sticks on the Sabbath) are clearly in the wrong if one upholds the Torah as the standard. Here in this story Jesus, not the Pharisees, is the one going beyond what is written.

It is important to note at this point that Luke's presentation of the Sermon on the Mount leaves out Jesus' statement about not coming to abolish the Law and the Prophets. Luke does, however, add part of Jesus' statement from chapter 5 of Matthew, but we will come back to that momentarily. In chapter 6 of Luke, the Sermon on the Plain is preceded by the story of the calling of the twelve, the healing of the man on the Sabbath, which we have just looked at, and the story of Jesus and his disciples going through grain fields and plucking grains

225 Lewis, C.S. Lewis Bible.

to eat on the Sabbath. Important for understanding Luke's version of the Sermon on the Mount is this last story found in verses 1-5 and the very last bit of Luke's Sermon on the Plain in verses 46-49. We'll first look at the hungry Jesus and his disciples.

As the story goes, some Pharisees confronted Jesus and his disciples because they were walking through grain fields and freely eating some grain heads on the Sabbath, which according to those accusers was unlawful. In response to this accusation of breaking the law, Jesus essentially says, "Don't you remember that David broke the law?" Apparently, David had entered the house of God and being hungry and on the run, he and his companions had eaten some bread of the presence, which according to the Torah only the priests can eat.

Said another way, what Jesus is doing is giving *King David's actions* as precedence for breaking the law. If the great King David can break the law, then surely the "Son of Man"[226] who is "Lord of the Sabbath"[227] can break the law. In the narrative, Luke presents Jesus as someone with the authority to do so. This story comes right before Jesus heals the man on the Sabbath. It is almost as if after having declared that he can break the law because he is the Lord of the Sabbath, he then doubles-down by declaring it through his actions in the healing of the man on the Sabbath.

At the very end of Luke's Sermon on the Plain account, verses 46-49, Jesus presents his own words and teaching, and thus himself, as the rock upon which to build our lives. As it is sandwiched between these two stories—Jesus declaring that he can break the law because he is the Lord of the Sabbath and ending his sermon by declaring himself the foundation of life—Luke does not need to include the same saying of Jesus that Matthew does in which Jesus declares that he has not come to abolish the scriptures. He does not need to do so because Jesus, within the gospel of Luke, is being presented as the one upon which to orient and establish our lives. The life of a Christian is Christocentric rather than scriptural-centric.

226 Lewis, *C.S. Lewis Bible*, Lk 6:1-5.

227 Ibid., Lk 6:1-5.

In the case of Luke's accounting of Jesus' words found in Matthew 5:18, we will quickly examine this text to see if it contradicts what I have just said. In Luke 16:16-17, it reads, "The law and the prophets were in effect until John came; since then the good news of the kingdom of God is proclaimed, and everyone tries to enter it by force. *But it is easier for heaven and earth to pass away, than for one stroke of a letter in the law to be dropped.*"[228] In Luke's version of this excerpt, he doesn't say it is impossible but that it's easier. Now maybe I'm taking a shot in the dark, but I'll suggest that, at least in Luke's version, we need to view this in the context of what the early church believed Jesus was doing. It was their belief that this current heaven and earth will pass away into the renewed and fully healed version of heaven and earth— that Christ as the Lord of all was making all things new.

So, Luke could be suggesting that just as this current heaven and earth will give way to the new heaven and new earth there are aspects of the Torah and Prophets which do not accurately represent God's nature and are in fact seen as invalid considering Jesus and his work. Said another way, the Torah and Prophets as we know them now, pre-resurrection, will pass away just as the current heaven and earth pass away and will be transformed into a new creation.

Considering Luke 24, in which Jesus shows the disciples how the scriptures speak about him—the scriptures as they were known, pre-resurrection, did pass away. The veil has been lifted, and they [the scriptures], like the ragged disciples, have been transformed by the resurrected Christ. Although, considering the previous verse, "The law and the prophets *were in effect*,"[229] Jesus may be making a hyperbolic statement about the stubbornness by which the religious leaders were holding onto the Law and the Prophets as the foundation to their faith and practice. This seems especially apt since in this verse

---

228 Lewis, C. S. *The C.S. Lewis Bible: NRSV: New Revised Standard Version* (London: HarperCollins, 2010). In Matthew's version of this saying of Jesus, it is worded slightly different. In chapter 5 verse 18, it reads, "For truly I tell you, until heaven and earth pass away, not one letter, not one stroke of a letter, will pass from the law until all is accomplished."

229 Ibid.

Luke might be suggesting that the Law and Prophets are no longer in effect. Considering what we saw in chapter 6 of Luke, I find these options more likely than to say that Jesus fully upheld every aspect of the scriptures.

According to the commands of the Torah and its precedents, Jesus and the healed man should have faced the death penalty for working on the Sabbath. Instead, as we have just seen, Jesus claims his authority (of which he has 100%), even over the Sabbath. We thus see from all of this that Jesus' approach to the scriptures is not congruent with popular notions of inspiration. It fits much more nicely with the participatory theology that says the writings of the Torah and the rest of the scriptures were a human response (a sometimes flawed one) to a Divine Revelation, rather than a revelation in and of itself. Otherwise, the claim of Jesus' divinity made by Christians would make little sense, since we wouldn't expect God to contradict his own revelation. If Jesus is divine and he contradicts scripture, it cannot be divine revelation.

Besides the witnesses behind these gospels, we find that there were also other followers of Jesus that seemed to have understood him as doing the exact opposite. The author of Ephesians [230] says this bluntly in 2:15, *"He has abolished the law [Torah] with its commandments and ordinances, that he might create in himself one new humanity in place of the two, thus making peace."*[231] However, I think it's possible that the author of Ephesians and Jesus are speaking of two different things when they speak of Torah.

Regarding Matthew 5:18, Origen explains that the "one dot" in Greek is an iota, or in Hebrew a yod, both of which are the first letter in Jesus' name. Making this connection, Origen says that Jesus is referring to himself when he speaks about the Law.

> "So, Jesus will be the one dot, the Word of God in the law, which does not pass from the law until all is accomplished. But the iota might also be (as he himself says) the ten commandments of the law,

---

230 Roughly written somewhere between 70-80 C.E.

231 Lewis, *C.S. Lewis Bible*.

for everything else passes away, but these do not pass away. But neither does Jesus pass away; if he "falls to the ground" he does so willingly, in order to bear much fruit. Again, the "one iota" or "one dot" has mastery over things both in heaven and on earth."[232]

In stating that Jesus' definition of the Torah and Prophets is himself—or rather, is himself incarnated in and through the scriptures—Origen solves the dilemma of Jesus contradicting himself. What the Ephesians passage, along with Origen's quote and concern revealed in his statement, shows us is that some early Christians thought it was more problematic for Jesus to contradict himself than it was for Jesus to contradict scripture. It also reveals to us that the Torah was not beyond question and criticism.

Derek Flood, in his book *Disarming Scripture*, makes the case that Jesus does in fact mean the actual Torah. He points out that the Greek word translated as "fulfill" can either mean fulfilling all the commands and requirements of the Torah or, more likely considering what Jesus does a few verses later, can mean fulfilment in the sense of bringing something to its intended purpose and thus perfecting or completing it.

As I noted earlier, many of the Mosaic laws, such as "eye for eye" were intended to limit the violence one could inflict upon another in revenge. According to Flood, it is in this sense that we can take Jesus to be fulfilling the intended purpose of those laws, to limit violence. Of course, as we have seen, Jesus would take this to another level in commanding no retaliation at all. He would, in this sense, fulfil the intended goal of those laws to limit violence.[233]

Another solution to this dilemma of Jesus seemingly contradicting himself (a dilemma largely, but not only, produced by the assumption that God's inspiration is synonymous with God's authorship[234]) is

---

[232] Manlio Simonetti and Thomas C. Oden, eds., *Matthew 1-13* (Downers Grove, IL: InterVarsity Press, 2001).

[233] Derek Flood, *Disarming Scripture: Cherry-Picking Liberals, Violence-Loving Conservatives, and Why We All Need to Learn to Read the Bible Like Jesus Did* (San Francisco, CA: Metanoia Books, 2014), 23-27.

[234] Jesus' contradiction of certain scriptures is only problematic from a Christian point of view if the Bible is assumed to be the very Word of God. Under this theological

found later on in the gospel of Matthew. There it records Jesus having a conversation about which commandment was the most important. This gives us vital insight into Jesus' view of the Torah and scriptures.

> "When the Pharisees heard that he had silenced the Sadducees, they gathered together, and one of them, a lawyer, asked him a question to test him. 'Teacher, which commandment in the law is the greatest?'[235] He said to him, "You shall love the Lord your God with all your heart, and with all your soul, and with all your mind." This is the greatest and first commandment. And a second is like it: "You shall love your neighbor as yourself." *On these two commandments hang all the law and the prophets.'*"[236] (Emphasis mine.)

Luke records the same interaction, but this time with the religious leader giving the answer,

> "One day an expert in religious law stood up to test Jesus by asking him this question: 'Teacher, what should I do to inherit eternal life?' Jesus replied, 'What does the law of Moses [the Torah] say? *How do you read it?*' The man answered, "You must love the Lord your God with all your heart, all your soul, all your strength, and all your mind." And, "Love your neighbor as yourself." 'Right!' Jesus told him. 'Do this and you will *live!*'"[237](Emphasis mine.)

Considering these passages, one could easily conclude that when Jesus says Torah, he isn't referring to the historical flesh and blood text itself but a particular interpretation of it. That is a certain way

---

framework, the whole of the scriptures must maintain a theological unity and cannot be contradicted by Jesus lest the whole Christian fundamentalist project collapse. If the Bible is not the very Word of God, there is less of a dilemma from Jesus' contradiction of certain scriptures. There remains, however, the problem of Jesus contradicting himself.

235 The fact that it is assumed there is a greatest commandment implies that there are lesser commandments, and therefore not all of scripture is of equal value.

236 Lewis, *C.S. Lewis Bible*, Mt 22:23-40.

237 *Every Man's Bible: New Living Translation* (Colorado Springs, CO: Tyndale House, 2004), Lk 10:25-28.

of reading the text, one which places a hermeneutical lens in front of it creating the correct interpretation of the scriptures. Consequently, Jesus asks, "*How do you read it?*"[238] (Emphasis mine.)

Church Father Augustine also seemed to interpret these passages with Jesus in a similar manner. For Augustine, the rule for interpreting all of scripture was whether a particular interpretation led one to love God and their neighbor. If the interpretation did not lead the reader to love God and their neighbor, it cannot be a true or a legitimate interpretation. As we will see further on, Jesus himself is the hermeneutical lens through which we correctly interpret scripture, and not only scripture, but tradition, experience, reason, politics, our relationships—indeed all of creation—and through him all things orient themselves to him.

Dan Lioy points to the heart of the discussion when he says, "A pivotal interpretative issue concerns whether Jesus was taking umbrage with the Mosaic Law recorded in the Old Testament or the Pharisaic interpretation of the same."[239] While he argues for the latter position, he points out what it all comes down to. This position, that Jesus is merely "taking umbrage with Pharisaic interpretation," might be too hasty. For instance, biblical scholar Kenneth Bailey, commenting on Luke 4, believes Jesus's reading of the scroll containing Isiah 61 is carefully edited by Jesus as he reads. There are points of the Isaiah text that are changed, interrupted, or even left out. The last verse in the Isaiah passage, which reads, "and the day of vengeance of our God," has completely been cut out.[240]

According to Bailey, our English versions often translate this text as if Jesus' audience was pleased in the beginning, only to turn on him later. However, he points out, "It is possible to understand the Greek text as describing a congregation which is upset *from the beginning.*"[241]

238 Ibid., Lk 10:25-28.

239 Dan Lioy, *Jesus as Torah in John 1-12* (Eugene, OR: Wipf & Stock Publishers, 2007).

240 Kenneth E. Bailey, *Jesus Through Middle Eastern Eyes* (Downers Grove, IL: IVP Academic, 2008), 151.

241 Ibid., 150.

The text may also be translated as, "And all witnessed against him."[242] Why would they be upset? Well, a likely reason is that Jesus reads the first half of the verse about proclaiming the year of the Lord's favor while leaving out the second half of verse 2 that talks about the day of God's vengeance. In other words, the audience in his hometown held the same perspective as reflected in the text of Isaiah—God is on the side of the Jews and part of the messianic deliverance will include his violent revenge upon the gentiles.

Jesus rejects this attitude by omitting it. While Isaiah is not part of the Torah, it gives us some insight that Jesus may not have been comfortable with seeing certain parts of the Hebrew scriptures as fully expressing the will and nature of God. Indeed, we've already observed that Jesus disagreed with certain passages from the Torah, such as the commands concerning the taking of oaths. It makes little sense that Jesus would play so fast and loose with scripture if he himself did not have all authority, and if these scriptures were his own word.[243]

As we saw with Origen, there was a motivation to explain why and how Jesus was not contradicting himself. This of course raises the question of authority as has been hinted at, not so subtly, throughout this book. Who has primary authority, Jesus or the scriptures? If Jesus must harmonize with the scriptures, as many in the evangelical and fundamentalists traditions believe, then scripture has the primary authority. This is summed up in the common mantra, "The Scriptures have all authority," found in many churches today. I may have the skills of a sixth grader[244] when it comes to math, but I'm pretty sure "all authority" means 100%.[245] Which would be another way of saying, if the Bible has all authority, then Jesus has none.

---

242 Ibid., 151.

243 If scripture is God's Word, and Jesus is God, then scripture is also Jesus' Word since he is God.

244 Funnily enough, I am being quite literal since the fact is I can't even do fractions. I have massive holes in my early education due to the childhood trauma I experienced.

245 When I say that Jesus, and therefore God, have all authority, I really do mean it. But I do not mean to say that God is limited in exercising God's authority through things outside of Godself. God can of course use things like scripture and tradition to

Yet, if Jesus is allowed to counter commands from the Torah and exchange them with his own commands, as it seems from his statements, "You have heard it said ... *but I* say to you,"[246] then clearly Jesus has the primary authority—or rather, to be precise, he has all authority. If we are to believe his own statements, both here and in Matthew 28:18, "*All authority* in heaven and on earth has been given to me,"[247] then this is the conclusion we must come to. He does not share his authority, but he is the absolute authority. We see this same affirmation in the ancient church into the second century.

Ignatius of Antioch, in his epistle to the Philadelphians, retells an encounter with what appeared to be Jewish-Christians in which they claimed "the Hebrew Scriptures ("the charters") determine the meaning of the Christian preaching (the "gospel")."[248] He responded, "To me the charters are Jesus Christ, the inviolable charters is his cross, and death, and resurrection, and the faith which is through them."[249] In Ignatius, we see a commitment to the same view that is recorded in the book of Matthew and Luke: that Jesus is the foundation and authority upon which his followers ground themselves. In other words, for Ignatius, it isn't the scriptures [Old Testament] that determine the meaning of the story of Jesus, but Jesus—since he has all authority—determines the meaning of the scriptures [Old Testament].

---

mediate the authority of Christ, but they are only vehicles of that authority, not the passenger who's riding in the vehicle. Jesus is a King (go figure), and *he* distributes his own authority through the many vehicles that make up God's creation. So, I would say, and have said in my other writings, that God exercises God's authority through various vehicles: scripture, tradition, the Church, etc. However, that authority is never intrinsic to the thing itself. It's always God's authority by nature. So, in that sense, God has all authority, even when he hitches a ride with scripture, it is still by nature God's authority. Because it is part of God's nature, it can never be separated from Godself.

246 Lewis, *C.S. Lewis Bible.*

247 Ibid.

248 Andrew Louth, ed., *Early Christian Writings, trans. M. Staniforth, 2nd ed.* (London, England: Penguin Books, 1987), 95.

249 Ibid., 95.

Dan Lioy points out the three main perspectives on Jesus' relationship to the Law. Some believe that Jesus came to abolish the law, to supersede or abrogate it, such as we saw with the author of Ephesians. Others believe that he radicalized the demands of the Torah and raised the standard of its requirements, and as a byproduct nullified some long-lasting commands. Lastly, there are those who believe Jesus produced demands that moved beyond the Law and indeed went in different directions from the Law. Lioy rejects these options as contradictions of Jesus' claim that he did not come to abolish the Torah and the Prophets. But as we've seen, the evidence does not support taking Jesus' statement here at face value, as if he means the actual flesh and blood scriptures. It is untenable since he contradicts a number of commands time and again.

Of course, we need not believe Jesus contradicted himself or that Jesus upheld the Torah and Prophets (Hebrew scriptures) as the fullest authority on the nature of God and his will. Taking the trajectory of Origen as he says, "So Jesus will be the one dot, the Word of God in the law which does not pass from the law until all is accomplished,"[250] we may say that the Torah and Prophets of which Jesus speaks in the deepest sense is himself. (We will discuss this further below.) This allows his statements to remain true and uncontradicted while also making sense of the places in which he clearly contradicts the Torah and rejects certain passages of scripture.

Now that we've discussed Jesus' relationship to Torah, it's time to look at his hermeneutic. We'll do so by focusing on Luke 24:27 and 24:44-45.

"Then beginning with Moses and all the prophets, he interpreted to them the things about himself in all the scriptures.[251] Then he said to them, "These are my words that I spoke to you while I was still with you—that everything written about me in the law of Moses, the

---

250 Manlio Simonetti and Thomas C. Oden, eds. *Matthew 1-13* (Downers Grove, IL: InterVarsity Press, 2001).

251 Lewis, *C.S. Lewis Bible*.

prophets, and the psalms must be fulfilled." Then he opened their minds to understand the scriptures."[252]

This passage is often used to support what I have been calling popular notions of inspiration and the faith statement that scripture is the "very Word of God,"[253] serving as our absolute foundation for the Christian faith. *This view places the identity of God and Jesus as subject to the witness of scripture.* But as we will see, this passage actually undermines that position.

Pointedly, Matthew Barrett, a professor at Midwestern Baptist Theological Seminary writes, "Unquestionably, Jesus knew that the entire Old Testament spoke of him and what he had accomplished."[254] Depending on how this is interpreted, I think all Christians should affirm this. However, when considering the context Barrett gives this statement within his book, it is implied that *Jesus is submitting to the scriptures.* What he is fulfilling must be fulfilled because of the authority of the scriptures. Barrett continues, "The New Testament writers believed the same,"[255] that Paul, as one example, testified Christ was raised on the third day *according to the scriptures.*

The next line clarifies Barrett's understanding of the phrase "according to the scriptures" as everything conforming to them, including Jesus: "Indeed, the apostolic testimony to the gospel and the resurrection of Christ is entirely *dependent upon the inspiration of the Old Testament.*"[256] Said another way, the work of Jesus entirely depends on the Bible as the Word of God. It seems the thrust behind Barrett's argument is not establishing the truth of Christ, but rather the truth of the scriptures and how Christ by extension fits into that.

---

252 Ibid.

253 Matthew Barrett, *God's Word Alone: The Authority of Scripture* (Grand Rapids, MI: Zondervan, 2016), 206.

254 Ibid., 210.

255 Ibid., 211.

256 Ibid., 211.

This same understanding of scripture as being the baseline upon which Jesus orients himself is found among Craig Keener's work. He states, "Every stratum of Gospel tradition reports his appeal to the Old Testament to define his mission." Keener proceeds by claiming that while Jesus may have had many disagreements regarding the interpretation of scripture "he agrees with them concerning its authority."[257] Here again we see an understanding of "in accordance with the scriptures" to mean a *scripturalformativity*,[258] one that even Christ must center his life around. From this perspective, Jesus appeals to the scriptures because it is also his authority. It defines his mission.

The Reformation Study Bible, put out by R.C. Sproul's Ligonier Ministries, includes a footnote regarding Luke 24:44, which reads: "Everything ... must be fulfilled. Notice the word 'must.' It is no accident that Scripture is fulfilled, for it reveals the purposes of God."[259] Here "everything must be fulfilled"[260] because scripture is the source that reveals God's purposes. In this way, Christ and the events surrounding him *had to happen* according to the scriptures; there was no choice or possibility to the contrary. This way of understanding the scriptures seems to suggest that they have some sort of gravitational pull around which everything must orient and submit itself. This way of thinking defines "in accordance with the scriptures" as an affirmation of scripture's intrinsic authority, one upon which even Christ must submit to.

However, it's not so cut and dry. "In accordance with the scriptures" could mean a lot of things. Those mentioned above seem to believe it means the scriptures themselves are the rule of faith by which we measure all things. When read in its own first century

---

257 Craig S. Keener, *The IVP Bible Background Commentary: New Testament* (Downers Grove, IL: InterVarsity Press, 1993), 258.

258 I believe this is a term I have coined. It means that all things must conform to the ultimate authority of scripture.

259 *The Reformation Study Bible: English Standard Version* (Lake Mary, FL: Ligonier Ministries, 2005), 1505.

260 Ibid., 1505.

hermeneutical context, however, it becomes clear that what we are dealing with here is not a statement of the centrality and intrinsic authority of scripture, but with a particular way of reading scripture. *It is the hermeneutic of a person and the events surrounding his life that serve as a foundation stone through which we see the scriptures.* Eastern Orthodox patristic scholar and priest John Behr has written, "The Christian Gospel, the revelation of Jesus Christ, was essentially a Christocentric reading of scripture."[261] Paul himself remarks about this in 2 Corinthians 3:14 when he writes, "Indeed, to this very day, when they hear the reading of the old covenant, that same veil is still there, *since only in Christ is it set aside.*"[262] Or as Rowan Greer has written, "According to Luke, the risen Lord reveals the true meaning of scripture."[263] Said another way, the phrase we find in Paul's letter to the Corinthians and the Nicene Creed, "in accordance with the scriptures," does not mean that the Christ event (his birth, life, passion, death, resurrection and ascension) happened as determined by the scriptures—as if the scriptures were the primary authority that shaped his life or as if they were pulling the strings behind the scenes.

Rather, when read and transformed by Christ, who is our sole authority (Matthew 28:19), they come to be about him, "newly filled with unexpected meaning."[264] In this way, what has happened—his birth, life, death, resurrection, and ascension—*is* in accordance with the scriptures, or more technically, *in accordance with a Christocentric reading of the scriptures.* He is not only our Lord but also the Lord of the scriptures, and as such, the scriptures must also bow their knee to Christ and be transformed into his image. The Christocentric

261 John Behr, trans., *On the Apostolic Preaching* (Crestwood, NY: St. Vladimir's Seminary Press, 1997), 11.

262 Coogan, et al., *New Oxford Annotated Bible.*

263 James L. Kugel and Rowan A. Greer, *Early Biblical Interpretation* (Philadelphia: Westminster Press, 1986), 136.

264 Richard Hays, "Figural Exegesis and the Retrospective Re-Cognition of Israel's Story," *Bulletin for Biblical Research* 29, no. 1 (2019): 39, doi.org/10.5325/bullbiblrese.29.1.0032.

reading of scripture found in the early church is therefore rooted in the Lordship of Christ.

This Christocentric view places the witness of scripture as subject to the identity of God as revealed in Jesus. In other words, the meaning of the scriptures and what they say is determined, shaped, and transformed by the person of Christ who is the full revelation of God. This is rooted in the Christ experience itself. The author of Matthew 17:5 wrote, "While he was still speaking, suddenly a bright cloud overshadowed them, and from the cloud a voice said, 'This is my Son, the Beloved; with him I am well pleased; listen to him!'"[265] The three disciples with Jesus wanted to make dwellings for all three prophets: Jesus, Elijah, and Moses, but the latter were taken away; God spoke *in the absence of the other two, commanding them to listen to Jesus.*

According to the New Oxford Annotated Bible, "Moses and Elijah symbolize, respectively, the Law and the Prophets."[266] Thus, it would seem Matthew is presenting Jesus as having priority over the Hebrew scriptures.[267] It is noteworthy to point out that we can say the same of Luke's account of the transfiguration in 9:28-36. The issue of authority comes up in the book of Matthew time and time again; until finally, at the culmination of the book, Jesus proclaims he has all authority on heaven and earth.[268]

However, even so, Jesus does not simply instruct his disciples to do away with the scriptures—instead, he teaches them how to read the scriptures anew in light of *who he is.* That seems to be what's going on in Luke 24 in particular. Hays writes, "Surely this figural correspondence is the sort of thing Luke means when he tells us that the mysterious risen Jesus explains to the befuddled travelers on the road to

265 Coogan, et al., *New Oxford Annotated Bible.*

266 Ibid., 1807.

267 To be sure, I am not saying that Christ rids us of scripture but that he, as the foundation of our faith, is the proper nexus for reading scripture.

268 The Gospel of Matthew ends with a final declaration of Christ's authority—Matthew 28:18—but the affirmation of this authority is throughout: 7:29, (arguably 8:9), 9:6, 9:8, 10:1, 21:23, and 21:24-27. The issue of Christ having authority is also prevalent in Luke 4:32-36, 5:24, 7:8, 9:1, 10:19, and 20:2-8.

Emmaus 'the things concerning himself in *all* the scriptures.'"[269] Jesus is essentially teaching them to read the scriptures through himself as the interpretative filter. Jesus is the lens or window through which we see the scriptures rightly. We find evidence that the disciples began enacting this type of new reading in the so-called predictive prophecy of Acts 2.

During Peter's sermon, he quotes Psalm 16 from the Septuagint as a predictive prophecy about Christ's resurrection. The original meaning of that psalm, however, is a prayer for protection, not of predictive prophecy. This description as "predictive prophecy" is in itself a retrospective rereading of the psalm through the hermeneutical lens of the resurrected Christ.[270] What we are seeing through all of this is that Jesus' way of reading scripture, and how he taught his disciples to, was to approach the text backwards in light of Jesus' Crucifixion and Resurrection, filling it with new meaning. Their understanding then became rooted in Jesus' authority rather than any intrinsic authority of scripture. At this level inspiration is found in the postproduction exegetical work of the Holy Spirit. Inspiration is found in its interpretation rather than in the text itself.

Considering all this, we can say that if Jesus declared himself as the one who holds all authority, rejected certain commands from the Torah, and placed himself as the foundation stone of the faith and as the scripture's correct hermeneutical lens, then what we end up with is an approach and relationship to scripture that does not fit within popular notions of inspiration, which make the Bible the Word of God. Instead, while Jesus may not fully articulate a participatory theology of revelation, his theology and practice of scripture sure fits better with it. If scripture is a response to Divine Revelation and Jesus is God, then we shouldn't be surprised at Jesus' sometimes fast and loose approach to those same scriptures.

---

269 Richard Hays, "Figural Exegesis and the Retrospective Re-Cognition of Israel's Story," *Bulletin for Biblical Research* 29, no. 1 (2019): 36. doi.org/10.5325/bullbiblrese.29.1.0032.

270 Ibid., 41.

However, if Jesus affirms God as the author of the Torah, then his actions are contradictory to his words. Through developing this view of the Torah as a response attempting to flesh-out a Divine Revelation, it brings us to a different place. Assuming Jesus doesn't see the Torah as the direct product of God, as our evidence seems to suggest, then he can delegate some of its individual laws as less than good, even sometimes evil.

REVELATION IS THE WORD [CHRIST] OF GOD: EARTHLY TORAH AND HEAVENLY TORAH

Taking in the trajectory's full breadth, let us further explore the theological implications of all this. Among the rabbis, it was widely thought that the Torah existed before the world[271]and that God used the Torah as the blueprint for creation.[272] In Christian thought, we find a similar or parallel notion. Yet instead of a preexistent Torah, there we find a preexistent Christ. In Saint Maximus the Confessor's *The Cosmic Mystery of Christ*, a similar point is made about a blueprint being used for creation.[273] For Maximus, however, it is Christ rather than the Torah who is that blueprint. The notion of prophecy as translation is reminiscent of an understanding of revelation that differentiates between the Torah known in our world and a Torah that exists beyond our world.

Said another way, they conceived of a *heavenly Torah and an earthly Torah*. This view of the Torah is largely associated with the Kabbalah tradition; however, it is also found in Talmudic and Midrashic literature.[274] Questions circulated among rabbis, such as how closely related was this preexistent Torah to our earthly Torah and are they identical? We need not explore these questions in depth, as Sommer does

---

271 Sommer, *Revelation And Authority*,113-118. See for example: Midrash Tehillim 93:3; Bereshit Rabbah 1:4; b. Nedarim 39b

272 Ibid.,113-118. See for example: m. Avot 3:18; Bereshit Rabbah 1:1.

273 Maximus, *On the Cosmic Mystery*.

274 Sommer, *Revelation and Authority*, 113.

an excellent job. Our point here is that this conception of heavenly and earthly Torah can bring us further along in our discussion of how Jesus' understanding of scripture fits well with participatory theologies of revelation.

If the heavenly Torah and earthly Torah are not completely identical, then one may say the earthly Torah is in some sense a reflection of the heavenly version. This is what I want to explore. What if Christ the Logos [Word of God] is the heavenly Torah? What if Christ is the very embodiment and essence of the commands to love God and your neighbor as yourself? In other words, I want to propose that Christ is the heavenly Torah, of which the earthly Torah was a human response to; in this way, he is the fulfillment, the full embodiment of what earthly Torah was and is reflecting. So, when Christ said that he had not come to abolish the Law and the Prophets but to fulfill them, this is how we should read it. He is their fulfillment because he is the true scriptures to which they were merely shadows of. In this way, I think we can say that the earthly Torah is our fleshing-out and response to Christ, the heavenly Torah. He is the Divine Revelation to which our scriptures respond.

Following the theological interpretive method of the historic church, the authors of the New Testament, Jesus, and all first century Jews, I offer—rather than a historical interpretation—a new take on Exodus 31:18. There it says, "When God finished speaking with Moses on Mount Sinai, he gave him the two tablets of the covenant, tablets of stone, *written with the finger of God.*"[275] The first set of tablets, which are recorded as having been written down by the finger of God, symbolically represent the heavenly Torah, which is Christ.

The first set of tablets is broken, just as Christ is later broken on the cross. In Exodus 34:1; 4, "The Lord said to Moses, 'Cut two tablets of stone like the former ones, and I will write on the tablets the words that were on the former tablets, which you broke ... *So Moses cut two tablets of stone like the former ones;* and he rose early in the morning and went up on Mount Sinai, as the Lord had commanded him, and

[275] Lewis, C.S. Lewis Bible, Ex 31:18.

took in his hand the two tablets of stone."[276](Emphasis mine.) Later on, the scriptures say that Moses—rather than God—wrote on the new stone tablets. These new tablets made and written on by Moses symbolically represent the earthly Torah, the human response and fleshing-out of God's heavenly Torah, which is Christ.

As odd as this might sound, this concept may not be completely foreign to the New Testament. Hebrew 10:1 says, "Since the law [Torah] has only a shadow [skia] of the good things to come and not the true form of these realities." In other words, the Torah, as given by Moses to the people, contains a shadow of things to come and is not the "true form of these realities." That is the realities to which it is pointing us. Earlier, the author of Hebrews in 8:5 had said something similar about the tabernacle built by Moses in the desert: "They offer worship in a sanctuary that is a sketch [hupodeigma] and shadow [skia] of the heavenly one; for Moses, when he was about to erect the tent [tabernacle], was warned, 'See that you make everything according to the pattern that was shown you on the mountain.'" Following this, in chapter nine verse 11, the author of Hebrews reiterates the point by contrasting that Christ has come and entered not *a tent made with human hands but a better and perfect tabernacle.*

It speaks of a heavenly tent of which the earthly one was a mere reflection. The author of Hebrews talks about how necessary it is for this earthly tabernacle to be purified in blood as it was by Moses since the earthly tabernacle was only a sketch or copy [hupodeigma] of the true one, of which it was a reflection. The words translated as shadow and sketch denote that there is something beyond Israelites that is casting these shadows. The author even wrote that this copy of the tabernacle was something made by humans, which was a way of calling it an idol.

Saint Basil of the fourth century in his book *On the Holy Spirit* suggests that the mystery of God is a great light, something that we as finite human beings must slowly adjust our eyes to; therefore, God gently guided and accommodated us, met us where we were, and slowly "trained us to see the shadows of bodies [its reflections] and to look at the sun in water [its reflection], so that we not be blinded by wrecking ourselves on the vision of pure light."[277] What St. Basil is saying is that instead of revealing the real thing in and of itself immediately, God had to meet us in our infantile minds and slowly prepare us to see the real thing. This God did by showing us the shadow or reflection of the real thing.

Directly preceding this line and reflecting on Hebrews 10:1, St. Basil writes, "According to the same logic, the Law, 'being a shadow of things to come' (Heb 10.1), and the prefiguring of the Prophets, *a reflection of the truth*, are intended as a school for the eyes of the heart, so that the change from these things to the wisdom hidden in mystery will be easy for us."[278] Now that we have been prepared by the shadow and reflections of the mystery of God, we can now set our eyes on the thing itself that casted the shadow. But let us not so quickly depart from Basil's thoughts here. Knowing that Christ is the truth (John 14:6), the law, which according to Basil was a "reflection of the truth,"[279] is indeed a reflection of Christ.

Twentieth century Jewish theologian Rosenzweig said in a letter to Martin Buber[280] in 1925, "The primary content of revelation is revelation itself. 'He came down' [on Sinai]—this already concludes the revelation; 'He spoke' is the beginning of interpretation."[281] Here Rosenzweig seems to identify God's presence with God's revelation and says the phrase "he spoke" is the beginning of the human's response to the revelatory event that is God's presence. Christianity also holds similar notions to both parts of this. Regarding God's presence as revelation, Karl Barth said,

---

277 Basil, St. *On the Holy Spirit.* Translated by Stephen Hildebrand. Yonkers, NY: St. Vladimir's Seminary Press, 2011. Pg 65.

278 Ibid. Pg. 65.

279 Ibid. Pg. 65.

280 Another twentieth century Jewish theologian

281 Sommer, *Revelation and Authority*, 104. Rosenzweig, OJL, 118.

"What God speaks is never known or true anywhere in abstraction from God Himself. It is known and true in and through *the fact that He Himself says it, that He is present in person in and with what is said by Him ... God's revelation in proclamation and Scripture, we must understand it in its identity with Himself. God's revelation is Jesus Christ, the Son of God."*[282]

Where Karl Barth went further than Rosenzweig was in declaring that God's self presence of Revelation is Christ Himself, the Word of God. All of this that we've been looking at helps us begin to make sense of how Jesus handled the Torah.

Jesus sees himself as a greater authority to Torah. Because from a Christian perspective, as we saw in Hebrews, he is the good thing to come. As St. Basil said, he is the truth of which the Law and Prophets were a reflection, the reality of which the Torah was but a shadow, a response, a reflection and interpretation of him. This seems to be the case since he commands his listeners to follow his own commands rather than the Torah. If he is the heavenly Torah, he must point people to himself in the same way in which the earthly Torah points to him. When God speaks, Christ is what is spoken; it is not merely words, but the Word. It is Christ himself, the heavenly Torah, who spoke to the prophets and to whom they responded.

"All who believe and are assured that *grace and truth came through Jesus Christ,* and who know Christ to be the truth, according to his saying, *I am the truth,* derive the knowledge which leads human beings to love a good and blessed life from no other source than from the very words and teaching of Christ. And by the words of Christ we mean not only those which he spoke when he became human and dwelt in the flesh; for even before this, Christ, the Word of God, was in Moses and the Prophets. For without the Word of God how could they have been able to prophesy of Christ?"[283]

282 Karl Barth, *The Doctrine of the Word of God.* Vol. 1, 2 vols. (Peabody, Massachusetts: Hendrickson Publishers, 2010), 137.

283 John Behr, trans. *Origen: On First Principles: A Reader's Edition* (Oxford, UK: Oxford University Press, 2019), 5.

Christ has been working among his people since the beginning of Creation, and they have been responding to him since the beginning of their creation. Heschel taking the phrase "God spoke" in a special sense says,

> *"Indicative* words ... stand in a fluid relation to ineffable meanings and, instead of describing, merely intimate something which we intuit but cannot fully comprehend ... Their function is not to call up a definition in our minds but to introduce us to a reality which they signify ... Words used in this sense must neither be taken literally nor figuratively but responsively ...They are not portraits but *clues,* serving us as guides, suggesting a line of thinking. This is our situation in regard to a statement such as "God spoke."[284]

All of this could be appropriated to be about Christ, the Word, the Heavenly Torah, the very blueprint and cosmic mystery of all reality and our interactions and response to that ineffable meaning and Word. The whole of the Hebrew and Christian Scriptures, nay, the whole of the Jewish and Christian traditions, which includes their scriptures,[285] may be said to be a response to this heavenly Torah.[286] They are a grasping for the ungraspable, struggling to find human words to describe the ineffable object that is the Son of God.

Tying this all together, we can say that Christ is the heavenly Torah, the one to whom the Torah and prophets were a response, shadow, and reflection of. He is not a revelation of God, even the fullest among many—but revelation is God. Christ is himself revelation, as he is himself God. He is the revelation and truth to which our

---

284 Heschel, *God In Search Of Man,* 181-183.

285 Most, if not all, of the New Testament, the Christian Scriptures, were indeed written by Jews, and it thereby could be said in a very real way that they are also Jewish scriptures in that they are Jewish. Although Judaism does not recognize them as their scriptures, I say this not to undervalue the Jewish tradition or undermine the differences between our two faiths, but rather to honor the origins of the Christian faith as an extension of the Jewish faith, and to honor much of the things held in common between the two.

286 Although the two religions would clearly differ in what this response is to—in this case heavenly Torah being Christ.

faithful spiritual and biological ancestors were responding to. He is the fulfillment of the earthly temple because he is the heavenly temple upon which the earthly temple was based and was but a copy of. In this sense, he is also the fulfillment of the Law and Prophets because he is the heavenly Torah of which they were mere shadows of. And since Christ is heavenly Torah, he is the standard by which the earthly Torah is judged. In this way, he is able to both fulfill the Law and the Prophets as the true scripture himself and contradict them since they are but shadows of himself.

Considering all that we have discussed in this chapter, I suggest that not only are participatory theologies of revelation acceptable for the follower of Jesus, but that these theologies account for Jesus' own interactions with scripture much better than do popular notions of inspiration. In addition, participatory theologies of revelation fit better with who we as Christians witness Jesus to be.

Lastly, with all that I have said in this chapter, I should note to the reader, particularly if the reader is anti-Jewish, that while I stress the discontinuities between Jesus and much of the Jewish theology and expectations of the time, my work does not recognize a complete break from the Jewish theology, expectations and background of Jesus. There certainly are continuities between Jesus, the Christian faith, and the Jewish faith and its theologies. The affirmation of Christian orthodoxy is that in Jesus, God became fully human while remaining God, which disallows for a complete break with the Jewish faith.

Not only *was and is* Jesus human, he *was and is* a Jewish human. As Beth Jones has written, "Jesus does not come among us as a generic human being; he comes as we do, with particulars. Jesus' particularity includes his maleness, his Jewishness, his location in first-century Palestine, and what Markus Bockmuehl calls his 'bloody historical concreteness.' If any proposal for doctrine tries to offer us a non-Jewish Jesus, something has gone seriously wrong."[287] The Christian faith can thus never completely reject the Jewish people and religion in which our faith was born.

---

[287] Jones, *Practicing Christian Doctrine,* 137.

Indeed, our faith is a continuation of their faith rather than a break from it. Much of the work that I do here engages Jewish sources and Jewish theologies. The fact that these theologies work in an entangled partnership witnesses to the continuity that exists between our two faiths because of the Christian's faith in an *eternal Jewish Messiah*. The first followers of Jesus, who were all Jewish, were not rejecting their Judaism. Rather what set them apart from their fellow Jews of the time was that they believed that Jesus was the centralizing factor of their Jewish faith rather than the Torah or Temple.

Now we move on to our next chapter on participatory views found within the Christian tradition.

CHAPTER FIVE

PARTICIPATORY VIEWS FOUND WITH THE CHRISTIAN TRADITION

As I wrap this book up, since I'm writing from a Christian perspective, we must address whether we find the theology I've been advocating within the Christian tradition itself. To an extent, I have already done this. In chapter 2, I've shown where we could detect seeds of essential kenosis within the Bible, early Christian tradition, and later within the writing of Protestant reformers like Jacob Arminius and John Wesley. In chapter 3, I tried to show where I believe we find participatory theologies of revelation both in the Old and New Testament. In addition to the ways in which I've already expanded, I'd like to focus on this task specifically in regards to participatory theologies. I'll do so by adding just a few more examples that represent various traditions within the Christian umbrella. Throughout this book, I have been constructing a proposal for a doctrine of inspiration, and here I will finish the work of doing so. But first, I'd like to lay out a couple of preliminary notes on the need for this discussion.

It is too often the case that our brothers and sisters within the fundamentalist tradition of Christianity present the loudest voice. Often claiming exclusive rights to the notion, they are the only true inheritors of historical Christianity. This repeatedly manifests itself with the attitude that they represent the whole of Christianity rather than only one stream within a very large Christian ocean. Such Christians regularly give the false impression to the culture and church at large that their viewpoints and dogmas are the only Christian ones—that what they believe is what all Christians, everywhere, in all places, and in all times have believed.

It is one of the major contributing factors to why many who leave the fundamentalist tradition leave Christianity altogether. When presented with the false notion that a fundamentalist understanding of Christianity is Christianity in its entirety, upon subsequently rejecting it, their only option is often atheism.[288] But Christianity, like many of the world's religions, is extremely diverse, far from being the monolithic faith that many both inside and outside the church think it is.

However, Christianity existed before the birth of fundamentalism, one hundred and fifty years ago, before Evangelicalism, two-hundred and fifty years ago, and before Protestantism, five hundred years ago. For this reason and for our purposes here, we embark on further exploring some alternative viewpoints within the broader Christian tradition. It is important that Christians be skeptical of anything that cannot show at least some roots or seeds in the past.

A fig tree does not produce thorns, just as a thorn bush does not produce figs. The seed of a Douglas fir tree may look very different from its full-grown version, but we know despite differences in appearance the tree came from the seed and is therefore in continuity with it. If some doctrine cannot show itself to have roots or even seeds going back to Christ himself, it is not legitimately Christian.[289] With all that said, we can begin.

Let's start off with Dennis R. Bratcher, an ordained Nazarene minister and Wesleyan theologian. From his essay in the book *Rethinking the Bible,* he seems to exhibit participatory theologies of revelation of

---

288 Of course, in reality, they have many more options than atheism, both inside and outside of the Christian faith. But in my experience, it is often the case that they choose atheism more often than not. I think this is because fundamentalism often presents itself and atheism as the only two options.

289 That being said, wherever we find truth, we find Christ for He is The Truth. So, there may be true things to be found outside the Church, but true things will never be found outside of Christ.

his own. There he writes, "I do not understand the Bible to be *direct* revelation ... Scripture is *the witness* that the community of faith has given *about revelation.*"[290] (Emphasis mine.) Earlier he claimed that God is revelation,[291] and that scripture is the witness to and response of that God. He continues by explaining that the gospel writers were witnessing to what they had observed with their eyes and heard with their ears.[292] Said another way, according to Bratcher what we have in scripture is a response to revelation which is distinguishable from the revelation itself.

He furthers his conversation about revelation by claiming that scripture is a collection of fleshed-out experiences with God produced by those ancient faith communities. If all that left doubt in the mind about his use of participatory theologies, his next statement leaves us little room to think otherwise. "God is revealed to us today through *interpreted* events. God revealed God-self in history (events), and the community of faith *interpreted those events* in what we now have as Scripture."[293] This means that what is interpreted—the human response to revelation—is influenced by the people encountering the revelation. Their interpretations to that divine encounter are shaped by their language, culture, personalities, and so forth. Considering Bratcher's statements above, it seems clear he's working with participatory theologies of revelation at some level. Whether he's conscious of that is another question to which I have no answer.

While we see participatory theology in the Protestant tradition represented above by Bratcher, we also find it in the Eastern Orthodox tradition and elements of it in the Roman Catholic Church. Eastern Orthodox New Testament scholar Veselin Kesich has written,

---

290 Dennis R Bratcher, *Rethinking the Bible: Inerrancy, Preaching, Inspiration, Authority, Formation, Archaeology, Postmodernism, and More,* ed. Richard P. Thompson and Thomas Jay Oord (Nampa, ID: SacraSage Press, 2018), 55.

291 This is a similar statement to what we've seen Karl Barth make.

292 Bratcher references the following Scriptures: Luke 1:1-4; 7:22; John 21:24-25; 3:32.

293 Bratcher, *Rethinking the Bible,* 56.

"In the incarnation the Word of God became flesh, and in the Bible the words of God became human language. The words of Scripture are simultaneously *the record of God's revelation and an expression of human response to God's actions.* These words inevitably consist of both divine and human elements. *The truth of God becomes incarnate in the reception and contemplation of it by human beings.*"[294] (Emphasis mine.)

Within the Eastern Orthodox perspective of Kesich, there is a divine element. Yet it seems to be that the human words of the Bible are a response to that divine element and indeed become a body, so to speak, for that divine element to incarnate. It is not, in his words, equated to that revelation. Instead, the Bible is a record of and a human response to the God of whom it witnesses.

Reminiscent of what we will see as Lewis' conception of *little incarnation*, Kesich seems to share a similar view: it is in our responses, our "reception and contemplation,"[295] as he calls it, that God's truth (or Christ himself knowing that He is the Truth)[296] is incarnated into our responses. Scripture, as the record of and human response to God's action, again, is where God incarnates God's self. I might suggest that we can see Origen's influence here; in that, like Origen, Kesich's language is evocative of scripture as an incarnation of the Word.

Later on, in speaking about accepting modern historical-critical methods of studying the Bible, he makes a comment that further illustrates his view of scripture. Kesich explains, "To reject the historical-critical method would be to reduce or even to neglect the importance of *the human response to the Word of God.*"[297] Here he calls the Bible a response to the Word of God, whom from the Orthodox perspective is Christ, thus in doing so distinguishes the human response from the Word itself.

---

294 Kesich, *Gospel Image of Christ*, 45.

295 Ibid., 45.

296 John 14:6

297 Kesich, *Gospel Image of Christ*, 46.

Regarding the four gospels, further on in his book Kesich says, "Their unique characteristics underline the intensity of the individual *responses of their authors to God's final revelation*, as well as the validity of their common inspiration."[298] This all fits into what we have been calling participatory theologies of revelation. God reveals God's self, and the authors of scripture respond to that revelation within their human interpretations.

Gregory of Nyssa, a forerunner of the Orthodox Church, said a similar thing. "*Moved by divine inspiration instead of by demonic power*, he uttered such words as were a clear prophecy of better things which would later come to pass ... Leaving divination aside, he *acted as an interpreter of the divine will*."[299] (Emphasis mine.) What Gregory is saying is that divine inspiration does not work like demonic possession or divination and that the prophet needs to translate or interpret the will of God. Unlike demonic power, where the Spirit of the Lord is, there is freedom. While Gregory claims this particular prophecy was accurate and would come to pass, the prophet nonetheless interpreted the communication that he received. There's a difference between good interpretations and bad ones, just as we saw in 1 Kings 22. The prophet was and is still in need of interpreting the will of God. He wasn't simply an empty vessel but acted with the freedom that is required by the act of interpretation.

The Roman Catholic perspective is more of a mixed bag. On the one hand, there seem to be ideas about the Bible that lend itself to participatory notions of revelation. On the other hand, some of the Catholic Church's statements in the magisterium would seem to curb the possibility of a Catholic participatory theology of revelation. The late Daniel J. Harrington, a Catholic New Testament scholar, briefly discusses some of these ideas in his book *The Bible and the Believer*, co-authored with Peter Enns and Marc Zvi Brettler. There Harrington writes, "Catholics believe the Bible was written by human authors under the guidance of the Holy Spirit. It is the word of God in human

---

298 Kesich, *Gospel Image of Christ*.

299 Gregory, The Life of Moses (San Francisco, CA: HarperOne, 2006), 29.

language, that is, '*the word of God in the words of men*.'"[300] If you recall from my discussion on Kesich, the language he used, "*the words of God became human language*,"[301] is almost identical to that used by Harrington and the Catholic tradition here, "*the word of God in the words of men.*"[302]

Said another way, God's words are translated into human language. Of course, anyone familiar with language translation will acknowledge that translation always includes interpretation. Something we saw in the concept of prophecy as translation in chapter 3. In reality, this could be understood in two radically different ways. *It could mean that humans have translated God's words.* The statement "The word of God in the words of men"[303] could be understood in this first sense. But it also could be taken in a second sense *to mean that God's self does the translation in much the same way as a human whose first language was Thai would translate her own words into Japanese.* If it's understood in this second sense, then the phrase would mean the Bible is not a response to divine revelation, since God would be the one translating, but that it is divine revelation. Based on Harrington's surrounding statements, one could easily understand the phrase in the first sense.

Furthermore, Harrington also made the claim that unlike Protestants and Muslims, Catholics are "not a religion of 'the book.'"[304] Rather, "Catholicism is more a religion of a person."[305] In addition to these statements, he explains the Catholic view of the Bible as primarily *a witness* to the person of Jesus, the Word of God. Further on, he says that to the Catholic people the scriptures are regarded "as a privileged witness" to revelation and a vehicle for further revelation.

300 Marc Zvi. Brettler, Peter Enns, and Daniel J Harrington, *Bible and the Believer: How to Read the Bible Critically and Religiously* (New York, NY: Oxford University Press, 2012), 87.

301 Kesich, *Gospel Image of Christ*, 45.

302 Zvi et al., *Bible and the Believer*, 87.

303 Ibid., 87.

304 Ibid., 85.

305 Ibid., 85.

As we will see with C. S. Lewis here shortly, Harrington also is fond of the imagery of a *vehicle* when discussing the function of scripture.

Here he claims that Scripture is a vehicle by which we can encounter and know the God revealed by Jesus, who is the Word of God. The next statement by Harrington makes me wonder how much of an influence Lewis had on him. There he writes, "The Bible, in turn, can serve as a vehicle that can move individuals and communities in certain positive directions."[306] This would seem to distinguish between the Word as Jesus or revelation and the Bible as a vehicle or witness to that Word/revelation.

Lastly, Harrington references the Catholic statement of Dei Verbum 13 as the theological impetus for their understanding of the Bible and its inspiration: "For the words of God, expressed in human language, have become like unto human speech, just as the Word of the eternal Father, when he took on himself the flesh of human weakness, became like unto human beings."[307] The analogy of incarnation we see used here (an analogy we will see with Lewis, as well as Origen) certainly has its limits. It is not, as far as I am able to discern, a statement declaring that the words of scripture are therefore equal to God. In other words, it's not saying that the scriptures share full divinity as the Son does with the Father. All of this would seem to leave open the possibility for participatory theologies of revelation.

Yet when one looks at some of his other comments on the same pages, one could take the second meaning, that God is the one doing the translation, as what's intended by the phrase. The trouble may lie in the Catholic emphasis upon, and love of paradox, of "both and's."[308] Thus, the Catholic Church could have both meanings in mind. Quoting Dei Verbum ii, Harrington writes, "We must acknowledge the Books of Scripture as teaching firmly, faithfully, and without error the truth that God wished to be recorded in the sacred writings for

---

306 Zvi et al., *Bible and the Believer*, 88.

307 Ibid., 88-89.

308 I actually think this is generally a positive thing from which Protestants could learn a lot. However, in this particular instance, I think it is a hindrance.

the sake of our salvation."[309] This statement by the teaching office of the church [the magisterium] would seem to limit such views of the inspiration of the Bible from fully entering participatory notions of revelation. Since the process of human beings responding within their human interpretive frameworks doesn't allow for the product [the scriptures] to be without errors on any topic, even regarding matters of salvation. Thus, it doesn't seem like the Catholic tradition is willing to give us what we may say is a full participatory theology of revelation. Nonetheless, we see seeds of it in their theology, and maybe one day those will germinate.

Continuing on, as we saw from earlier, Origen says something that suggests he doesn't believe the Bible to be the Word of God. I want to propose this leaves room for, if not outright leads toward a trajectory of participatory theologies of revelation. If revelation and the Word of God (something I equate) are distinguished from scripture, then what you have is participatory theologies of revelation. All that is left at that point is a human response to the divine Word. So here we see Origen write,

> "The things which are spoken through a prophet are not always to be taken as spoken by God. And even though through Moses God spoke many things, nevertheless Moses commanded other things by his own authority [the bill of divorce is given as an example] … *And Paul also shows things in his letters, when he says concerning some things:* 'The Lord says and not I,' and concerning others, 'These things moreover I say, not the Lord' (1 Cor. 7) (Kalin, 'Argument from Inspiration,' 103-4)."[310]

Clearly from Origen's point of view, although Moses and Paul were certainly inspired and Christ the Word certainly spoke to them, inspiration and God's Word are not synonymous. In Origen's mind, inspiration did not prevent Moses and Paul from saying things of their own accord that ended up in scripture. If Moses and Paul are

309 Zvi et al., *Bible and the Believer*, 87.

310 Allert, *High View of Scripture*, 183.

thus speaking on their own in what became scripture, what we have at least at some level, is humans responding to God's revelation, which as we have seen is essentially a participatory theology of revelation. Of course, regarding Origen and his words here, this is admittedly somewhat speculative. I am more so taking what Origen has said and drawing what I believe to be the logical outcome of his thinking. Founded on this, I believe participatory theology to be implicit in his writing, at least here in the above passage.

However, what might be clearer for us, when it comes to Origen, is his view that scripture serves as a body, a type of incarnation that the Word of God takes up for himself. What's more participatory than that? Humans encounter the Word of God and write their own reflections concerning those encounters. Then that very Word, whom those writings are about, comes to dwell in and through those texts as a way to further encounter us. Recorded in the Philokalia, an anthology of Gregory the theologian and Basil the Great's favorite selections from Origen, we find a succinct statement regarding this concept: "The garments of the Word are the phrases of Scripture; these words are the clothing of the divine thoughts."[311] Just as the eternal Son of God would one day take up human flesh through his mother, Mary, so did the Word embody himself in and through the words of scripture.

We should expect nothing less than this. Since God does not change, whatever God does is what God has in some sense always done. So, if God incarnates into humanity and creation, then God must have in some sense always have been incarnated into his creation. Jesus' incarnation—God becoming fully human—is of course a unique, special, one might say a fuller incarnation, since God actually ontologically joined our humanity by becoming human. This is the only time in which God actually became the thing in which God incarnated in and through. Yet God has always been an incarnational

---

311 *Philokalia, The Philocalia of Origen*, ed. J.A. Robinson (Cambridge: Cambridge University Press, 1893); ed., French trans., introduction and notes M. Harl, *Origene: Philocalie, 1-20; Sur les Ecritures*, SC 302 (Paris: Cerf, 1983); trans. G. Lewis (Edinburgh: T. and T. Clark, 1911).

God. So, for God to use the words of scripture to embody God's self should not surprise us.

So far in this book, I've been trying to put together a fairly complex puzzle. Each piece of that puzzle has been important. The first piece was the theology of essential kenosis. The second piece was a participatory theology of revelation. What I argued was the natural entailment of essential kenosis. The third piece was Jesus as the heavenly Torah, the Word of God, Revelation itself, that to which the earthly Torah and Prophets responded. Here I would like to end the chapter by taking the idea of participatory revelation and Christ as that revelation further into the context of a Christian incarnational theology. This is the last piece of the puzzle called an *essentially kenotic incarnational participatory theology of inspiration*. Lewis, a Christian from the Anglican tradition, is the last piece of our puzzle, and he continues what we just saw with Origen.

The very concept of the incarnation of God, what C. S. Lewis calls the "central miracle asserted by Christians,"[312] could be understood as a participatory act. In Lewis' book *Reflections on the Psalms*, he discusses poetry in particular and human speech more broadly as a little incarnation of God. There Lewis writes,

"It seems to me appropriate, almost inevitable, that when that great Imagination which in the beginning, for Its own delight and for the delight of men and angels and of beasts, had invented and formed the whole world of Nature, *submitted to express Itself in human speech, that speech should sometimes be poetry. For poetry too is a little incarnation*, giving body to what had been before invisible and inaudible."[313]

Here Lewis says that God submitted himself to communicate in human words and that sometimes those human words are poetry; he finds poetry to be also a little incarnation. In fact, for Lewis, as well as for Origen, these words give body to the bodiless God and make

312 Lewis, *C.S. Lewis Bible*, 1137.

313 C.S. Lewis, *Reflections on the Psalms* (San Francisco, CA: Harper One, 2017), 6.

the invisible and incomprehensible God comprehensible and visible. For him to say "poetry too" implies, based on the structure of his sentence, that human speech too is a little incarnation of God. Lewis is not saying that God is the author of human speech or poetry, but that God incarnates God's self *into human speech*, thus his phrase "*little incarnation.*"

That this is Lewis' meaning seems clear from what he says later in his book when discussing allegorical readings of scripture. While some may point to his statement on page 22 of the book in which he declares that "scripture is in some-though not all parts of it in the same sense-the word of God."[314] To suggest that Lewis means that the words themselves of scripture are God's very words rather than human words picked up by God through incarnation would be a mistake. For even in the statement itself, he qualifies it by stating that it is God's word "in some sense."[315]

Notice he also uses a lowercase "w" when denoting it as God's word. There's a level of nuance here that should give us pause. In his letter to Mrs. Johnson dated to November 8, 1952, he states unequivocally that "it is Christ Himself, not the Bible, who is the true word of God. The Bible, read in the right spirit and with the guidance of good teachers, will bring us to Him."[316] Here we pick up another hint of what he means when he says that the Bible is in some sense the word of God. It would seem that to Lewis the word of God, in an ontological sense, is Christ, not the Bible. But the Bible can—given the right conditions—bring us to him. To understand how reading the Bible in the right way will bring Christ to us, we need to explore some of Lewis' statements further.

On page 37 of his book, addressing the morally pungent cursing found in some psalms, he writes, "Though hideously distorted by the human instrument, something of the Divine voice can be heard in these passages." The way he words this statement harps back to

---

314 Ibid., 22.

315 Ibid., 22.

316 Lewis, *C.S. Lewis Bible*, 1188.

the language he used earlier about human speech being a little incarnation. In chapter 10, he writes about scripture as a whole. There he clarifies up until this point, he has been discussing the historical meaning of the psalms, what the author intended in his own context, but here he makes an important caveat.

This is not the way they have been read by most Christians for most of church history. Here Lewis states, "Instead they have been believed to contain a second or hidden meaning, an 'allegorical' sense."[317] Essentially, he is saying that Christians have approached the Bible with what New Testament scholar Richard Hays terms as a figural retrospective reading of scripture. They have been reading the Bible backwards in light of the crucified and risen Christ. Lewis continues by saying that "in light of later events,"[318] a new meaning becomes apparent to the reader.

For Christians, these later events include the passion, death and resurrection of Jesus. And it is through these that they read the Old Testament scriptures. Although one might, at this point, think these "new meanings" could really just be old meanings that were part of God's multifaceted authorship of scripture, which remained hidden until the events of the passion. While this may be the case for some church fathers, with Lewis, someone acquainted with historical criticism, it seems like it would be hard for him to deny both the humanness of the original meaning and the divinity of the new retrospective reading.

Unlike the church fathers who lived before the rise of historical criticism, Lewis had to grapple with a way to hold both: how the church has interpreted scripture until the eighteenth and nineteenth century, what we call the allegorical hermeneutic, and the historical method of reading scripture that we are so familiar with today. Suggesting that the new meanings were originally put there in the words of the Bible by God as the author doesn't account for the historical method of reading scripture that had taken hold by Lewis' time.

---

317 Lewis, *Reflections on the Psalms*, 115.

318 Ibid., 116.

So, considering all of that, Lewis' concept of "little incarnation" reaches its culmination by the end of his book. "Generalizing this, I take it that the whole of the Old Testament consists of the same sort of material as any other literature-chronicle, poems, moral and political diatribes, romances, and what not; but all taken into the service of God's word."[319] Admitting that the whole of the scriptures are indeed human literature, something historical criticism has taught us and has become undeniable, he heads toward how he thinks all of this human literature is taken up to serve God's word. On the next page he writes, "The human qualities of the raw materials show through. Naivety, error, contradiction, even (as in the cursing psalms) wickedness are not removed. The total result is not 'the Word of God' in the sense that every passage, itself gives impeccable science or history. *It carries the Word of God.*"[320] (Emphasis mine.) Shortly thereafter, he calls the human material that carries that Word an "untidy and leaky vehicle."[321]

The language of vehicle seems to be important to Lewis and carries the connotation of incarnation. Something we also saw with Origen, Daniel Harrington, and Veselin Kesich. In a letter to Lee Turner, dated July 19th, 1958, he discusses the notion of scripture's inspiration. There he says he believes some of our ancestors took inspiration to mean that God controlled the minds of the biblical authors or, at minimum, dictated to them as if they were secretaries.[322] Lewis states that the Bible denies these ideas of inspiration and discusses Paul as an example of someone who clearly says he's writing for himself.[323]

He also mentions the prophets and their encounters with God, saying, "*their own reactions* to them would be absurd if they were not

---

319 Ibid., 129.

320 Ibid., 130.

321 Ibid., 130.

322 This is part of what I have termed popular notions of inspiration in this book.

323 Something we discussed in an earlier chapter

writing for themselves,"[324] a statement clearly in line with participatory thinking. Lastly, in this passage from his letter, he uses the incarnation as an analogous example for the process of inspiration. Just as in Christ a human body is assumed and therefore becomes the vehicle of the divine nature, "so in Scripture a mass of human legend, history, moral teaching, etc. are taken up and made the vehicle of God's Word."[325] Considering all this, it would seem that for Lewis, scripture, as human words, are taken up incarnationally by the Word of God, who is Christ.

We will now attend to how Lewis' understanding of "little incarnation" is a sort of a participatory theology of revelation. As we have seen for Lewis, scripture itself, and its production, seem to remain human, just as any other literature we might find from the ancient world or today. The inspiration of scripture seems to be less in the writing process itself, which is human, and more in the exegetical process, whereby Christ takes it up as a vehicle, which brings him to us in the opening of the scriptures. From a sacramental perspective, this is also how Christ brings himself to us in the bread and wine. In the participatory models of revelation, scripture remains a product of the human authors themselves, while being a response to the revelation that those same authors are encountering. This is what we find in Lewis's model of incarnational inspiration.

In Lewis' model, what I'm calling a participatory incarnation of inspiration, God takes the entire process a step further. Christ reveals himself to the authors of scripture who then write their responses to that revelation. This initial response is what we call scripture. God continues this participatory act of revealing God's self through a back-and-forth dialogical process, even after scripture's production. At this point, the second person of the Trinity, whom we know to be the Word of God, enters *scripture, which was our human response* to that Word/Revelation. Wrapping himself in scripture as a sort of warm blanket *made of our words*, he uses those very responses to Revelation

324 Lewis, *C.S. Lewis Bible*, 1247.

325 Lewis, *C.S. Lewis Bible*, 1247.

as a vehicle for further bringing himself [Revelation] to us and for an opportunity for us to further respond to that revelation. So, it's not as if scripture is our only response to God, but we continue to respond to the Revelation, who is the Word, that comes to us through the text. We can sum the process up this way: God presents God's self, and our initial response to that is scripture. God then responds to our initial response by entering the text. Then, we respond to God in and through the text, and the process goes on and on. Said another way, it's God's response to our response [scripture], by taking up our response as a vehicle for himself, in order to make it his own response to us. If that doesn't get your engines revved up, I don't what will!

So not only do we see Lewis engaging with what I have called participatory theologies of revelation, he takes it a step beyond by creating a participatory incarnation of inspiration in which the process of participatory theology continues, even in the exegetical process, beyond the production of the text itself. If theology was ever going to bring tears to your eyes, it would be now. And all the theology nerds said Amen.

In this chapter, we have briefly touched on participatory theologies of revelation in the Christian tradition, knowing that I have discussed some of this already in earlier parts of the book. Although this is just a short sampling, I hope that you have been given enough to see this as a legitimate alternative to popular ways of thinking about revelation and inspiration. The book as a whole is meant to be a conversation starter rather than a dissertation covering as much as possible. I could not write such a book at this time (although maybe one day I will), nor would I want to at this moment. This book, for all its flaws, is meant to involve more than just academics, and thus it is fairly short. Now, it is time to move on to the last chapter.

CHAPTER SIX

IMPLICATIONS AND THE ROLE OF SCRIPTURE NOW

Finally, we have made it to the last chapter. If you have stuck with me this far, I thank you. I am honored that you have opened your ears to listen to me. I do not take this for granted. However, having gotten this far, you could be a little disoriented from the hike up to the peak. So, in this last chapter, I'd like to give you a good breather. While much of what I have done might seem as if I was merely tearing down assumptions, I hope it's clear that throughout this book I've been building something or rather excavating something that was already there to take its place.

We will end by explaining how the essential kenosis view of inspiration and revelation solves each of the six dilemmas I outlined in chapter 1. While this should already be clear if I did my job right, explicitly and briefly connecting the dots will hopefully and helpfully sum it all up for you. I will then proceed by pointing out what I think the main implications are of this book. Lastly, I will attempt to show you how scripture is still beautiful, useful, and beneficial to the Christian faith. I hope as a result you will open the scriptures and encounter the crucified and risen Christ.

SIX DILEMMAS ANSWERED

1. The Problem of Evil

As we saw here, popular notions of inspiration fall ill to the problem of evil. Most popular renditions of inspiration identify the product of inspiration with God's Word, requiring a God who at some level can control the biblical authors, editors, compliers, and so forth. The problem is if there is such a God with this kind of controlling power, then why does God not prevent genuine evil in the world? If God could control the authors of scripture to produce his Word, then why does God not prevent terrible events like the Holocaust? The theologies of God that underlie popular notions of inspiration have tried to answer this question but have failed again and again, leaving many people with the belief that their only options are to think that God is not good, not all-powerful, or that there is no God.

My solution solves this issue by explaining that God does not control the authors of scripture. Since the ability to control goes beyond the bounds of God's nature, God also cannot control free creatures to prevent such evil tragedies as the Holocaust. The essential kenosis view of inspiration I have tried to argue for here presents a theology of God that simply is not susceptible to the problem of evil in the ways that underlying theologies of popular notions of inspiration are. Through essential kenosis, we can maintain that God is all-powerful because God is not barred from being fully God and that God is all-loving because God's very nature is uncontrolling Love that always seeks the good and betterment of all in relationship with God.

2. Inerrancy

Among the problems we discussed that the doctrine of inerrancy presents was that it assumes a God who can control a problem. Along with that, it also creates cognitive dissonance between the teachings of Jesus and the Old Testament and suggests a synonymous relationship between God and the Bible. If Jesus teaches non-violence, but the narratives of genocide in the Old Testament teach that violence is not only sometimes acceptable but indeed at times is commanded by God, we are left with the choice of trying to harmonize these texts rather than submit fully to Jesus. This leads into our last problem of ultimately equating God and the Bible.

An essentially kenotic participatory theology of inspiration provides a solution to these issues by showing how scripture is ontologically different from God, since God cannot control creatures, which he would need to do in order to produce a text we could call the inerrant Word of God. What we have because of an uncontrolling God is a human interpreted response [our Bible] to the Word of God [the Son of God].

Thus, we need not harmonize the historical meaning of violent passages in scripture with the teachings of Jesus but may fully give him our due allegiance. This leads to a Christocentric reading of scripture that transforms all of scripture into a witness to him and his teachings. Rather than interpret scripture on its own merits, we can interpret scripture through the lens of the risen Christ. These problematic texts die to themselves and become resurrected. By bending the knee to Christ, they are born anew and are given a new beautiful Christocentric meaning.

3. Apparent Attributions of Scripture

As we noted here, the fundamentalists of the early twentieth century rejected the non-mosaic authorship of the Torah since to them this would imply that God lied; in their view, the Torah clearly attributes its authorship to Moses. Although this perspective is not totally consistently adopted, as they also believe God to be the author of scripture. We also saw that, according to this same logic, if God was the author of scripture God would be a liar because scripture attributes its authorship to humans. Of course, I also tried to show how attributions of authorship in the ancient world differed radically from our own.

My view of inspiration laid out in this book, however, skirts the whole question of apparent authorship. If God cannot control, it results in scripture becoming a response to revelation rather than God authoring it, and therefore the human attribution of authorship would be truthful. According to my view, even if someone had lied about who actually wrote a particular text, say about Moses being the author (again something I think misunderstands the attribution of authorship in the ancient world), we would not need to panic since it is not the Word of God. It thus does not distort the truthful character of God.

4. The Generality of Inspiration

As we saw in this section, the problem of the ancient church's broad use of the concept of inspiration gives common notions of inspiration a run for their money. If inspiration really means authorship, we should expect to see this understanding of inspiration among the earliest Christians. But if this was their understanding of what it meant for something to be inspired, then what we would find is that the ancient church believed many things outside of canonized scripture to be God's Word. This is not what we found to be the case. We also noted that the theory of inspiration popularly held today fails to account for how God speaks outside of the Bible. Lastly, we saw that the modern view of inspiration is in exceptional discontinuity with the earliest Christian use and understanding of inspiration outside of the New Testament.

The implications of my arguments in this book solve these issues by simply not falling prey to the problems through rejecting a definition of inspiration that is equated with authorship. These are only problems if one believes inspiration means authorship. However, as I have argued, inspiration and authorship are not synonymous. God cannot control free creatures in order to write the Bible; rather, the scriptures are a product of a human interpretation of revelation. That leaves room for a lot of things to be inspired outside of canonized scripture. And this is exactly what we find in the ancient church's conception and use of inspiration, many things being called inspired. My solution also solved the dilemma of discontinuity by sharing a view of inspiration that is broad enough to include all of the things the early church called inspired.

Earlier, I had said that inspiration was found on two levels: at the level of interpretation and the level of influence among the various authors, editors, and compilers of scripture. God can and does influence all of creation, and God can use all of that creation as a vehicle for Christ to deliver a Christocentric meaning to the "reader." Thus, it is not problematic for things outside of scripture to be inspired (since it does not mean authorship) as the ancient church clearly believed.

5. The Bible is God's Word-Authorship and Inspiration seen as Synonymous

Starting with my examination of Greg Boyd's *Cross Vision*, we discussed more extensivelyy what I think is the biggest problem for popular ideas of inspiration—that authorship is viewed as synonymous with inspiration, meaning that inspiration is equated as God's Word. Among the issues with seeing the Bible as God's Word, we saw that because God does not change and is eternal whatever Word God speaks must also be eternal; otherwise, a newly spoken word would be a change in God. It would also mean that scripture holds full equality with God. And as I pointed out, only God has equality with God.

Ultimately, this leads to scripture and God being one and the same, which is problematic if one holds to Trinitarian theology, as I do. We also saw that if scripture is God's Word, then Christ cannot have a superior authority to scripture since it would be Jesus' Word as well. This is extremely problematic if Jesus contradicts scripture at all, which we addressed earlier in this book. Therefore, it is absurd to say that Jesus could have a superior authority over his own Word. We also discussed the problematic nature of equating God's Word with the Bible, considering the lack of evidence that the New Testament authors and the ancient church equated the two.

My solution solves this issue by making it impossible for the Bible to be the Word of God. The Word of God, as I have argued, is Jesus Christ, who is the Son of God. Within the framework of an essentially kenotic participatory incarnational theology of revelation, the Bible is a human interpretation or shadow of the heavenly Torah, the Word of God. This is because God cannot control free creatures, and thus what is produced as scripture is a solely human product. In this sense, Jesus, as heavenly Torah, is the fulfillment of the earthly Torah and Prophets because he is the one of whom they were mere sketches and copies of. This also solves the seeming contradiction of Jesus' claim to be the fulfilment of the scriptures while clearly contradicting some of them. This simply sidesteps all the problems associated with declaring the Bible to be the Word of God since the Bible is indeed not the Word of God.

6. Granting Accommodation Theory: Allowing Our Misunderstandings

Last, we discussed Boyd's accommodation theory of inspiration and why that was insufficient. If you recall, from Boyd's perspective, when we see violent portrayals of God in the Old Testament, in light of the Cross, we see God to be accommodating the misunderstandings of an ancient Near Eastern tribal warrior society. Said another way, God really doesn't command or even desire his followers to commit ethnic genocide (thank God!), yet God accommodated those views by allowing the biblical authors to believe them; therefore, we have them now recorded in the biblical narrative.

The point I take issue with wasn't so much the concept of accommodation as it was Boyd's idea that God could have done otherwise. Said another way, the problem is that if God could have corrected the ancient Hebrews in their misunderstandings and thus prevented morally repugnant actions, why didn't God do so? Here again the problem of evil rears its head. The heart of the issue is, from Boyd's point of view, God could choose not to accommodate.

The essential kenosis approach shared in this book solves this dilemma by suggesting that God cannot control free creatures, and thus God must always accommodate. Therefore, when say the ancient Israelites believed that they were commanded to kill men, women, and children, and steal their land,[326] God could not necessarily prevent such a tragedy because God cannot control people and cannot

---

326 Historically, there was probably no invasion of Canaan by Hebrews from Egypt. The mainstream view in archaeology is that the evidence suggests the majority of what became Israel was probably occupied by Canaanites who were already living in the land. Thus, they are the indigenous peoples of the land.

control people's culturally embedded ideas of who God is and what God desires.

Therefore, God is not culpable for failing to inform the ancient Israelites that killing men, women and children is morally reprehensible because God could not necessarily do so. Nor is God morally culpable for other instances in which humans commit evil based on misunderstandings of God. Of course, God can influence, persuade, and teach people in order to move them away from their misunderstandings to better conceptions of who God is. But that can take time, and people are stubborn. There's no on-or-off switch that God can use to correct people's distorted views.

IMPLICATIONS

Considering all that I have said in this book, I want to summarize what I believe the implications of my book are. Of course, these are what *I believe* are the implications. You may read the book and come to different, or even contradictory, implications than those I lay out. There might even be more implications than what I am suggesting here or am aware of. But for the sake of brevity, these will have to be enough.

If what I have said about essential kenosis and participatory theologies of revelation is true, then the origin of scripture—what initiated its creation in the first place—is God, in the sense that God provided God's revelation first, and human beings freely responded to that self-revealed God. The scriptures are a product and result of that response. On this level, they have human beings as their sole creators, but if God had not revealed God's self, there would be no human response, no scriptures. This is the first implication.

Second, from the theology outlined in this book, the inspiration of scripture is not found in the text itself. That is, the original meaning is not placed into the author's pen by God, but we find at least a twofold nature of inspiration: 1) inspiration is found in the postproduction exegetical work of the Holy Spirit, in its interpretation, and 2) it is found in the experience of the authors who wrote the words. Their lives are shaped by God, and therefore the scriptures they wrote are indirectly shaped by God. In both ways, we can say that scripture is fully inspired by God without claiming that God wrote scripture.

Third, scripture cannot be the primary means by which we measure our theology and faith. Said another way, considering all that I have written, the doctrine of *sola scriptura*[327] is null and void. Sola scriptura, however, is something that the progenitor of essential kenosis, Thomas Jay Oord, affirms. Of course, from what I can tell, he affirms more of a classical reformation understanding of sola scriptura. Martin Luther the progenitor of sola scriptura did not believe his doctrine excluded the use of tradition for theological reflection or faith practice. He did however believe that scripture was supreme to tradition. Considering this, sola scriptura would be better translated and understood as scripture supreme.

Luther also didn't believe the Bible was the Word of God since scripture itself taught that Christ, not the Bible, is the Word of God. He believed in the doctrine of scripture supreme, not because he thought the Bible was the Word of God, but because he believed that tradition had been corrupted—something understandable considering the corruption of the Roman Catholic Church of his time. Scripture, in his opinion, thus served as a more reliable witness to Christ, the Word of God, than did tradition.

Yet considering the evidence throughout this book I see no reason to believe that tradition is less reliable, since 1) scripture is a type of tradition, and 2) tradition is also a human response to Christ. The reliability of the scriptures, traditions, reason, experience, and there various witnesses is not found in there human limits and fallibilities or

---

327 Commonly, this is misunderstood to mean the Bible alone. That is that one cannot draw from sources outside of scripture, such as tradition, reason, or so forth, for theological reflection or praxis. While some hold this to be the meaning of sola scriptura, the doctrine, as originally formulated by Martin Luther, means something like "scripture supreme." While scripture is supreme to all other sources of theological reflection and praxis, one may faithfully draw from such sources as tradition, reason, or experience, as long as those sources don't, in any given case, contradict scripture. If one finds a contradiction between say tradition and scripture, one shall therefore side with the opinion of scripture. For further thoughts on and a clear definition of the doctrine of sola scriptura see my article on the matter. http://misfitstheology.com/2020/04/15/what-is-supreme-about-sola-scriptura/

lack thereof. It is found in the reliability and trustworthiness of Christ who takes up those instruments to serve as his vehicle to bring himself to us in the opening of the scriptures, in the living out of tradition, the use of reason, and the lived experiences of the community of the Church. In the postproduction of those items, we find the action of the Holy Spirit enacted in the christo-formative work of transforming them into worthy witnesses and conduits for Jesus.

The fourth and final implication I want to suggest, the one I've beat like a dead horse,[328] is that the Bible cannot be, in any ontological sense, the Word of God. The Word of God was the Son of God, is the Son of God, and will forever be the Son of God—and no other may claim that title. Nothing else can ever take his place. His own Nature, and that of creation, has made sure of that.

A DEFINITION OF AN ESSENTIALLY KENOTIC INCARNATIONAL PARTICIPATORY THEOLOGY OF INSPIRATION

The doctrine of essential kenosis says that God's very nature is uncontrolling love. The natural entailment of this is participatory theologies of revelation, which state that scripture is a human response, interpretation, and witness to Divine Revelation. Scripture is not to be identified with that revelation. Rooted in a historically orthodox position, my theory suggests that Christ [who is Revelation] not only is freely responded to by human beings, thus resulting in our scriptures, but Christ also enters into our responses to him through a little incarnation.

Scripture thus serves as a vehicle for Christ, and when read through him as a hermeneutical lens, we encounter the Son of God through the opening of the scriptures. Inspiration happens at two levels: 1) we find it in the postproduction exegetical work of the Holy Spirit, involved in the scripture's interpretation through scripture being used as a vehicle for the risen Christ brought to us through the Holy Spirit and 2) we find it in the experience of the authors who wrote the

---

328 I did this so that the dead horse does not come back as a Zombie to kill humanity.

words. Their lives are shaped by God, and therefore the scriptures they wrote are indirectly shaped by God.

THE ROLE OF SCRIPTURE NOW

The basic assumption and affirmation of the Christian and Jewish faith *is that God speaks*. For Christians, it is always the Son of God who is spoken. Throughout this book, I have not denied this vividly important affirmation; I have only denied particular understandings of this belief. Considering all the implications I just listed, perhaps the biggest question following this conclusion is "What now?" Is there any part of scripture left for the Christian? Yes, all of it! But we'll get to that in a few moments.

If scripture is not and never will be the Word of God, if it is not the foundation for our faith and beliefs, then what is the role of scripture? It's important to reiterate that throughout this book my goal has not been to discredit scripture. My aim has rather been to discredit views of the Bible that have given a certain Godhood to scripture. So, the problem isn't scripture; the Bible overall is good and useful. The issue is us. We are the problem.

We have set up scripture as our God, and we have fallen into idolatry. It leaves us blinded to the wonderful witness of the scriptures to Christ. I mean this book to do two things: firstly, to take the Bible away from you, and secondly, to give the Bible back to you. This time they are not meant as an idol to replace God, but as a good and useful collection of scriptures that serve as a vehicle to bring Christ to you. Here in the very last part of the book, I wish to give you back the Bible that, until now, it seems I have taken away from you.

First some preliminary notes: I find that given the climate we currently find ourselves in, it's necessary to address a topic that I have up to this point not touched on at all. Some books written to serve as alternative views to popular notions of inspiration in the last couple of years have taken this denial of popular beliefs about inspiration to mean that the traditional views of sexuality are null and void. While they may not say this explicitly, this seems to be the logic. If the Bible is not the Word of God, then non-traditional views of sexuality are permissible. Indeed, some of these books include whole chapters devoted to a progressive sexual ethic.

But please don't misunderstand me; I'm not actually affirming traditional views of sexuality here. That's not my point. I'm not going to tell you if I have a traditional or progressive conception of sexuality. Rather, what I'm trying to get across here is the view I have proposed allows room for multiple perspectives on multiple issues. Indeed our source of unity is Christ rather than the Bible. If the Bible is not the Word of God or the supreme authority in matters of doctrine or faith, it does not follow that we must accept progressive views of sexuality. Yet it also does not follow that we must accept traditional views of sexuality. *My concern here is not whether Christians take a progressive or conservative stance. I worry that this issue will continue to tear apart the church, and I do not want my work to be a source of further division.*

The conversation about human sexuality and all the complexities that come along with that may use scripture as a jumping off point for theological and doctrinal reflection on the issues. Yet from my perspective regardless of what the Bible says about homosexuality being positive or negative, either position may or may not be true. My point is that in my view the Bible does not decide whether homosexuality is created by God or something unnatural.

People with traditional or progressive views of sexuality may still hold to my view of inspiration. Because scripture is not the rule of faith—that which we must measure our beliefs and behaviors against—it means that scripture is not the determining factor of what's included in historical orthodoxy. This is the reason one could have a progressive or traditional view of sexuality and still be a historically Orthodox Christian because it's not a matter of orthodoxy and neither is our doctrine of scripture.

As I have argued elsewhere, orthodoxy is important. It doesn't simply mean "right belief," but also "right worship," and it is intricately and eternally tied to orthopraxy, which means "right behavior." To be orthodox means to embody who God is, to worship God rightly by how you shape your thoughts, attitudes, and behaviors.

Often among some churches, both conservative and progressive, the requirements of orthodoxy include declaring your stance on scripture, homosexuality, church politics, etc., but the only doctrines that are matters of orthodoxy are doctrines of God because, as the definition of right worship implies, the church's worship has always been intricately tied to orthodoxy. Since we worship God alone, God alone is our measure of what makes you orthodox. It's the doctrines of who God is: the Trinity and Christology (the full humanity and full divinity of Jesus, the virgin birth, and the bodily resurrection).

At this point, I should clarify that although I believe there are doctrines that make you orthodox and that all Christians *should believe and live these out*, that doesn't mean that you have to believe in the sense of intellectual head knowledge in order to be healed (what most term "saved"). The idea that you must have certain knowledge to be healed [saved] is from the heresy of *Gnosticism*,[329] by which many Americans are afflicted. It's not head knowledge that heals you and brings you into right relationship with God, creation, and our neighbors.

It's relational knowledge—following Jesus—which as C. S. Lewis has pointed out doesn't require someone to realize on an intellectual and conscious level that they even know Christ or that they are in fact

---

329 Gnosticism is the early church heresy still prevalent today that teaches a number of things. The first is that physical matter, creation, is evil. This includes our bodies, which act as a prison to our true selves, found in the form of our spirit or soul. The goal of the Gnostic, or their concept of salvation, is to escape from the body and physical world to a spiritual dimension. The way for our souls to escape from our evil bodies and the evil physical world is through secret knowledge that "saves" us. The result is that we don't need to take care of our bodies or those of our neighbors, nor do we need to steward and care for the world because it's all evil; we're just waiting for our souls to be saved by our knowledge of the truth and to be taken away to that spiritual place in the sky. Sound familiar? Yeah, most American Christians actually are Gnostics, theologically. This is why many Christians don't care about their physical health or the health of the planet—or the social welfare of those in need. Their primary concern is to "save" people's souls by giving them the right propositional knowledge so that they can escape this evil world and go to heaven. In reality, the first Christians and those who wrote the New Testament believed that physical matter, like our bodies and the rest of creation is good, although broken, because it was created by a good God. Instead of believing that salvation was their souls going to heaven, they believed that Jesus had reclaimed his kingship through his victory over death, sin and evil in the bodily resurrection. They also believed that through Christ God was healing creation and that one day our bodies would also be resurrected like Jesus. Then, after Christ judges the living and the dead, after he makes all things right, we would live with God on Earth as the new garden of Eden in our new immortal bodies.

following Jesus. In a letter to Mrs. Johnson dated November 8, 1952, he writes, "I think that every prayer which is sincerely made even to a false god or to a very imperfectly conceived true God, is accepted by the true God and that Christ saves many who do not think they know Him."[330] Said another way, true relational knowledge of Christ is a deeper knowledge than simply affirming some propositional belief, and it is the kind of knowledge that is available to all since God is present to all.

It is precisely these doctrines of the Trinity and Christology which are foundational to our faith whether we believe them or not. It is because God *is* three persons in one God that Love exists.[331] God is Love because God is Trinity. Or said in the inverse, God is Trinity because God is Love. This is why your right behavior, or orthopraxy, goes hand in hand with orthodoxy. You cannot hate your neighbor and be a Trinitarian. And you cannot love your neighbor, unless at a deeper level than mere intellect, you are a Trinitarian.

While sexuality is not a matter of orthodoxy, love certainly is. Therefore, conservatives and liberals are not off the hook, and one cannot exclude a person or group from the church without dismissing love and thereby, God. While the church may hold different positions on homosexuality, we are commanded to love homosexuals and include them in our communities. The same goes for those in the church who hold progressive stances; they are commanded to love and include in their communities those with conservative stances on homosexuality. And vice versa, conservatives are commanded to love and include in their communities those with progressive views on this topic.

---

330 Lewis, *C.S. Lewis Bible*, 1100.

331 Often the Trinity is misunderstood to be three ways in which God reveals God's self. But in reality, this isn't what the tradition has taught. The three persons and their interrelationship are what constitutes the very being of God. Said another way, God does not reveal God's self as Father, Son, and Holy Spirit; God *is Father, Son and Holy Spirit, all perfectly unified in one God*. In addition, God doesn't give self-revelation as something separate from God's self—God is Revelation. God is omnipresent, and therefore all things become conduits for God's revealing presence.

Nobody is excluded from the command to love their neighbor, enemy, and Christian brothers and sisters, and therefore nobody is excluded from the community. Bigotry is a term often tossed at conservatives, but it is a charge that could be made to both traditionalists and progressives. *To exclude anyone from the community is bigoted: gays, conservatives, or liberals. Even more important, it is unloving and therefore a denial of the Trinity who is Love. Simply put it is heresy.*

Finally, we've made it to the very end. I want to leave you with a brief description of the place the scriptures have in our faith.

As the scriptures serve as a vehicle for Christ, they bring us into an encounter with the crucified and risen Jesus through the mediation of the Holy Spirit. When I sit down on a Sunday morning among the gathered Eucharistic community [the church] to hear scripture read, it is among the people of Christ, his body, that the scriptures are opened, and the bread is broken. Here, it is that Christ once again becomes incarnate in and through us as his body, the scriptures, and the bread and wine.

It is among the community of his followers that we most readily hear the voice of Christ echoing through the scriptures. There, we hear the scriptures spoken as the church has done since Jesus himself stood in the synagogue reading the scroll of Isaiah and since the twelve apostles and their progeny heard the scriptures read during the Eucharistic meals.

In hearing the scriptures, for those who have hearts to hear, Christ is found incarnating himself into those softly spoken words. There, Christ comes to rest in our very lives, not merely as individuals but as a community dedicated to hearing the voice of Christ as we follow him into his kingdom here on Earth, while he works and calls us to join him in that work of healing all of creation. It is in this community and through the opening of the scriptures and the traditions of the Church that we find a common language. Here, in the community scripture, is one apparatus of which we use to teach one another, correct one another, and train one another in right relationship with God, our neighbors, and all of creation. When I sit down to read the scriptures, I know that Christ sits with me eagerly awaiting his opportunity to once again enter those words and speak himself to me.

Eastern Orthodox priest and scholar Andrew Louth also once wrote about the scriptures as a way to encounter Christ. There he said concerning the scriptures, "But all this is more than record: it is through the Scriptures that Christ continues to encounter humankind; to read the Bible as Scripture is to be open to encounter with Christ. The same applies *mutatis mutandis* to the writings of the Fathers, the history of the Church and its councils, the lives of the saints: all these are ways of encountering Christ, or of understanding the lineaments of such an encounter. And what makes this a possibility is prayer; it is prayer that creates beings capable of hearing the voice of Christ."[332]

And lastly, it is through prayer, our communications with God—spoken, silent, rote, or spontaneous—and lives of loving service to the King of Kings through the loving of our neighbor and creation that we are formed into the type of people that can hear that voice of Christ incarnated into the scriptures, traditions, and even all of creation.

Indeed, the author of 2 Timothy 3:16 was right when they wrote, "All scripture is inspired by God and is useful for teaching, for reproof, for correction, and for training in righteousness, so that everyone who belongs to God may be proficient, equipped for every good work."[333]

---

332 Andrew Louth, *Introducing Eastern Orthodox Theology* (Downers Grove, IL: InterVarsity Press, 2013), 7.

333 Lewis, *C.S. Lewis Bible*, 2 Tm 3:16-17.

GLOSSARY

Ancient Near Eastern: Essentially the ancient Near East is what today we would typically call the Middle East.

Church Fathers: Depending on who you are asking, the term church fathers is referring to Christians that lived from either the second through the fourth centuries or the second through the eighth centuries. It is more or less interchangeable with the term patristic.

Documentary Hypothesis of the Torah: The documentary hypothesis is what biblical scholars call the theory that the Torah was not written by Moses but instead consisted of multiple sources, scribes, editors, and compilers.

Ethnocentric: Ethnocentric means to place one's own ethnic group and culture as inherently superior to others.

Exegesis: This simply means interpretation.

Etymology: This is the study of the origin of words, their use, and their historical development, as well as how they have been used throughout their existence.

Evangelical: While there are different definitions of an evangelical, David Bebbington's definition is seen as sort of the standard one by which others must respond. And I think he has the most accurate definition. There are four central tenets to the definition of an evangelical. The Four Pillars of evangelicalism are 1) biblicism, 2) conversionism, 3) activism, 4) crucentrism. Biblicism is the idea that Bible has some kind of authority. Conversionism is the idea that one must be converted. Activism is the idea that Christians must be active in social justice and evangelism. Crucentrism is the idea that the faith is centrally focused on the Cross.

Fallibility: This refers to ability for humans to be wrong, err, or make mistakes.

Finitude: This means to be limited to such an extent that there are things beyond our comprehension.

Fundamentalists: There are five main pillars of fundamentalism: 1) the inerrancy of the Bible, 2) penal substitutionary atonement, 3) the virgin birth of Jesus, 4) the bodily resurrection of Jesus, and 5) the historical accuracy of the miracles performed by Jesus. The last three of these pillars are held by all historic Orthodox Christians, and therefore these beliefs do not make fundamentalism distinct as a tradition. Neither does the second pillar, since penal substitutionary atonement is historically a broadly Protestant doctrine. Therefore, in my view, the one doctrine that is new to the fundamentalist movement, and therefore that distinguishes them as a distinct tradition, is a belief in scripture's inerrancy. I would therefore broadly define someone as a fundamentalist as someone that subscribes to inerrancy.

Gnosticism: Gnosticism is the early church heresy, still prevalent today, which teaches a number of things. The first is that physical matter, creation, is evil. This includes our bodies, which act as a prison to our true selves, found in the form of our spirit or soul. The goal of the Gnostic, or their concept of salvation, is to escape from the body and physical world to a spiritual dimension. The way for our souls to escape from our evil bodies and the evil physical world is through secret knowledge that "saves" us. The result is that we don't need to take care of our bodies or those of our neighbors, and we don't need to steward and care for the world because it's all evil. Gnostics were just waiting for their souls to be saved by knowledge of the truth and to be taken away to that spiritual place in the sky. Sound familiar? Yeah, most American Christians actually are Gnostics, theologically. This is why many Christians don't care about their physical health or the health of the planet—or the social welfare of those in need. Their primary concern is to "save" people's souls by giving them the right propositional knowledge so that they can escape this evil world and go to heaven. In reality, the first Christians and those who wrote the New Testament believed that physical matter, like our bodies and the rest of creation is good, although broken, because it was created by a good God. Instead of believing that salvation was their souls going to heaven, they believed that Jesus had reclaimed his kingship through his victory over death, sin and evil in the bodily resurrection. They also believed that through Christ God was healing creation and that one day our bodies would also be resurrected like Jesus. Then, after Christ judges the living and the dead, after making all things right, we would live with God on Earth as the new garden of Eden in our new immortal bodies.

Hermeneutic: Hermeneutic is the art of interpretation.

Historical Criticism: Historical criticism is a modern historical way of studying the Bible. Historical criticism explores the origins of ancient texts in order to better understand them in their own historical and social contexts.

Immutable: Immutable is the classical term that means God does not change.

Inerrancy: While there are different variations, inerrancy is the belief that the Bible is God's Word and therefore is without any errors.

Infallibility: This is the idea that scripture will not fail to accomplish its goal.

Marcionite: Maricon was a heretic who believed the God revealed in Jesus was a different God than Yahweh, whom he thought was an evil god but not the creator God; he thus rejected the Old Testament as Christian scripture. It's also important to note that Christians were not oblivious to the wildly different depictions of God found between the Old and New Testaments. Their answer more or less was to read the Old Testament allegorically. As a result, they did not see the Old Testament as literally teaching that Yahweh was hungry for violence.

To read it in such literal terms seemed nonsensical to them. Maricon, however, did read it literally, and this is what led him to believe that Yahweh was a different God than the one revealed in Jesus. It was thus his way of reading scripture that ultimately set Maricon apart from the mainstream Orthodox Church.

Omnibenevolent: Omnibenevolent means that God is all good.

Omnipotent: Omnipotent means that God is all powerful.

Ontological: Ontology is essentially an academic term for nature. Specifically, it is a branch in the philosophy of metaphysics that investigates the nature of being. So, when I use the word "ontology" or "ontological," I use it to refer to the inherent nature of something, its essence, what it is that makes it that thing.

Original Autographs: An original autograph is the actual piece of parchment or scroll that, say for example, the apostle Paul used to write his letter to the Corinthians. There are absolutely no original autographs that have survived to this day. All we have are copies of copies. That doesn't necessarily mean we don't have a good idea of what the original autographs actually said. Sometimes we do. There are scholars who devote their lives to the task of discerning what the original autographs said. This is what is called textual criticism.

Patristic: Depending on whom you are asking, the term patristic is referring to Christians that lived from either the second to the fourth centuries or the second to the eighth centuries. It is more or less interchangeable with the phrase church fathers.

Protestantism: Roger Olson, a Baptist historical theologian, says that there were three shared doctrines between all branches of the Protestant Reformation (Anabaptist, Reformed, Lutheran, and Anglican) that made them distinct from the Catholic Church as Protestants. Those were 1) sola scriptura, 2) justification by grace alone through faith alone, and 3) the priesthood of all believers.[334]

Pseudepigraphy: The attribution of authorship by the author to someone who isn't the author.

Scripturalformativity: I believe this is a term I have coined. It means that all things must conform to the ultimate authority of scripture.

Second Temple Hermeneutics: The Second Temple period is the time between the rebuilding of the second temple in 520-515 B.C.E. (after the destruction of the first temple) and the destruction of the second temple by the Romans in 70 C.E. During this period, a creative type of interpretation began to flourish. This method of reading the Bible was rooted in the present moment. Since the the original writings of these texts predated the readers of scripture by a few hundred years, it became paramount to those viewing scripture to read according to their own situations. The question for them when reading scripture became "What does this mean to us and for our situation?" They were not really concerned about the author's intention or what these texts would have meant to the original audience since that was a moot point for people living in a time so far removed and in new post-exilic scenarios. Furthermore, since they had no scholars who were dedicated to discovering the original meanings and social contexts of the texts, it would have been nearly an impossibility to have such a concern. Second Temple hermeneutics is therefore the creative reading of the text that developed during the Second Temple period.

Sola Scriptura: Commonly, this is misunderstood to mean the Bible alone. This means that one cannot draw from sources outside of scripture, such as tradition, reason or so forth, for theological reflection or praxis. While some hold this to be the meaning of sola scriptura, the doctrine as originally formulated by Martin Luther means something like "scripture supreme." While scripture is supreme to all other

---

334 Roger E. Olson, *The Story of Christian Theology: Twenty Centuries of Tradition and Reform* (Downers Grove, IL: InterVarsity Press Academic, 1999), 370.

sources of theological reflection and praxis, one may faithfully draw from such sources as tradition, reason, or experience, as long as those sources don't, in any give case, contradict scripture. If one finds a contradiction between say tradition and scripture, one shall therefore side with the opinion of scripture.

Stenographer-Dictation Theory: The stenographer or dictation theory of inspiration states that what was written down was written down exactly how God wanted it to be since God was using the authors as direct writing utensils.

Theological Unity of Scripture: The theological unity of scripture is a doctrine that asserts because God inspired scripture (often understood to mean God is the author of scripture) all of scripture's theology is consistent. In this sense, what scripture teaches in one area cannot contradict what scripture teaches in another. For example: If the Old Testament teaches that God commands genocide, then the New Testament cannot teach something that is contrary. This is why often many Christians do not affirm that Jesus taught non-violence because it would contradict other parts of the Old Testament. So, while this is the modern fundamentalist understanding of the doctrine of the theological unity of scripture, it's important to note that the early church also believed in a sort of theological unity of scripture. The main difference of how such theological unity was obtained was through the use of a Christocentric allegorical interpretation of the Bible. In other words, while the historical meaning wasn't always simply dismissed, it wasn't the main meaning to be found in the biblical text. The primary meaning was the allegorical meaning that spoke about Jesus. When read in this way, all of the scriptures spoke about Jesus and therefore were unified theologically.

Traditional Christianity: What I am calling traditional or historic Orthodox Christianity is Christianity that more or less has historically affirmed the creeds (Apostles, Nicene and so forth), specifically the four doctrines of the *Trinity*, the *full humanity* and *full deity of Jesus,* his *bodily resurrection*, and his *virgin birth.*

APPENDIX

THE GENERALITY OF INSPIRATION IN THE PATRISTIC PERIOD

Justin Martyr (100-165 AD)

In his book Second Apologies (150-160 AD)
In this work, Justin makes the claim that stoics, poets, Plato, historians, the writers of the scriptures, etc., spoke according to their participation in the eternal Logos [Word] of God [Jesus Christ]. What he calls the "spermatic word," or "implanted word." "I confess that I both boast and with all my strength strive to be found a Christian; not because the teachings of Plato are different from those of Christ, but because they are not in all respects similar, as neither are those of the others, Stoics, and poets, and historians. *For each man spoke well in proportion to the share he had of the spermatic word, seeing what was related to it* ... Whatever things were rightly said among all men, are the property of us Christians. For next to God, we worship and love the Word [Jesus Christ] who is from the unbegotten and ineffable God, since also He became man for our sakes, that, becoming a partaker of our sufferings, He might also bring us healing. *For all the writers were able to see realities darkly through the sowing of the implanted word that was in them.* For the seed and imitation imparted according to capacity is one thing, and quite another is the thing itself, of which

there is the participation and imitation according to the grace which is from Him."[335]

Although he doesn't use the word inspiration, when seen in the context of the patristic world, particularly alongside the view that it was the Word [Christ] who spoke to or inspired the prophets, inspiration seems to be what he has in mind here. For instance, Irenaeus held this belief, "that the Scriptures are indeed perfect, since they were spoken by the Word of God and His Spirit."[336] And so did Origen, "And by the words of Christ we mean not only those which he spoke when he became human and dwelt in the flesh; for even before this, *Christ, the Word of God, was in Moses and the Prophets.* For without the Word of God [Christ] how could they have been able to prophesy of Christ?"[337] Even Justin Martyr says this, "And that the prophets are inspired by no other than the Divine Word, even as you, as I fancy will grant."[338] In this way, Justin Martyr seems to be saying that more than just the authors of scripture are being influenced by and responding to the Logos of God [The Son of God].

Irenaeus (115-202 AD)

From his book Against Heresies
5.8.1 (ANF 1:533): "But we do now receive a certain portion of His Spirit, tending towards perfection, and preparing us for incorruption, being little by little accustomed to receive and bear God."[339]

Life of Abercius (The author is unknown)

"Life of Abercius (4th century; Symeon Metaphrastes relayed it in the 10th century)

---

335 Martyr, *First and Second Apologies*, 72-73.

336 Willis, ed., *Teachings of the Church Fathers*, 84.

337 Behr, *Origen: On First Principles*, 5.

338 Martyr, *First and Second Apologies*, 28.

339 Allert, *High View of Scripture*, 188.

76: characterizes the epitaph Abercius (late 2nd AD), a bishop Hierapolis, composed for himself as an inspired (theopneuston) inscription."[340]

Eusebius of Caesarea (260-340 AD)

In his book Ecclesiastical History
6.29.3 (NPNF 2 1:275): Eusebius shares the story of the inspired election of a new bishop: "Thereupon all the people, as if *moved by one Divine Spirit* with all eagerness and unanimity cried out that he [Fabianus] was worthy, and without delay they took him and placed him upon the episcopal [Made him Bishop] seat."[341]

In his book Oration in Praise of Constantine
11.3 (NPNF 2 1:595): "Those, indeed, who are enlightened in heavenly knowledge by the power of the Divine Spirit, well understand the cause, and justly admire and bless thee for that counsel and resolution which Heaven itself inspired. On the other hand the ignorant and spiritually blind regard these designs with open mockery and scorn, and deem it a strange and unworthy thing indeed that so mighty a prince should waste his zeal on the graves and monuments of the dead."[342] This shows that according to Eusebius, the Spirit's activity of imparting knowledge was not restricted to the authors of scriptural texts nor to the era of the apostles in the first century.

In his book the Life of Constantine
1.11.2 (NPNF 2 1:485): Here Eusebius states that he was inspired while writing the *Life of Constantine*. "Let me implore then the help of God, and may *the inspiring aid of the heavenly Word be with me*, while I commence my history from the very earliest period of his life."[343]

---

340 Ibid., 188.

341 Ibid., 186.

342 Ibid., 186.

343 Ibid., 186.

Here again we see the notion that the Word [Christ] is the aid of inspiration rather than being the product of inspiration.

3.26.6 (NPNF 2 1:527): In reaction to a church's building that was built at the supposed tomb of Christ by Constantine, Eusebius claims that he undertook its construction, "acting … under the guidance of the divine Spirit."[344]

3.48 (NPNF 2 1:532): Here Eusebius states that Constantine as a result of "being filled … with Divine wisdom"[345] was committed to eradicating evil in Constantinople.

In his work Constantine's Oration to the Assembly of the Saints
2 (NPNF 2 1:562): In this work, Eusebius incorporates a sermon ascribed to Constantine. Whoever the actual preacher is they do not restrict inspiration to the scriptures. "May the mighty inspiration of the father and of his Son … be with me in speaking these things."[346]

18 (NPNF 2 1:574): After giving the impression of his general disapproval towards the Erythraean Sibyl, the writer presents an acrostic: "On the occasion, however, having rushed into the sanctuary of her vain superstition, *she became really filled with inspiration from above, and declared in prophetic verses the future purposes of God*; plainly indicating the advent of Jesus by the initial letters of these verses, forming an acrostic in these words: Jesus Christ, Son of God, Saviour, Cross. The verses themselves are as follows."[347]

26 (NPNF 2 1:580): "When men commend my services, which owe their origin to the inspiration of Heaven, do they not clearly establish the truth that God is the cause of the exploits I have performed?"[348]

344 Ibid., 186.

345 Ibid., 186.

346 Ibid., 187.

347 Ibid., 187.

348 Ibid., 187.

Gregory of Nazianzus (lived 329 AD-389 AD)

From his work Orations

21.33 (NPNF 2 7:279): "Here too was shown in a very high degree the simple-mindedness of Athanasius, and the steadfastness of his faith in Christ. For, when all the rest who sympathized with us were divided into three parties, and many were faltering in their conception of the Son, and still more in that of the of the Holy Ghost, (a point on which to be only slightly in error was to be orthodox) and few indeed were sound upon both points, he was the first and only one, or with the concurrence of but a few, to venture to confess in writing, with entire clearness and distinctness, the Unity of Godhead and Essence of the Three persons, and thus to attain in later days, *under the influence of inspiration to the same faith in regard to the Holy Ghost, as had been bestowed at an earlier time on most of the Fathers in regard to the Son.* This confession, a truly royal and magnificent gift, he presented to the Emperor, opposing to the unwritten innovation, a written account of the orthodox faith, so that an emperor might be overcome by an emperor, reason by reason, treatise by treatise."[349]

The Council of Ephesus (431 AD)

The Synodical Epistle (Acta conciliorum oecumenicorum, p. 70, line 11): In this epistle the condemnation of the declared heretic Nestorius is described as "their inspired (theopneustos) decision."[350]

THE WORD OF GOD IN PATRISTIC THOUGHT

Justin Martyr (100-160 AD)

In his work First and Second Apologies

349 Ibid.,187.

350 Ibid.,185.

"… the Father of the universe has a Son; who also, being the first-begotten Word of God, is even God."[351]

"We have been taught that Christ is the first-born of God, and we have declared above that He is the Word of whom every race of men were partakers."[352]

"For not only among the Greeks did reason (Logos) prevail to condemn these things through Socrates, but also among the Barbarians were they condemned by Reason (or the Word, the Logos) Himself, who took shape, and became man, and was called Jesus Christ…"[353]

The Epistle to Diognetus (120-200 AD)

The author of the Epistle to Diognetus states, "The Almighty Himself, the Creator of the universe, the God whom no eye can discern, *has sent down His very own Truth from heaven, His own holy and incomprehensible Word*, to plant it among men and ground it in their hearts."[354]

Irenaeus (115-202 AD)

Irenaeus, in his book *Against Heresies,* wrote "that the Scriptures are indeed perfect, since they were spoken by the Word of God and His Spirit."[355] He does not equate scripture and the Word but declares that the Word of God is the one who spoke forth the scripture, which is different from saying scripture is the Word.

Irenaeus in another book writing about the Holy Trinity, identifies Jesus as the Word by saying, "And the second article [Second person of

---

351 Martyr, *First and Second Apologies,* 53.

352 Ibid., 37.

353 Ibid., 4.

354 Louth, *Early Christian Fathers,* 146.

355 Willis, ed. *Teachings of the Church Fathers,* 84.

the Trinity]: *the Word of God, the Son of God, Jesus Christ...*"[356] A couple pages later in the same book he says, *"... for those who bear the Spirit of God are led to the Word, that is to the Son ..."*[357] Once more, he says, *"... resting upon the Son of God, that is [on]the Word in His human advent ..."*[358] Lastly he writes, *"This God, then, is glorified by His Word, who is His Son ..."*[359] Clearly Irenaeus believed Jesus was the Word of God.

Tertullian (155,160-220 AD)

Against Praxeas

"... this one only God has also a Son, His Word, who proceeded from Himself, by whom all things were made, and without whom nothing was made."[360]

Hippolytus (170-235 AD)

In his book *The Apostolic Tradition*, Hippolytus writes, "Thus after this proof it is clear that the Son of God is proclaimed at the beginning; through these psalms is betokened the Word, the Wisdom, the only-begotten Son of the Father."[361]

Origen (185-254 AD)

On First Principles

---

356 Irenaeus, *On the Apostolic Preaching*, trans. John Behr (Crestwood, NY: St. Vladimir's Seminary Press, 1997), 43.

357 Ibid., 44.

358 Ibid., 45.

359 Ibid., 46.

360 Willis, ed. *Teachings of the Church Fathers*, 91.

361 Hippolytus and Alistair C. Stewart, *On the Apostolic Tradition* (Yonkers, NY: St. Vladimir's Seminary Press, 2015), 223.

"And by the words of Christ we mean not only those which he spoke when he became human and dwelt in the flesh; for even before this, *Christ, the Word of God,* was in Moses and the Prophets. For without the Word of God how could they have been able to prophesy of Christ?"[362]

"For the Son is the Word ..."[363]

As we saw from earlier, Origen says something that suggests he doesn't believe the Bible to be the Word of God. "The things which are spoken through a prophet are not always to be taken as spoken by God. And even though through Moses God spoke many things, nevertheless Moses commanded other things by his own authority [the bill of divorce is given as an example]. ... *And Paul also shows things in his letters, when he says concerning some things: "The Lord says and not I,' and concerning others, 'These things moreover I say, not the Lord'* (1 Cor. 7)' (Kalin, 'Argument from Inspiration,' 103-4)."[364]

Athanasius (298-373 AD)

On The Opinion of Dionysius
"'In the beginning was the Word' (Jn. 1:1), the Virgin at the consummation of the ages conceived, and the Lord has become man. And He who is indicated by both statements is one Person, for 'the Word was made flesh' (ib. 14) ... And he that writes of the human attributes of the Word knows also what concerns His Godhead ... while a human body lay in the tomb, it was raised as God's body by the Word Himself."[365]

---

362 Behr, *Origen: On First Principles,* 5.

363 Ibid., 25.

364 Allert, *High View of Scripture,* 183.

365 Willis, ed. *Teachings of the Church Fathers,* 316-317.

Letter to Epictetus
"For what the human Body of the Word suffered, this the Word, dwelling in the body, ascribed to Himself, in order that we might be enabled to be partakers of the Godhead of the Word ... the Word, being by Nature God"[366]

Hilary of Poitiers (315-368 AD)

From his work On The Trinity
"Hence, this is the true faith of human blessedness: to acknowledge Him as God and man, to proclaim Him as the Word and as the flesh, to know of God that He is man, and to know of the flesh that it is the Word ... Hence, the man Jesus Christ, the only-begotten God, who through the flesh and the Word is the Son of Man as well as the Son of God, has assumed a true manhood according to the likeness of our manhood without sacrificing His divinity."[367]

Basil The Great (330-379 AD)

In his work On The Holy Spirit
"... and so they make *God the Word* inferior and abolish the Holy Spirit."[368]

"You would learn from the preceding words that this verse has been said of the Word of God, the maker of all creation."[369]

"... the Word and Maker, the Only-begotten God..."[370]

---

366 Ibid.,312.

367 Ibid., 313.

368 Basil, *On The Holy Spirit*, trans. Stephen M. Hildebrand (Yonkers, NY: St. Vladimir's Seminary Press, 2011), 32.

369 Ibid., 34.

370 Basil, *On the Holy Spirit*, 48.

John Chrysostom (347-407 AD)

Homilies On St. John

"The assumption of true flesh...for by an Union and Conjoining God the Word and the Flesh are One, not by any confusion or obliteration of substances, but by a certain union ineffable, and past understandings ..."[371]

St. Vincent of Lerins (died 450 AD)

In his work Commonitory

"From this unity of Person it follows, by reason of a like mystery, that, since *the flesh of the Word was born of an undefiled mother, God the Word Himself* is most catholicly believed ..."[372]

THE WORD OF GOD IN NEW TESTAMENT THOUGHT

Oftentimes when we hear the phrase "Word of God," we assume the Bible is what's being referred to. And so, when we read the phrase "Word of God" in scripture, particularly the New Testament, we read it through that lens and thus assume what the authors of scripture are referring to is the Bible.

This appendix is a guide for every time the phrase "Word of God" is used in the New Testament. Or said another way, it is an appendix of every occurrence of the Greek words *logos, rhema*, as well as the Greek word *graphe* that we translate as scripture. My goal ultimately is to point to the one in whom our faith is founded upon. "For no one can lay any foundation other than the one that has been laid; that foundation is Jesus Christ." (1 Corinthians 3:11 NRSV). In others words it's all about Jesus, Jesus, Jesus!

That being said, I will comment on a few of these verses that contain occurrences of each word, logos, rhema, and graphe. Based on my

371 Willis, *Teachings of the Church Fathers*, 314.

372 Ibid., 319.

previous elaboration, it seems unnecessary to comment on each and every verse. Particular instances where it is abundantly clear the phrase *Word of God* is not a reference to scripture, I have not commented, as it would seem patronizing. I believe the reader is intelligent enough to discern that on their own. I will, however, comment on particular verses that I think help shine light on the goal of this appendix or on passages that I think have been misunderstood. Lastly, while I will not comment on each verse, I will certainly locate the Greek word (either logos, graphe, or rhema) for you in order to aid your discernment of what the word is referring to. Where I have not been able to locate the exact word that has been translated as logos, rhema, or graphe, I have paraphrased how it is translated in other translations.

There are different forms of the Greek word logos, graphe, and rhema, for the sake of simplicity I will always just say logos, graphe, and rhema.

All scripture is quoted from the New Revised Standard Version unless otherwise stated.[373]

NEW TESTAMENT USAGE OF LOGOS (λόγος)

Matthew

Matt 5:32 "But I say to you that anyone who divorces his wife, except on the ground [*logos*] of unchastity, causes her to commit adultery; and whoever marries a divorced woman commits adultery." (Here we can see from the context of the passage that the word being translated from logos here is being used to denote a reason, justification, or as translated here the grounds for enacting a divorce. It is clear it is not referring to scripture.)

Matt 5:37 "Let your word [*logos*] be 'Yes, Yes' or 'No, No'; anything more than this comes from the evil one." (Here we can see that logos means your actual words, what you have spoken. When you give someone your word, let that be more than enough rather than need-ing to resort to an oath.)

Matt 7:24 "Everyone then who hears these words [*logos*] of mine and acts on them will be like a wise man who built his house on rock." (This verse is coming at the end of the Sermon on the Mount and thus is clear that the words Jesus is referring to here are his own words spoken in the sermon, his teaching.)

Matt 7:26 "And everyone who hears these words [*logos*] of mine and does not act on them will be like a foolish man who built his house on sand." (See note on Matt 7:24.)

Matt 7:28 "Now when Jesus had finished saying [*logos*] these things, the crowds were astounded at his teaching" (See note Matt 7:24.)

Matt 8:8 "The centurion answered, 'Lord, I am not worthy to have you come under my roof; but only speak the word [*logos*], and my servant will be healed.'" (Here the word which the centurion requests Jesus speak is clearly his actual spoken words and not scripture.)

Matt 8:16 "That evening they brought to him many who were pos-sessed with demons; and he cast out the spirits with a word [*logos*], and cured all who were sick." (See note on Matt 8:8. In other words, he spoke, and the demons fled.)

Matt 10:14 "If anyone will not welcome you or listen to your words [*logos*], shake off the dust from your feet as you leave that house or town." (Jesus is speaking of their message (also what logos is some-times translated as here) to mean the gospel message, that which they're going into these villages to proclaim. Repent for the Kingdom is near. It's not a reference to scripture, particularly because before the printing press people didn't have Bibles to carry around in their back pockets. The scriptures were written on separate scrolls that were rare and expensive to obtain; they were not something that was just carried around from town to town.)

Matt 12:32 "Whoever speaks a word [*logos*] against the Son of Man will be forgiven, but whoever speaks against the Holy Spirit will not be forgiven, either in this age or in the age to come."

Matt 12:36 "I tell you, on the day of judgment you will have to give an account for every careless word [*logos*] you utter."

Matt 12:37 "for by your words [*logos*] you will be justified, and by your words [*logos*] you will be condemned."

Matt 13:19-23 "When anyone hears the word [*logos*] of the kingdom and does not understand it, the evil one comes and snatches away what is sown in the heart; this is what was sown on the path. As for what was sown on rocky ground, this is the one who hears the word [*logos*] and immediately receives it with joy; yet such a person has no root, but endures only for a while, and when trouble or persecution arises on account of the word, [*logos*] that person immediately falls away. As for what was sown among thorns, this is the one who hears the word, [*logos*] but the cares of the world and the lure of wealth choke the word, [logos] and it yields nothing. But as for what was sown on good soil, this is the one who hears the word [*logos*]and understands it, who indeed bears fruit and yields, in one case a hundredfold, in another sixty, and in another thirty." (This passage is a parable about the gospel message (repent for the kingdom is near); therefore, the logos here is the gospel message not scripture.)

Matt 15:6 "So, for the sake of your tradition, you make void the word [*logos*] of God." (See comments in chapter 1 under section heading, The Bible is God's Word-Authorship and Inspiration Seen as Synonymous.)

Matt 15:12 "Then the disciples approached and said to him, "Do you know that the Pharisees took offense when they heard what you said? [*logos*]"

Matt 15:23 "But he did not answer her at all. And his disciples came and urged him, saying, 'Send her away, for she keeps shouting after us.'" (In other translations, it says something like (I'm paraphrasing) he did not answer her with a word.)

Matt 18:23 "For this reason the kingdom of heaven may be compared to a king who wished to settle accounts [*logos*] with his slaves."

Matt 19:1 "When Jesus had finished saying [*logos*] these things, he left Galilee and went to the region of Judea beyond the Jordan."

Matt 19:11 "But he said to them, 'Not everyone can accept this teaching, [*logos*] but only those to whom it is given.'"

Matt 19:22 "When the young man heard this word, [*logos*] he went away grieving, for he had many possessions."

Matt 21:24 "Jesus said to them, 'I will also ask you one question [*logos*]; if you tell me the answer, then I will also tell you by what authority I do these things.'"

Matt 22:15 "Then the Pharisees went and plotted to entrap him in what he said [*logos*]."

Matt 22:46 "No one was able to give him an answer, nor from that day did anyone dare to ask him any more questions." (I'm paraphrasing, but other translations will say something like nobody could answer him with a word.)

Matt 24:35 "Heaven and earth will pass away, but my words [*logos*] will not pass away."

Matt 25:19 "After a long time the master of those slaves came and settled accounts [*logos*] with them."

Matt 26:1 "When Jesus had finished saying [*logos*] all these things, he said to his disciples"

Matt 26:44 "So leaving them again, he went away and prayed for the third time, saying the same words [*logos*]."

Matt 28:15 "So they took the money and did as they were directed. And this story [*logos*] is still told among the Jews to this day."

Mark

Mark 1:45 "But he went out and began to proclaim it freely, and to spread the word [*logos*], so that Jesus could no longer go into a town openly, but stayed out in the country; and people came to him from every quarter."

Mark 2:2 "So many gathered around that there was no longer room for them, not even in front of the door; and he was speaking the word [*logos*] to them."

Mark 4:14-20 "The sower sows the word [*logos*]. These are the ones on the path where the word [*logos*] is sown: when they hear, Satan immediately comes and takes away the word [*logos*] that is sown in them. And these are the ones sown on rocky ground: when they hear the word [*logos*], they immediately receive it with joy. But they have no root, and endure only for a while; then, when trouble or persecution arises on account of the word [*logos*], immediately they fall away. And others are those sown among the thorns: these are the ones who hear the word [*logos*], but the cares of the world, and the lure of wealth, and the desire for other things come in and choke the word [*logos*], and it yields nothing. And these are the ones sown on the good soil: they hear the word [*logos*] and accept it and bear fruit, thirty and sixty and a hundredfold."

Mark 4:33 "With many such parables he spoke the word [*logos*] to them, as they were able to hear it"

Mark 5:36 "But overhearing what [*logos*] they said, Jesus said to the leader of the synagogue, 'Do not fear, only believe.'"

Mark 7:13 "thus making void the word [*logos*] of God through your tradition that you have handed on. And you do many things like this." (See comments in chapter 1 under section heading, The Bible is God's Word-Authorship and Inspiration Seen as Synonymous.)

Mark 7:29 "Then he said to her, 'For saying [*logos*] that, you may go—the demon has left your daughter.'"

Mark 8:32 "He said all this [*logos*] quite openly. And Peter took him aside and began to rebuke him."

Mark 8:38 "Those who are ashamed of me and of my words [*logos*] in this adulterous and sinful generation, of them the Son of Man will also be ashamed when he comes in the glory of his Father with the holy angels."

Mark 9:10 "So they kept the matter [*logos*] to themselves, questioning what this rising from the dead could mean."

Mark 10:22 "When he heard this [*logos*], he was shocked and went away grieving, for he had many possessions."

Mark 10:24 "And the disciples were perplexed at these words [*logos*]. But Jesus said to them again, 'Children, how hard it is to enter the kingdom of God!'"

Mark 11:29 "Jesus said to them, 'I will ask you one question [*logos*]; answer me, and I will tell you by what authority I do these things.'"

Mark 12:13 "Then they sent to him some Pharisees and some Herodians to trap him in what he said [*logos*]."

Mark 13:31 "Heaven and earth will pass away, but my words [*logos*] will not pass away."

Mark 14:39 "And again he went away and prayed, saying the same words [*logos*]."

Mark 16:20 "And they went out and proclaimed the good news everywhere, while the Lord worked with them and confirmed the message [*logos*]by the signs that accompanied it."

Luke

Luke 1:2 "just as they were handed on to us by those who from the beginning were eyewitnesses and servants of the word [*logos*]"

Luke 1:4 "so that you may know the truth concerning the things [*logos*] about which you have been instructed."

Luke 1:20 "But now, because you did not believe my words [*logos*], which will be fulfilled in their time, you will become mute, unable to speak, until the day these things occur."

Luke 1:29 "But she was much perplexed by his words [*logos*] and pondered what sort of greeting this might be."

Luke 3:4 "as it is written in the book of the words [*logos*] of the prophet Isaiah, 'The voice of one crying out in the wilderness: "Prepare the way of the Lord, make his paths straight."'" (This may be an instance in which logos is used in reference to the scriptures, however I would contend that more likely logos here is being used to reference Isaiah's own words rather than scripture as an entity itself. His words are recorded in scripture, but it is those words, not scripture as a whole that is being referred to.)

Luke 4:22 "All spoke well of him and were amazed at the gracious words [*logos*] that came from his mouth. They said, 'Is not this Joseph's son?'"

Luke 4:32 "They were astounded at his teaching, because he spoke [*logos*] with authority."

Luke 4:36 "They were all amazed and kept saying to one another, 'What kind of utterance [*logos*] is this? For with authority and power he commands the unclean spirits, and out they come!'"

Luke 5:1 "Once while Jesus was standing beside the lake of Gennesaret, and the crowd was pressing in on him to hear the word [*logos*] of God"

Luke 5:15 "But now more than ever the word [*logos*] about Jesus spread abroad; many crowds would gather to hear him and to be cured of their diseases."

Luke 6:47 "I will show you what someone is like who comes to me, hears my words [*logos*], and acts on them."

Luke 7:7 "therefore I did not presume to come to you. But only speak the word [*logos*], and let my servant be healed."

Luke 7:17 "This word [*logos*] about him spread throughout Judea and all the surrounding country."

Luke 8:11-13 "Now the parable is this: The seed is the word [*logos*] of God. The ones on the path are those who have heard; then the devil comes and takes away the word [*logos*] from their hearts, so that they may not believe and be saved. The ones on the rock are those who, when they hear the word [*logos*], receive it with joy."

Luke 8:15 "But as for that in the good soil, these are the ones who, when they hear the word [*logos*], hold it fast in an honest and good heart, and bear fruit with patient endurance."

Luke 8:21 "But he said to them, 'My mother and my brothers are those who hear the word [*logos*] of God and do it.'"

Luke 9:26 "Those who are ashamed of me and of my words [*logos*], of them the Son of Man will be ashamed when he comes in his glory and the glory of the Father and of the holy angels."

Luke 9:28 "Now about eight days after these sayings [*logos*] Jesus took with him Peter and John and James, and went up on the mountain to pray."

Luke 9:44 "Let these words [*logos*] sink into your ears: The Son of Man is going to be betrayed into human hands."

Luke 10:39 "She had a sister named Mary, who sat at the Lord's feet and listened to what he was saying [*logos*]."

Luke 11:28 "But he said, 'Blessed rather are those who hear the word [*logos*] of God and obey it!'"

Luke 12:10 "And everyone who speaks a word [*logos*] against the Son of Man will be forgiven; but whoever blasphemes against the Holy Spirit will not be forgiven."

Luke 16:2 "So he summoned him and said to him, 'What is this that I hear about you? Give me an accounting [*logos*] of your management, because you cannot be my manager any longer.'"

Luke 20:3 "He answered them, 'I will also ask you a question [*logos*], and you tell me'"

Luke 20:20 "So they watched him and sent spies who pretended to be honest, in order to trap him by what he said [*logos*], so as to hand him over to the jurisdiction and authority of the governor."

Luke 21:33 "Heaven and earth will pass away, but my words [*logos*] will not pass away." (His words here are in reference to his own teaching, not to scripture.)

Luke 22:61 "The Lord turned and looked at Peter. Then Peter remembered the word [*logos*] of the Lord, how he had said to him, 'Before the cock crows today, you will deny me three times.'"

Luke 23:9 "He questioned him at some length, but Jesus gave him no answer." (Other translations say something like he questioned Jesus with many words.)

Luke 24:17 "And he said to them, 'What are you discussing with each other while you walk along?' They stood still, looking sad." (Other translations say something like what are these words or matters of which you are discussing.)

Luke 24:19 "He asked them, 'What things?' They replied, 'The things about Jesus of Nazareth, who was a prophet mighty in deed and word [*logos*] before God and all the people'"

Luke 24:44 "Then he said to them, 'These are my words [*logos*] that I spoke to you while I was still with you—that everything written [*graphe*] about me in the law of Moses, the prophets, and the psalms must be fulfilled.'"

John

John 1:1 "In the beginning was the Word [*logos*], and the Word [*logos*] was with God, and the Word [*logos*]was God."

John 1:14 "And the Word [*logos*] became flesh and lived among us, and we have seen his glory, the glory as of a father's only son, full of grace and truth."

John 2:22 "After he was raised from the dead, his disciples remembered that he had said this; and they believed the scripture [*graphe*] and the word [*logos*] that Jesus had spoken."

John 4:37 "For here the saying [*logos*] holds true, 'One sows and another reaps.'"

John 4:39 "Many Samaritans from that city believed in him because of the woman's testimony [*logos*], 'He told me everything I have ever done.'"

John 4:41 "And many more believed because of his word [*logos*]."

John 4:50 "Jesus said to him, 'Go; your son will live.' The man believed the word [*logos*] that Jesus spoke to him and started on his way."

John 5:24 "Very truly, I tell you, anyone who hears my word [*logos*] and believes him who sent me has eternal life, and does not come under judgment, but has passed from death to life."

John 5:38 "and you do not have his word [*logos*] abiding in you, because you do not believe him whom he has sent."

John 6:60 "When many of his disciples heard it, they said, 'This teaching [*logos*] is difficult; who can accept it?'"

John 7:36 "What does he mean by saying [*logos*], 'You will search for me and you will not find me' and 'Where I am, you cannot come'?"

John 7:40 "When they heard these words [*logos*], some in the crowd said, 'This is really the prophet.'"

John 8:31 "Then Jesus said to the Jews who had believed in him, 'If you continue in my word [*logos*], you are truly my disciples'"

John 8:37 "I know that you are descendants of Abraham; yet you look for an opportunity to kill me, because there is no place in you for my word [*logos*]."

John 8:43 "Why do you not understand what I say? It is because you cannot accept my word [*logos*]."

John 8:51-52 "Very truly, I tell you, whoever keeps my word [*logos*] will never see death. The Jews said to him, 'Now we know that you have a demon. Abraham died, and so did the prophets; yet you say, "Whoever keeps my word [*logos*] will never taste death."'"

John 8:55 "though you do not know him. But I know him; if I would say that I do not know him, I would be a liar like you. But I do know him and I keep his word [*logos*]."

John 10:19 "Again the Jews were divided because of these words [*logos*]."

John 10:35 "If those to whom the word [*logos*] of God came were called 'gods'—and the scripture [*graphe*] cannot be annulled" (See comments in section 5 of chapter 1. I think a similar thing could be said here. That even if here Jesus is equating scripture and the Word, he could be using their own theology against them rather than saying this is what he believes.)

John 12:38 "This was to fulfill the word [*logos*] spoken by the prophet Isaiah: 'Lord, who has believed our message, and to whom has the arm of the Lord been revealed?'"

John 12:48 "The one who rejects me and does not receive my word [*logos*] has a judge; on the last day the word [*logos*] that I have spoken will serve as judge"

John 14:23-24 "Jesus answered him, 'Those who love me will keep my word [*logos*], and my Father will love them, and we will come to them and make our home with them. Whoever does not love me does not keep my words [logos]; and the word [*logos*] that you hear is not mine, but is from the Father who sent me.'"

John 15:3 "You have already been cleansed by the word [*logos*] that I have spoken to you."

John 15:20 "Remember the word [*logos*] that I said to you, 'Servants are not greater than their master.' If they persecuted me, they will persecute you; if they kept my word [*logos*], they will keep yours also."

John 15:25 "It was to fulfill the word [*logos*] that is written in their law, 'They hated me without a cause.'" (Here logos just means words, just as I would say the words in this book. It's not a reference to the Word of God. It is not a claim that the words in the scriptures are authored by God.)

John 17:6 "I have made your name known to those whom you gave me from the world. They were yours, and you gave them to me, and they have kept your word [*logos*]."

John 17:14 "I have given them your word [*logos*], and the world has hated them because they do not belong to the world, just as I do not belong to the world."

John 17:17 "Sanctify them in the truth; your word [*logos*] is truth." (See my comments on Augustine's commentary on this in section 5 of chapter 1.)

John 17:20 "I ask not only on behalf of these, but also on behalf of those who will believe in me through their word [*logos*]"

John 18:9 "This was to fulfill the word [*logos*] that he had spoken, 'I did not lose a single one of those whom you gave me.'"

John 18:32 "(This was to fulfill what Jesus had said [*logos*] when he indicated the kind of death he was to die.)"

John 19:8 "Now when Pilate heard this [*logos*], he was more afraid than ever." (This word is the statement that he heard.)

John 19:13 "When Pilate heard these words [*logos*], he brought Jesus outside and sat on the judge's bench at a place called The Stone Pavement, or in Hebrew Gabbatha."

John 21:23 "So the rumor [*logos*] spread in the community that this disciple would not die. Yet Jesus did not say to him that he would not die, but, 'If it is my will that he remain until I come, what is that to you?'"

Acts

Acts 1:1 "In the first book [*logos*], Theophilus, I wrote about all that Jesus did and taught from the beginning" (Here is one of the few instances that logos is used to refer to a book. However other translations say account rather than book. I find it odd that the NRSV translates it as book since it rarely is translated to mean book.)

Acts 2:22 "You that are Israelites, listen to what I have to say [*logos*]: Jesus of Nazareth, a man attested to you by God with deeds of power, wonders, and signs that God did through him among you, as you yourselves know—"

Acts 2:40-41 "And he testified with many other arguments [*logos*] and exhorted them, saying, 'Save yourselves from this corrupt generation.' So those who welcomed his message [*logos*] were baptized, and that day about three thousand persons were added."

Acts 4:4 "But many of those who heard the word [*logos*] believed; and they numbered about five thousand."

Acts 4:29 "And now, Lord, look at their threats, and grant to your servants to speak your word [*logos*] with all boldness"

Acts 4:31 "When they had prayed, the place in which they were gathered together was shaken; and they were all filled with the Holy Spirit and spoke the word [*logos*] of God with boldness."

Acts 5:5 "Now when Ananias heard these words [*logos*], he fell down and died. And great fear seized all who heard of it."

Acts 5:24 "Now when the captain of the temple and the chief priests heard these words [*logos*], they were perplexed about them, wondering what might be going on."

Acts 6:2 "And the twelve called together the whole community of the disciples and said, 'It is not right that we should neglect the word [*logos*] of God in order to wait on tables.'" (Word is in reference to the preaching of the gospel.)

Acts 6:4 "while we, for our part, will devote ourselves to prayer and to serving the word [*logos*]."

Acts 6:5 "What they said [*logos*] pleased the whole community, and they chose Stephen, a man full of faith and the Holy Spirit, together with Philip, Prochorus, Nicanor, Timon, Parmenas, and Nicolaus, a proselyte of Antioch."

Acts 6:7 "The word [*logos*] of God continued to spread; the number of the disciples increased greatly in Jerusalem, and a great many of the priests became obedient to the faith."

Acts 7:22 "So Moses was instructed in all the wisdom of the Egyptians and was powerful in his words [*logos*] and deeds."

Acts 7:29 "When he heard this [*logos*], Moses fled and became a resident alien in the land of Midian. There he became the father of two sons."

Acts 8:4 "Now those who were scattered went from place to place, proclaiming the word [*logos*]." (Again, the proclaiming of the gospel message is what's in mind here.)

Acts 8:14 "Now when the apostles at Jerusalem heard that Samaria had accepted the word [*logos*] of God, they sent Peter and John to them."

Acts 8:21 "You have no part or share in this [*logos*], for your heart is not right before God."

Acts 8:25 "Now after Peter and John had testified and spoken the word [*logos*] of the Lord, they returned to Jerusalem, proclaiming the good news to many villages of the Samaritans."

Acts 10:29 "So when I was sent for, I came without objection. Now may I ask why you sent for me?" (Other translations say something like what reason [*logos*] have you sent me.)

Acts 10:36 "You know the message [*logos*] he sent to the people of Israel, preaching peace by Jesus Christ—he is Lord of all."

Acts 10:44 "While Peter was still speaking, the Holy Spirit fell upon all who heard the word [*logos*]."

Acts 11:1 "Now the apostles and the believers who were in Judea heard that the Gentiles had also accepted the word [*logos*] of God."

Acts 11:19 "Now those who were scattered because of the persecution that took place over Stephen traveled as far as Phoenicia, Cyprus, and Antioch, and they spoke the word [*logos*] to no one except Jews."

Acts 11:22 "News [*logos*] of this came to the ears of the church in Jerusalem, and they sent Barnabas to Antioch."

Acts 12:24 "But the word [*logos*] of God continued to advance and gain adherents."

Acts 13:5 "When they arrived at Salamis, they proclaimed the word [*logos*] of God in the synagogues of the Jews. And they had John also to assist them."

Acts 13:7 "He was with the proconsul, Sergius Paulus, an intelligent man, who summoned Barnabas and Saul and wanted to hear the word [*logos*] of God."

Acts 13:15 "After the reading of the law and the prophets, the officials of the synagogue sent them a message, saying, 'Brothers, if you have any word [*logos*] of exhortation for the people, give it.'" (Here we see that the logos being mentioned is clearly distinguished from the scripture (the Law and the Prophets).)

Acts 13:26 "My brothers, you descendants of Abraham's family, and others who fear God, to us the message [*logos*] of this salvation has been sent."

Acts 13:44 "The next sabbath almost the whole city gathered to hear the word [*logos*] of the Lord."

Acts 13:46 "Then both Paul and Barnabas spoke out boldly, saying, 'It was necessary that the word [*logos*] of God should be spoken first to you. Since you reject it and judge yourselves to be unworthy of eternal life, we are now turning to the Gentiles.'"

Acts 13:48-49 "When the Gentiles heard this, they were glad and praised the word [*logos*] of the Lord; and as many as had been destined for eternal life became believers. Thus the word [*logos*] of the Lord spread throughout the region."

Acts 14:3 "So they remained for a long time, speaking boldly for the Lord, who testified to the word [*logos*] of his grace by granting signs and wonders to be done through them."

Acts 14:12 "Barnabas they called Zeus, and Paul they called Hermes, because he was the chief speaker [*logos*]."

Acts 14:25 "When they had spoken the word [*logos*] in Perga, they went down to Attalia."

Acts 15:6-7 "The apostles and the elders met together to consider this matter [*logos*]. After there had been much debate, Peter stood up and said to them, 'My brothers, you know that in the early days God made a choice among you, that I should be the one through whom the Gentiles would hear the message [*logos*] of the good news and become believers.'"

Acts 15:15 "This agrees with the words [*logos*] of the prophets, as it is written" (Again this seems to be about the words of the prophets themselves, which of course were recorded in scripture, but it's not saying that the scriptures are the word of God. It's not even calling the words of the prophets the Word of God; it's simply making a reference to the words of the prophets.)

Acts 15:24 "Since we have heard that certain persons who have gone out from us, though with no instructions from us, have said things [*logos*] to disturb you and have unsettled your minds"

Acts 15:27 "We have therefore sent Judas and Silas, who themselves will tell you the same things by word [*logos*] of mouth." (This word here is neither a reference to the gospel message or Christ, but logos is being used here to reference the edict made by the Christians in Jerusalem that gentile converts don't have to get circumcised. I bet you gentiles are glad. As for me, I'm more-old fashioned.)

Acts 15:32 "Judas and Silas, who were themselves prophets, said [*logos*] much to encourage and strengthen the believers."

Acts 15:35-36 "But Paul and Barnabas remained in Antioch, and there, with many others, they taught and proclaimed the word [*logos*] of the Lord. After some days Paul said to Barnabas, 'Come, let us return and visit the believers in every city where we proclaimed the word [*logos*] of the Lord and see how they are doing.'"

Acts 16:6 "They went through the region of Phrygia and Galatia, having been forbidden by the Holy Spirit to speak the word [*logos*] in Asia."

Acts 16:32 "They spoke the word [*logos*] of the Lord to him and to all who were in his house."

Acts 16:36 "And the jailer reported the message [*logos*] to Paul, saying, 'The magistrates sent word to let you go; therefore come out now and go in peace.'"

Acts 17:11 "These Jews were more receptive than those in Thessalonica, for they welcomed the message [*logos*] very eagerly and examined the scriptures [*graphe*] every day to see whether these things were so." (Here we see a clear distinction made between the scriptures and the logos or message. Also see notes in section 5 of chapter 1.)

Acts 17:13 "But when the Jews of Thessalonica learned that the word [*logos*] of God had been proclaimed by Paul in Beroea as well, they came there too, to stir up and incite the crowds."

Acts 18:5 "When Silas and Timothy arrived from Macedonia, Paul was occupied with proclaiming the word [*logos*], testifying to the Jews that the Messiah was Jesus."

Acts 18:11 "He stayed there a year and six months, teaching the word [*logos*] of God among them."

Acts 18:14-15 "Just as Paul was about to speak, Gallio said to the Jews, 'If it were a matter of crime or serious villainy, I would be justified [*logos*] in accepting the complaint of you Jews; but since it is a matter of questions about words [*logos*] and names and your own law, see to it yourselves; I do not wish to be a judge of these matters.'"

Acts 19:10 "This continued for two years, so that all the residents of Asia, both Jews and Greeks, heard the word [*logos*] of the Lord."

Acts 19:20 "So the word [*logos*] of the Lord grew mightily and prevailed."

Acts 19:38 "If therefore Demetrius and the artisans with him have a complaint [*logos*] against anyone, the courts are open, and there are proconsuls; let them bring charges there against one another."

Acts 19:40 "For we are in danger of being charged with rioting today, since there is no cause that we can give to justify this commotion." (Other translations say something like we have no explanation [*logos*] to give for it.)

Acts 20:2 "When he had gone through those regions and had given the believers much encouragement [*logos*], he came to Greece"

Acts 20:7 "On the first day of the week, when we met to break bread, Paul was holding a discussion with them; since he intended to leave the next day, he continued speaking [*logos*] until midnight."

Acts 20:24 "But I do not count my life of any value to myself, if only I may finish my course and the ministry that I received from the Lord Jesus, to testify to the good news of God's grace." (Other translations say something to the effect of consider my life of no account [*logos*].)

Acts 20:32 "And now I commend you to God and to the message [*logos*] of his grace, a message that is able to build you up and to give you the inheritance among all who are sanctified."

Acts 20:35 "In all this I have given you an example that by such work we must support the weak, remembering the words [*logos*] of the Lord Jesus, for he himself said, 'It is more blessed to give than to receive.'"

Acts 20:38 "grieving especially because of what he had said [*logos*], that they would not see him again. Then they brought him to the ship."

Acts 22:22 "Up to this point they listened to him, but then they shouted, 'Away with such a fellow from the earth! For he should not be allowed to live.'" (Other translations say something like up to this statement [*logos*] or word [*logos*] they listened to him.)

Romans

Rom 3:4 "By no means! Although everyone is a liar, let God be proved true, as it is written, 'So that you may be justified in your words [*logos*], and prevail in your judging.'"

Rom 9:6 "It is not as though the word [*logos*] of God had failed. For not all Israelites truly belong to Israel"

Rom 9:9 "For this is what the promise said [*logos*], 'About this time I will return and Sarah shall have a son.'"

Rom 9:28 "for the Lord will execute his sentence [*logos*] on the earth quickly and decisively."

Rom 13:9 "The commandments, 'You shall not commit adultery; You shall not murder; You shall not steal; You shall not covet'; and any other commandment, are summed up in this word [*logos*], 'Love your neighbor as yourself.'"

Rom 14:12 "So then, each of us will be accountable [*logos*] to God."

Rom 15:18 "For I will not venture to speak of anything except what Christ has accomplished through me to win obedience from the Gentiles, by word [*logos*] and deed"

1 Corinthians

1 Cor 1:5 "for in every way you have been enriched in him, in speech [*logos*] and knowledge of every kind"

1 Cor 1:17-18 "For Christ did not send me to baptize but to proclaim the gospel, and not with eloquent [*logos*] wisdom, so that the cross of Christ might not be emptied of its power. For the message [*logos*] about the cross is foolishness to those who are perishing, but to us who are being saved it is the power of God."

1 Cor 2:1 "When I came to you, brothers and sisters, I did not come proclaiming the mystery of God to you in lofty words [*logos*] or wisdom."

1 Cor 2:4 "My speech [*logos*] and my proclamation were not with plausible words [*logos*] of wisdom, but with a demonstration of the Spirit and of power"

1 Cor 2:13 "And we speak of these things in words [*logos*] not taught by human wisdom but taught by the Spirit, interpreting spiritual things to those who are spiritual."

1 Cor 4:19-20 "But I will come to you soon, if the Lord wills, and I will find out not the talk [*logos*] of these arrogant people but their power. For the kingdom of God depends not on talk [*logos*] but on power."

1 Cor 12:8 "To one is given through the Spirit the utterance [*logos*] of wisdom, and to another the utterance [*logos*] of knowledge according to the same Spirit"

1 Cor 14:9 "So with yourselves; if in a tongue you utter speech [*logos*] that is not intelligible, how will anyone know what is being said? For you will be speaking into the air."

1 Cor 14:19 "nevertheless, in church I would rather speak five words [*logos*] with my mind, in order to instruct others also, than ten thousand words [*logos*] in a tongue."

1 Cor 14:36 "Or did the word [*logos*] of God originate with you? Or are you the only ones it has reached?"

1 Cor 15:2 "through which also you are being saved, if you hold firmly to the message [*logos*] that I proclaimed to you—unless you have come to believe in vain."

1 Cor 15:54 "When this perishable body puts on imperishability, and this mortal body puts on immortality, then the saying [*logos*] that is written will be fulfilled: 'Death has been swallowed up in victory.'" (Here is another possible rare instance in which logos is being used to refer to scripture. I think it's more likely however that here it simply means words that are written in scripture rather than being a statement that these words are logos of God. In the same way that logos is used in other passages to merely refer to someone's speech.)

2 Corinthians

2 Cor 1:18 "As surely as God is faithful, our word [*logos*] to you has not been 'Yes and No.'"

2 Cor 2:17 "For we are not peddlers of God's word [*logos*] like so many; but in Christ we speak as persons of sincerity, as persons sent from God and standing in his presence."

2 Cor 4:2 "We have renounced the shameful things that one hides; we refuse to practice cunning or to falsify God's word [*logos*]; but by the open statement of the truth we commend ourselves to the conscience of everyone in the sight of God."

2 Cor 5:19 "that is, in Christ God was reconciling the world to himself, not counting their trespasses against them, and entrusting the message [*logos*] of reconciliation to us."

2 Cor 6:7 "truthful speech [*logos*], and the power of God; with the weapons of righteousness for the right hand and for the left"

2 Cor 8:7 "Now as you excel in everything—in faith, in speech [*logos*], in knowledge, in utmost eagerness, and in our love for you—so we want you to excel also in this generous undertaking."

2 Cor 10:10-11 "For they say, 'His letters are weighty and strong, but his bodily presence is weak, and his speech [*logos*] contemptible.' Let such people understand that what we say [*logos*] by letter when absent, we will also do when present."

2 Cor 11:6 "I may be untrained in speech [*logos*], but not in knowledge; certainly in every way and in all things we have made this evident to you."

Galatians

Gal 5:14 "For the whole law is summed up in a single commandment [*logos*], 'You shall love your neighbor as yourself.'"

Gal 6:6 "Those who are taught the word [*logos*] must share in all good things with their teacher."

Ephesians

Eph 1:13 "In him you also, when you had heard the word [*logos*] of truth, the gospel of your salvation, and had believed in him, were marked with the seal of the promised Holy Spirit"

Eph 4:29 "Let no evil talk [*logos*] come out of your mouths, but only what is useful for building up, as there is need, so that your words may give grace to those who hear."

Eph 5:6 "Let no one deceive you with empty words [*logos*], for because of these things the wrath of God comes on those who are disobedient."

Eph 6:19 "Pray also for me, so that when I speak, a message [*logos*] may be given to me to make known with boldness the mystery of the gospel"

Philippians

Phil 1:14 "and most of the brothers and sisters, having been made confident in the Lord by my imprisonment, dare to speak the word [*logos*] with greater boldness and without fear."

Phil 2:16 "It is by your holding fast to the word [*logos*] of life that I can boast on the day of Christ that I did not run in vain or labor in vain."

Phil 4:15 "You Philippians indeed know that in the early days of the gospel, when I left Macedonia, no church shared with me in the matter [*logos*] of giving and receiving, except you alone."

Phil 4:17 "Not that I seek the gift, but I seek the profit that accumulates to your account [*logos*]."

Colossians

Col 1:5 "because of the hope laid up for you in heaven. You have heard of this hope before in the word [*logos*] of the truth, the gospel"

Col 1:25 "I became its servant according to God's commission that was given to me for you, to make the word [*logos*] of God fully known"

Col 2:23 "These have indeed an appearance of wisdom in promoting self-imposed piety, humility, and severe treatment of the body, but they are of no value in checking self-indulgence." (Other translations say something like these matters [*logos*] or regulations [logos].)

Col 3:16-17 "Let the word [*logos*] of Christ dwell in you richly; teach and admonish one another in all wisdom; and with gratitude in your hearts sing psalms, hymns, and spiritual songs to God. And whatever you do, in word [*logos*] or deed, do everything in the name of the Lord Jesus, giving thanks to God the Father through him."

Col 4:3 "At the same time pray for us as well that God will open to us a door for the word [*logos*], that we may declare the mystery of Christ, for which I am in prison"

Col 4:6 "Let your speech [*logos*] always be gracious, seasoned with salt, so that you may know how you ought to answer everyone."

1 Thessalonians

1 Thess 1:5-6 "because our message of the gospel came to you not in word [*logos*] only, but also in power and in the Holy Spirit and with full conviction; just as you know what kind of persons we proved to be among you for your sake. And you became imitators of us and of the Lord, for in spite of persecution you received the word [*logos*] with joy inspired by the Holy Spirit"

1 Thess 1:8 "For the word [*logos*] of the Lord has sounded forth from you not only in Macedonia and Achaia, but in every place your faith in God has become known, so that we have no need to speak about it."

1 Thess 2:5 "As you know and as God is our witness, we never came with words [*logos*] of flattery or with a pretext for greed"

1 Thess 2:13 "We also constantly give thanks to God for this, that when you received the word [*logos*] of God that you heard from us, you accepted it not as a human word [*logos*] but as what it really is, God's word [*logos*], which is also at work in you believers."

1 Thess 4:15 "For this we declare to you by the word [*logos*] of the Lord, that we who are alive, who are left until the coming of the Lord, will by no means precede those who have died."

1 Thess 4:18 "Therefore encourage one another with these words [*logos*]."

2 Thessalonians

2 Thess 2:2 "not to be quickly shaken in mind or alarmed, either by spirit or by word [*logos*] or by letter, as though from us, to the effect that the day of the Lord is already here."

2 Thess 2:15 "So then, brothers and sisters, stand firm and hold fast to the traditions that you were taught by us, either by word [*logos*] of mouth or by our letter."

2 Thess 2:17 "comfort your hearts and strengthen them in every good work and word [*logos*]."

2 Thess 3:1 "Finally, brothers and sisters, pray for us, so that the word [*logos*] of the Lord may spread rapidly and be glorified everywhere, just as it is among you"

2 Thess 3:14 "Take note of those who do not obey what we say [*logos*] in this letter; have nothing to do with them, so that they may be ashamed."

1 Timothy

1 Tim 1:15 "The saying [*logos*] is sure and worthy of full acceptance, that Christ Jesus came into the world to save sinners—of whom I am the foremost."

1 Tim 3:1 "The saying [*logos*] is sure: whoever aspires to the office of bishop desires a noble task."

1 Tim 4:5-6 "for it is sanctified by God's word [*logos*] and by prayer. If you put these instructions before the brothers and sisters, you will be a good servant of Christ Jesus, nourished on the words [*logos*] of the faith and of the sound teaching that you have followed."

1 Tim 4:9 "The saying [*logos*] is sure and worthy of full acceptance."

1 Tim 4:12 "Let no one despise your youth, but set the believers an example in speech [*logos*] and conduct, in love, in faith, in purity."

1 Tim 5:17 "Let the elders who rule well be considered worthy of double honor, especially those who labor in preaching [*logos*] and teaching" (It should be noted that when the early church talks about preaching, they do not necessarily mean what we mean by preaching. They mean preaching the gospel message about Christ Crucified and Risen as the Lord of the New Creation. It means preaching Christ, not scripture; although scripture can be used to preach Christ.)

1 Tim 6:3 "Whoever teaches otherwise and does not agree with the sound words [*logos*] of our Lord Jesus Christ and the teaching that is in accordance with godliness"

2 Timothy

2 Tim 1:13 "Hold to the standard of sound teaching [*logos*] that you have heard from me, in the faith and love that are in Christ Jesus."

2 Tim 2:9 "for which I suffer hardship, even to the point of being chained like a criminal. But the word [*logos*] of God is not chained."

2 Tim 2:11 "The saying [*logos*] is sure: If we have died with him, we will also live with him"

2 Tim 2:15 "Do your best to present yourself to God as one approved by him, a worker who has no need to be ashamed, rightly explaining the word [*logos*] of truth."

2 Tim 2:17 "and their talk [*logos*] will spread like gangrene. Among them are Hymenaeus and Philetus"

2 Tim 4:2 "proclaim the message [*logos*]; be persistent whether the time is favorable or unfavorable; convince, rebuke, and encourage, with the utmost patience in teaching." (See my comments on this text in section 5 of chapter 1.)

2 Tim 4:15 "You also must beware of him, for he strongly opposed our message [*logos*]."

Titus

Titus 1:3 "in due time he revealed his word [*logos*] through the proclamation with which I have been entrusted by the command of God our Savior"

Titus 1:9 "He must have a firm grasp of the word [*logos*] that is trustworthy in accordance with the teaching, so that he may be able both to preach with sound doctrine and to refute those who contradict it."

Titus 2:5 "to be self-controlled, chaste, good managers of the household, kind, being submissive to their husbands, so that the word [*logos*] of God may not be discredited."

Titus 2:8 "and sound speech [*logos*] that cannot be censured; then any opponent will be put to shame, having nothing evil to say of us."

Titus 3:8 "The saying [*logos*] is sure. I desire that you insist on these things, so that those who have come to believe in God may be careful to devote themselves to good works; these things are excellent and profitable to everyone."

Hebrews

Heb 2:2 "For if the message [*logos*] declared through angels was valid, and every transgression or disobedience received a just penalty"

Heb 4:2 "For indeed the good news came to us just as to them; but the message [*logos*] they heard did not benefit them, because they were not united by faith with those who listened."

Heb 4:12-13 "Indeed, the word [*logos*] of God is living and active, sharper than any two-edged sword, piercing until it divides soul from spirit, joints from marrow; it is able to judge the thoughts and intentions of the heart. And before him no creature is hidden, but all are naked and laid bare to the eyes of the one to whom we must render an account [*logos*]." (Notice that the word here is referred to as a him and that he is to whom we must render an account. As far as I'm aware, the Bible doesn't have male chromosomes, and it is Christ who will come back to judge the living and the dead. See section 5 of chapter 1 for more details."

Heb 5:11 "About this we have much to say [*logos*] that is hard to explain, since you have become dull in understanding."

Heb 5:13 "for everyone who lives on milk, being still an infant, is unskilled in the word [*logos*] of righteousness."

Heb 6:1 "Therefore let us go on toward perfection, leaving behind the basic teaching [*logos*] about Christ, and not laying again the foundation: repentance from dead works and faith toward God"

Heb 7:28 "For the law appoints as high priests those who are subject to weakness, but the word [*logos*] of the oath, which came later than the law, appoints a Son who has been made perfect forever."

Heb 12:19 "and the sound of a trumpet, and a voice whose words made the hearers beg that not another word [*logos*] be spoken to them."

Heb 13:7 "Remember your leaders, those who spoke the word [*logos*] of God to you; consider the outcome of their way of life, and imitate their faith."

Heb 13:17 "Obey your leaders and submit to them, for they are keeping watch over your souls and will give an account [*logos*]. Let them do this with joy and not with sighing—for that would be harmful to you."

Heb 13:22 "I appeal to you, brothers and sisters, bear with my word [*logos*]of exhortation, for I have written to you briefly."

James

James 1:18 "In fulfillment of his own purpose he gave us birth by the word [*logos*] of truth, so that we would become a kind of first fruits of his creatures."

James 1:21-23 "Therefore rid yourselves of all sordidness and rank growth of wickedness, and welcome with meekness the implanted word [logos] that has the power to save your souls. But be doers of the word [logos], and not merely hearers who deceive themselves. For if any are hearers of the word [*logos*] and not doers, they are like those who look at themselves in a mirror"

James 3:2 "For all of us make many mistakes. Anyone who makes no mistakes in speaking [*logos*] is perfect, able to keep the whole body in check with a bridle."

1 Peter

1 Pet 1:23-25 "You have been born anew, not of perishable but of imperishable seed, through the living and enduring word [*logos*] of God. For

All flesh is like grass
    and all its glory like the flower of grass.
The grass withers,
    and the flower falls,
but the word of the Lord endures forever.

That word is the good news [*gospel*] that was announced to you."

1 Pet 2:8 "and 'A stone that makes them stumble, and a rock that makes them fall.' They stumble because they disobey the word [*logos*], as they were destined to do."

1 Pet 3:1 "Wives, in the same way, accept the authority of your hus-bands, so that, even if some of them do not obey the word [*logos*], they may be won over without a word [*logos*] by their wives' conduct"

1 Pet 3:15 "but in your hearts sanctify Christ as Lord. Always be ready to make your defense to anyone who demands from you an accounting [*logos*] for the hope that is in you"

1 Pet 4:5 "But they will have to give an accounting [*logos*] to him who stands ready to judge the living and the dead." (Remember the language of Hebrews 4:12-13? We must give account [*logos*] to Christ who is the logos.)

2 Peter

2 Pet 1:19 "So we have the prophetic message [*logos*] more fully confirmed. You will do well to be attentive to this as to a lamp shining in a dark place, until the day dawns and the morning star rises in your hearts." (See comments on this passage in section 5 of chapter 1.)

2 Pet 2:3 "And in their greed they will exploit you with deceptive words [*logos*]. Their condemnation, pronounced against them long ago, has not been idle, and their destruction is not asleep."

2 Pet 3:5 "They deliberately ignore this fact, that by the word [*logos*] of God heavens existed long ago and an earth was formed out of water and by means of water"

2 Pet 3:7 "But by the same word [*logos*] the present heavens and earth have been reserved for fire, being kept until the day of judgment and destruction of the godless."

1 John

1 John 1:1 "We declare to you what was from the beginning, what we have heard, what we have seen with our eyes, what we have looked at and touched with our hands, concerning the word [*logos*] of life—" (This is alluding back to John 1; both of these passages are speaking of Christ.)

1 John 1:10 "If we say that we have not sinned, we make him a liar, and his word [*logos*] is not in us."

1 John 2:5 "but whoever obeys his word [*logos*], truly in this person the love of God has reached perfection. By this we may be sure that we are in him"

1 John 2:7 "Beloved, I am writing you no new commandment, but an old commandment that you have had from the beginning; the old commandment is the word [*logos*] that you have heard."

1 John 2:14 "I write to you, children, because you know the Father I write to you, fathers, because you know him who is from the beginning. I write to you, young people, because you are strong and the word [*logos*] of God abides in you, and you have overcome the evil one."

1 John 3:18 "Little children, let us love, not in word [*logos*] or speech, but in truth and action."

3 John

3 John 10 "So if I come, I will call attention to what he is doing in spreading false charges [*logos*] against us. And not content with those charges, he refuses to welcome the friends, and even prevents those who want to do so and expels them from the church."

Revelation

Rev 1:2-3 "who testified to the word of God [*logos*] and to the testimony of Jesus Christ, even to all that he saw. Blessed is the one who reads aloud the words [*logos*] of the prophecy, and blessed are those who hear and who keep what is written in it; for the time is near."

Rev 1:9 "I, John, your brother who share with you in Jesus the persecution and the kingdom and the patient endurance, was on the island called Patmos because of the word [*logos*] of God and the testimony of Jesus."

Rev 3:8 "I know your works. Look, I have set before you an open door, which no one is able to shut. I know that you have but little power, and yet you have kept my word [*logos*] and have not denied my name."

Rev 3:10 "Because you have kept my word [*logos*] of patient endurance, I will keep you from the hour of trial that is coming on the whole world to test the inhabitants of the earth."

Rev 6:9 "When he opened the fifth seal, I saw under the altar the souls of those who had been slaughtered for the word [*logos*] of God and for the testimony they had given"

Rev 12:11 "But they have conquered him by the blood of the Lamb and by the word [*logos*] of their testimony, for they did not cling to life even in the face of death."

Rev 17:17 "For God has put it into their hearts to carry out his purpose by agreeing to give their kingdom to the beast, until the words [*logos*] of God will be fulfilled."

Rev 19:9 "And the angel said to me, 'Write this: Blessed are those who are invited to the marriage supper of the Lamb.' And he said to me, 'These are true words [*logos*]of God.'"

Rev 19:13 "He is clothed in a robe dipped in blood, and his name is called The Word [*logos*] of God."

Rev 20:4 "Then I saw thrones, and those seated on them were given authority to judge. I also saw the souls of those who had been beheaded for their testimony to Jesus and for the word [*logos*] of God. They had not worshiped the beast or its image and had not received its mark on their foreheads or their hands. They came to life and reigned with Christ a thousand years."

Rev 21:5 "And the one who was seated on the throne said, 'See, I am making all things new.' Also he said, 'Write this, for these words [*logos*] are trustworthy and true.'"

Rev 22:6-7 "And he said to me, 'These words [*logos*] are trustworthy and true, for the Lord, the God of the spirits of the prophets, has sent his angel to show his servants what must soon take place. "See, I am coming soon! Blessed is the one who keeps the words [*logos*] of the prophecy of this book.""

Rev 22:9-10 "but he said to me, 'You must not do that! I am a fellow servant with you and your comrades the prophets, and with those who keep the words [*logos*] of this book. Worship God!' And he said to me, 'Do not seal up the words [*logos*] of the prophecy of this book, for the time is near.'"

Rev 22:18-19 "I warn everyone who hears the words [logos] of the prophecy of this book: if anyone adds to them, God will add to that person the plagues described in this book; if anyone takes away from the words [*logos*] of the book of this prophecy, God will take away that person's share in the tree of life and in the holy city, which are described in this book."

NEW TESTAMENT USAGE OF RHEMA (ῥῆμα)

Matthew

Matt 4:4 "But he answered, 'It is written, "One does not live by bread alone, but by every word [*rhema*] that comes from the mouth of God.""

Matt 12:36 "I tell you, on the day of judgment you will have to give an account for every careless word [*rhema*] you utter"

Matt 18:16 "But if you are not listened to, take one or two others along with you, so that every word [*rhema*] may be confirmed by the evidence of two or three witnesses."

Matt 26:75 "Then Peter remembered what [*rhema*] Jesus had said: 'Before the cock crows, you will deny me three times.' And he went out and wept bitterly."

Matt 27:14 "But he gave him no answer, not even to a single charge [*rhema*], so that the governor was greatly amazed."

Mark

Mark 9:32 "But they did not understand what he was saying [*rhema*] and were afraid to ask him."

Mark 14:72 "At that moment the cock crowed for the second time. Then Peter remembered that Jesus had said [*rhema*] to him, 'Before the cock crows twice, you will deny me three times.' And he broke down and wept."

Luke

Luke 1:37-38 "For nothing [*rhema*] will be impossible with God. Then Mary said, 'Here am I, the servant of the Lord; let it be with me according to your word [*rhema*].' Then the angel departed from her."

Luke 1:65 "Fear came over all their neighbors, and all these things [*rhema*] were talked about throughout the entire hill country of Judea."

Luke 2:15 "When the angels had left them and gone into heaven, the shepherds said to one another, 'Let us go now to Bethlehem and see this thing [*rhema*] that has taken place, which the Lord has made known to us.'"

Luke 2:17 "When they saw this, they made known what had been told them about this child" (Other translations say something like made known the statement [*rhema*] or message [*rhema*].)

Luke 2:19 "But Mary treasured all these words [*rhema*] and pondered them in her heart."

Luke 2:29 "Master, now you are dismissing your servant in peace, according to your word [*rhema*]"

Luke 2:50-51 "But they did not understand what he said [rhema] to them. Then he went down with them and came to Nazareth, and was obedient to them. His mother treasured all these things [*rhema*] in her heart."

Luke 3:2 "during the high priesthood of Annas and Caiaphas, the word [*rhema*] of God came to John son of Zechariah in the wilderness."

Luke 5:5 "Simon answered, 'Master, we have worked all night long but have caught nothing. Yet if you say [*rhema*] so, I will let down the nets.'"

Luke 7:1 "After Jesus had finished all his sayings [*rhema*] in the hearing of the people, he entered Capernaum."

Luke 9:45 "But they did not understand this saying [*rhema*]; its meaning was concealed from them, so that they could not perceive it. And they were afraid to ask him about this saying [*rhema*]."

Luke 18:34 "But they understood nothing about all these things; in fact, what he said [*rhema*] was hidden from them, and they did not grasp what was said."

Luke 20:26 "And they were not able in the presence of the people to trap him by what he said [*rhema*]; and being amazed by his answer, they became silent."

Luke 22:61 "The Lord turned and looked at Peter. Then Peter remembered the word [*rhema*] of the Lord, how he had said to him, 'Before the cock crows today, you will deny me three times.'"

Luke 24:8-9 "Then they remembered his words [*rhema*], and returning from the tomb, they told all this to the eleven and to all the rest."

Luke 24:11 "But these words [*rhema*] seemed to them an idle tale, and they did not believe them."

John

John 3:34 "He whom God has sent speaks the words [*rhema*] of God, for he gives the Spirit without measure."

John 5:47 "But if you do not believe what he wrote, how will you believe what I say [*rhema*]?"

John 6:63 "It is the spirit that gives life; the flesh is useless. The words [*rhema*] that I have spoken to you are spirit and life."

John 6:68 "Simon Peter answered him, 'Lord, to whom can we go? You have the words [*rhema*] of eternal life.'"

John 8:20 "He spoke these words [*rhema*] while he was teaching in the treasury of the temple, but no one arrested him, because his hour had not yet come."

John 8:47 "Whoever is from God hears the words [*rhema*] of God. The reason you do not hear them is that you are not from God."

John 10:21 "Others were saying, 'These are not the words [*rhema*] of one who has a demon. Can a demon open the eyes of the blind?'"

John 12:47-48 "I do not judge anyone who hears my words [*rhema*] and does not keep them, for I came not to judge the world, but to save the world. The one who rejects me and does not receive my word [*rhema*] has a judge; on the last day the word that I have spoken will serve as judge"

John 14:10 "Do you not believe that I am in the Father and the Father is in me? The words [*rhema*] that I say to you I do not speak on my own; but the Father who dwells in me does his works."

John 15:7 "If you abide in me, and my words [*rhema*] abide in you, ask for whatever you wish, and it will be done for you."

John 17:8 "for the words [*rhema*] that you gave to me I have given to them, and they have received them and know in truth that I came from you; and they have believed that you sent me."

Acts

Acts 2:14 "But Peter, standing with the eleven, raised his voice and addressed them, "Men of Judea and all who live in Jerusalem, let this be known to you, and listen to what I say [*rhema*]."

Acts 5:20 "Go, stand in the temple and tell the people the whole message [*rhema*] about this life."

Acts 5:32 "And we are witnesses to these things [*rhema*], and so is the Holy Spirit whom God has given to those who obey him."

Acts 6:11 "Then they secretly instigated some men to say, 'We have heard him speak blasphemous words [*rhema*] against Moses and God.'"

Acts 6:13 "They set up false witnesses who said, 'This man never stops saying things [*rhema*] against this holy place and the law'"

Acts 10:22 "They answered, 'Cornelius, a centurion, an upright and God-fearing man, who is well spoken of by the whole Jewish nation, was directed by a holy angel to send for you to come to his house and to hear what you have to say [*rhema*].'"

Acts 10:37 "That message [*rhema*] spread throughout Judea, beginning in Galilee after the baptism that John announced"

Acts 10:44 "While Peter was still speaking, the Holy Spirit fell upon all who heard the word [*rhema*]."

Acts 11:14 "he will give you a message [*rhema*] by which you and your entire household will be saved."

Acts 11:16 "And I remembered the word [*rhema*] of the Lord, how he had said, 'John baptized with water, but you will be baptized with the Holy Spirit.'"

Acts 13:42 "As Paul and Barnabas were going out, the people urged them to speak about these things [*rhema*] again the next sabbath."

Acts 16:38 "The police reported these words [*rhema*] to the magistrates, and they were afraid when they heard that they were Roman citizens"

Acts 26:25 "But Paul said, 'I am not out of my mind, most excellent Festus, but I am speaking [*rhema*] the sober truth.'"

Acts 28:25 "So they disagreed with each other; and as they were leaving, Paul made one further statement [*rhema*]: 'The Holy Spirit was right in saying to your ancestors through the prophet Isaiah'"

Romans

Rom 10:8 "But what does it say? 'The word [*rhema*] is near you, on your lips and in your heart' (that is, the word [*rhema*] of faith that we proclaim)"

Rom 10:17-18 "So faith comes from what is heard, and what is heard comes through the word [*rhema*] of Christ. But I ask, have they not heard? Indeed they have; for 'Their voice has gone out to all the earth, and their words [*rhema*] to the ends of the world.'"

2 Corinthians

2 Cor 12:4 "was caught up into Paradise and heard things [*rhema*] that are not to be told, that no mortal is permitted to repeat."

2 Cor 13:1 "This is the third time I am coming to you. 'Any charge [*rhema*] must be sustained by the evidence of two or three witnesses.'"

Ephesians

Eph 5:26 "in order to make her holy by cleansing her with the washing of water by the word [*rhema*]"

Eph 6:17 "Take the helmet of salvation, and the sword of the Spirit, which is the word [*rhema*] of God."

Hebrews

Heb 1:3 "He is the reflection of God's glory and the exact imprint of God's very being, and he sustains all things by his powerful word [*rhema*]. When he had made purification for sins, he sat down at the right hand of the Majesty on high"

Heb 6:5 "and have tasted the goodness of the word [*rhema*] of God and the powers of the age to come"

Heb 11:3 "By faith we understand that the worlds were prepared by the word [*rhema*] of God, so that what is seen was made from things that are not visible." (This is clearly a statement about Christ since we know from John that it was through Christ as the Word that the world was made.)

Heb 12:19 "and the sound of a trumpet, and a voice whose words [*rhema*] made the hearers beg that not another word be spoken to them."

1 Peter

1 Pet 1:25 "but the word [*rhema*] of the Lord endures forever. That word is the good news that was announced to you." (Here the author is defining the word as the gospel message not the scriptures.)

2 Peter

2 Pet 3:2 "that you should remember the words [*rhema*] spoken in the past by the holy prophets, and the commandment of the Lord and Savior spoken through your apostles." (We tend to compress the prophets and apostles into scripture because of our preconceived notion that the role of the prophets and apostles was to write scripture. It is thus the word that was spoken to them, not the words they wrote down, that is being referred to here.)

Jude

Jude 17 "But you, beloved, must remember the predictions [*rhema*] of the apostles of our Lord Jesus Christ." (Being that our New Testament, as we know it today, was still coming together at this point, this probably is not a reference to scripture. Indeed, to assume it is so collapses the apostles into scripture. There's no indication here that scripture is what the author had in mind.)

NEW TESTAMENT USAGE OF GRAPHE (γραφή)

Matthew

Matt 21:42 "Jesus said to them, 'Have you never read in the scriptures [*graphe*]: "The stone that the builders rejected has become the cornerstone"; this was the Lord's doing, and it is amazing in our eyes'?"

Matt 22:29 "Jesus answered them, 'You are wrong, because you know neither the scriptures [*graphe*] nor the power of God.'" (See comments in chapter 1 under section heading The Bible is God's Word-Authorship and Inspiration Seen as Synonymous.)

Matt 26:54 "But how then would the scriptures [*graphe*] be fulfilled, which say it must happen in this way?" (On the concept of the scriptures being fulfilled see chapter 4.)

Matt 26:56 "'But all this has taken place, so that the scriptures [*graphe*] of the prophets may be fulfilled.' Then all the disciples deserted him and fled."

Mark

Mark 12:10 "Have you not read this scripture [*graphe*]: 'The stone that the builders rejected has become the cornerstone'"

Mark 12:24 "Jesus said to them, 'Is not this the reason you are wrong, that you know neither the scriptures [*graphe*] nor the power of God?'"

Mark 14:49 "Day after day I was with you in the temple teaching, and you did not arrest me. But let the scriptures [*graphe*] be fulfilled."

Luke

Luke 4:21 "Then he began to say to them, 'Today this scripture [*graphe*] has been fulfilled in your hearing.'" (See my discussion on what it means for Jesus to fulfill scripture in chapter 4.)

Luke 24:27 "Then beginning with Moses and all the prophets, he interpreted to them the things about himself in all the scriptures [*graphe*]."

Luke 24:32 "They said to each other, 'Were not our hearts burning within us while he was talking to us on the road, while he was opening the scriptures [*graphe*] to us?'"

Luke 24:45 "Then he opened their minds to understand the scriptures [*graphe*]"

John

John 2:22 "After he was raised from the dead, his disciples remembered that he had said this; and they believed the scripture [*graphe*] and the word that Jesus had spoken."

John 5:39 "You search the scriptures [*graphe*] because you think that in them you have eternal life; and it is they that testify on my behalf."

John 7:38 "and let the one who believes in me drink. As the scripture [*graphe*] has said, 'Out of the believer's heart shall flow rivers of living water.'"

John 7:42 "Has not the scripture [*graphe*] said that the Messiah is descended from David and comes from Bethlehem, the village where David lived?"

John 10:35 "If those to whom the word of God came were called 'gods'—and the scripture [*graphe*] cannot be annulled—"

John 13:18 "I am not speaking of all of you; I know whom I have chosen. But it is to fulfill the scripture [*graphe*], 'The one who ate my bread has lifted his heel against me.'"

John 17:12 "While I was with them, I protected them in your name that you have given me. I guarded them, and not one of them was lost except the one destined to be lost, so that the scripture [*graphe*] might be fulfilled."

John 19:24 "So they said to one another, 'Let us not tear it, but cast lots for it to see who will get it.' This was to fulfill what the scripture [*graphe*] says, 'They divided my clothes among themselves, and for my clothing they cast lots.'"

John 19:28 "After this, when Jesus knew that all was now finished, he said (in order to fulfill the scripture [*graphe*]), 'I am thirsty.'"

John 19:36-37 "These things occurred so that the scripture [*graphe*] might be fulfilled, 'None of his bones shall be broken.' And again another passage of scripture [*graphe*] says, 'They will look on the one whom they have pierced.'"

John 20:9 "for as yet they did not understand the scripture [*graphe*], that he must rise from the dead."

Acts

Acts 1:16 "Friends, the scripture [*graphe*] had to be fulfilled, which the Holy Spirit through David foretold concerning Judas, who became a guide for those who arrested Jesus—"

Acts 8:32 "Now the passage of the scripture [*graphe*] that he was reading was this: 'Like a sheep he was led to the slaughter, and like a lamb silent before its shearer, so he does not open his mouth.'"

Acts 8:35 "Then Philip began to speak, and starting with this scripture [*graphe*], he proclaimed to him the good news about Jesus."

Acts 17:2 "And Paul went in, as was his custom, and on three sabbath days argued with them from the scriptures [*graphe*]"

Acts 17:11 "These Jews were more receptive than those in Thessalonica, for they welcomed the message [*logos*] very eagerly and examined the scriptures [*graphe*] every day to see whether these things were so."

Acts 18:24 "Now there came to Ephesus a Jew named Apollos, a native of Alexandria. He was an eloquent man, well-versed in the scriptures [*graphe*]."

Acts 18:28 "for he powerfully refuted the Jews in public, showing by the scriptures [*graphe*] that the Messiah is Jesus."

Romans

Rom 1:2 "which he promised beforehand through his prophets in the holy scriptures [*graphe*]"

Rom 4:3 "For what does the scripture [*graphe*] say? 'Abraham believed God, and it was reckoned to him as righteousness.'"

Rom 9:17 "For the scripture [*graphe*] says to Pharaoh, 'I have raised you up for the very purpose of showing my power in you, so that my name may be proclaimed in all the earth.'"

Rom 10:11 "The scripture [*graphe*] says, 'No one who believes in him will be put to shame.'"

Rom 11:2 "God has not rejected his people whom he foreknew. Do you not know what the scripture [*graphe*] says of Elijah, how he pleads with God against Israel?"

Rom 15:4 "For whatever was written in former days was written for our instruction, so that by steadfastness and by the encouragement of the scriptures [*graphe*] we might have hope."

Rom 16:26 "but is now disclosed, and through the prophetic writings [*graphe*] is made known to all the Gentiles, according to the command of the eternal God, to bring about the obedience of faith—"

1 Corinthians

1 Cor 15:3-4 "For I handed on to you as of first importance what I in turn had received: that Christ died for our sins in accordance with the scriptures [*graphe*], and that he was buried, and that he was raised on the third day in accordance with the scriptures [*graphe*]." (See comments in chapter 4 on what it means for these things to have happened according to the Scriptures.)

Galatians

Gal 3:8 "And the scripture [*graphe*], foreseeing that God would justify the Gentiles by faith, declared the gospel beforehand to Abraham, saying, 'All the Gentiles shall be blessed in you.'" (I would care to wager that the phrase about scripture foreseeing is anthropomorphic and metaphorical.)

Gal 3:22 "But the scripture [*graphe*] has imprisoned all things under the power of sin, so that what was promised through faith in Jesus Christ might be given to those who believe."

Gal 4:30 "But what does the scripture [*graphe*] say? 'Drive out the slave and her child; for the child of the slave will not share the inheritance with the child of the free woman.'"

1 Timothy

1 Tim 5:18 "for the scripture [*graphe*] says, 'You shall not muzzle an ox while it is treading out the grain,' and, 'The laborer deserves to be paid.'"

2 Timothy

2 Tim 3:16 "All scripture [*graphe*] is inspired by God and is useful for teaching, for reproof, for correction, and for training in righteousness"

James

James 2:8 "You do well if you really fulfill the royal law according to the scripture [*graphe*], 'You shall love your neighbor as yourself.'" (See discussion on according to the scripture in chapter 4.)

James 2:23 "Thus the scripture [*graphe*] was fulfilled that says, 'Abraham believed God, and it was reckoned to him as righteousness,' and he was called the friend of God."

James 4:5 "Or do you suppose that it is for nothing that the scripture [*graphe*] says, 'God yearns jealously for the spirit that he has made to dwell in us'?"

1 Peter

1 Pet 2:6 "For it stands in scripture [*graphe*]: 'See, I am laying in Zion a stone, a cornerstone chosen and precious; and whoever believes in him will not be put to shame.'"

2 Peter

2 Pet 1:20 "First of all you must understand this, that no prophecy of scripture [*graphe*] is a matter of one's own interpretation" (See my discussion on this passage in section 5 of chapter 1.)

2 Pet 3:16 "speaking of this as he does in all his letters. There are some things in them hard to understand, which the ignorant and unstable twist to their own destruction, as they do the other scriptures [*graphe*]."

For more information about Gabriel Gordon
or to contact him for speaking engagements,
please visit *www.MisfitsTheology.com*

Many voices. One message.

Quoir is a boutique publisher
with a singular message: *Christ is all.*
Venture beyond your boundaries to discover Christ
in ways you never thought possible.

For more information, please visit
www.quoir.com

9 781938 480867